DATE DUE

MAY 1 7 1993		APR 1 6 1993	

Demco, Inc. 38-293

Encyclopedic Directory of
Ethnic
Newspapers and Periodicals

Encyclopedic Directory of

Ethnic
Newspapers and Periodicals
in the United States

Lubomyr R. Wynar

KENT STATE UNIVERSITY

1972

LIBRARIES UNLIMITED, INC., LITTLETON, COLO.

Library of Congress Card Number 70-185344
International Standard Book Number 0-87287-042-1

LIBRARIES UNLIMITED, INC.
P.O. Box 263
Littleton, Colorado 80120

PREFACE

This *Encyclopedic Directory of Ethnic Newspapers and Periodicals*
is the first comprehensive annotated guide to the current ethnic press in the
United States. The fact that American ethnic publications are continually
being published by various ethnic groups in many languages directly reflects
the multi-ethnicity of American society. The historian, sociologist, political
scientist, bibliographer and other scientists engaged in the multidimensional
analysis of American society and culture must closely explore the phenomena
of American ethnic groups and their press. Ethnic publications not only play
a significant role in ethnic life but also constitute important primary and
secondary sources for historical and sociological studies of the American
people and their culture.

The main objective of this Directory is to identify the number of
newspapers and periodicals published by various ethnic groups in the United
States in terms of bibliographical information and content.

The publication is intended primarily to serve both scholars engaged
in the study of ethnic groups and librarians involved in reference service and
the building of collections with ethnic materials. Until now bibliographical
control of the ethnic press has been neglected.

This directory consists of the following parts:

1. Preface
2. Bibliographical introduction
3. A survey article on the ethnic press in the United States
   and its bibliographical control
4. Forty-three sections listing 903 ethnic titles
5. Appendix (statistical analysis of individual ethnic
   presses)
6. Alphabetical index

It is hoped that this publication will fill an important gap in the reference
literature.

ACKNOWLEDGEMENTS

A number of persons have contributed, either directly or indirectly,
to the compilation of this directory. First of all, I would like to express my
gratitude to all the editors and publishers of ethnic newspapers and periodicals
who cooperated in the survey of the ethnic press by submitting relevant
information concerning their publications.

I would especially like to thank my graduate assistants and students at the School of Library Science, Kent State University, who assisted in this project, namely, Suzan Motylewicz, Vicky Zanca, Nancy Paterson, Mary Haag, Judy Rosenberg, Savitri Bhangsbha, and others.

I greatly appreciate the aid of those who assisted in the translation and content analysis of several non-English publications: Dr. Vitout Kipel, New York, Public Library; Mr. John Gadzow, Kent State University; Mr. Kalman Szekely, Bowling Green University; Mr. Amer Al-Kindilchie, Barberton Public Library; Mr. V. Lesniak, Akron; Professor Kenyon Rosenberg, Kent State University, Mr. Shige Jajiki, Kent State University, and many others.

Finally, I would like to express my appreciation to Dr. Guy Marco, Dean of the School of Library Science, Kent State University, who helped to establish the Center for the Study of Ethnic Publications at Kent State University.

L. R. W.

TABLE OF CONTENTS

BIBLIOGRAPHICAL INTRODUCTION

DATA AND SCOPE

The bibliographical information concerning the ethnic press was obtained from a survey of ethnic newspapers and periodicals in the United States conducted during the calendar years of 1970 through July 1971. For this purpose a special questionnaire was designed and distributed to all known publishers or editors of ethnic publications in this country. The content analysis of individual publications was based on both the editors' statements and *de visu* examination of individual titles of newspapers and periodicals housed at the Center for the Study of Ethnic Publications at Kent State University. In general the scope of this directory is limited to periodicals and newspapers currently published by 43 ethnic groups in the United States.

Only those groups are included which have continued to publish in the non-English (native) languages, with a total of 903 titles listed. Omitted are ethnic groups which publish entirely in English (e.g., Afro-American press, American Indian press, Irish American press, etc.). Also omitted are those non-English language professional and trade periodicals which are not published by ethnic groups but rather by American institutions (e.g., industries, universities, etc.) for a professional and trade clientele. These publications are not considered as constituting an "ethnic press."

ARRANGEMENT

Titles are arranged in alphabetical order under individual ethnic presses, which are listed as separate sections on the basis of language. The ethnic press unit contains two major parts. Part One includes publications printed entirely in non-English (native language) as well as those which are bi-lingual (one section published in the native language and the other section in English). Part Two lists titles published entirely in English.

The purpose of including titles printed entirely in English by individual ethnic groups is to compare the number of publications which appear in the native language or are bilingual to those which are published in English. Such a comparison can shed valuable light on the degree of retention of the native language within each group.

Within each part titles are arranged alphabetically. Exceptions to this arrangement are made for three presses—Arab, Spanish, and Jewish. The first two are arranged on the basis of linguistic principle only and are not subdivided into individual ethnic groups existing within either the Arab-speaking or the Spanish-speaking world (e.g., Iraqi, Syrian, Mexican, Puerto Rican, and others). The Jewish press is divided into four parts: 1) Hebrew and Hebrew-English publications; 2) Yiddish and Yiddish-English publications; 3) Jewish publications in German; and 4) Jewish publications in English.

The necessary cross-references in this respect will facilitate the use of this directory.

ENTRIES

All entries in the directory are numbered in consecutive numerical order. A complete entry provides information in the following sequence:

1. title of publication
2. translation of the title (unless the title is in English)
3. year of origin
4. editorial address
5. editor's name
6. language(s) used in publication
7. sponsoring organization
8. circulation
9. frequency
10. annual subscription rate
11. annotation

In some instances entries do not contain complete bibliographical information. A few publishers or editors failed to provide complete entries to some items in the questionnaire. Sometimes the circulation figure, the date of origin, or other relevant information was omitted. A sample entry is provided below.

132. DENNI HLASATEL.　　The Daily Herald.　　1891— .
　　1545 West 18th Street, Chicago, Illinois 60608
　　　Editor: Dr. Anton Hrebik　　Language: Czech
　　　Sponsor: Denni Hlasatel Printing and Publishing Company
　　　Circulation: 17,587　　Frequency: Daily　　Subscription: $20.00

　　General, international, and national news of interest to the Czech community.

TITLE

All titles are transliterated into the Latin alphabet. In cases where the transliteration was not provided by the editor, Library of Congress transliteration tables were used. All titles include English translations unless the title is in English or is exactly the same when translated.

ANNOTATION

Brief descriptive annotations are based on editors' statements and on *de visu* examination of the relevant title. The objective is to determine the scope, content, and purpose of the publication.

Annotations were not provided in cases where the titles and bibliographical information was self-explanatory, or when no statement of content was available.

STATISTICAL DATA

Statistical analysis of individual ethnic presses is included in an appendix. Additional statistical charts are presented in the introductory article, "The Ethnic Press in the United States and its Bibliographical Control."

INDEX

This index includes title entries arranged in straight alphabetical order with ethnic press designation. Figures cited after the entries refer to the item number assigned to the title.

The table of contents should serve as a subject index.

THE ETHNIC PRESS IN THE UNITED STATES
AND ITS BIBLIOGRAPHICAL CONTROL

It is rather difficult to trace the historical development of the ethnic press in the United States. Its origin goes back to the eighteenth century,[1] before the American War of Independence, and is directly related to the immigration process in the eighteenth and nineteenth centuries. Despite the importance of the ethnic press in the comprehension of the pluralistic character of American society, only marginal attention was focused on this topic. The only comprehensive study on the ethnic press was published by Robert E. Park in 1922,[2] in which he presented a thorough sociological and historical analysis of the so-called "immigrant press." However, one of his major hypotheses in regard to the disappearance of the American non-English press proved to be false.[3] It is true that during the whole 239 years of its existence the ethnic press in the United States was characterized by fluctuation. Many publications were started, then discontinued or merged with other periodicals. Many, however, continued to survive, so that today American ethnic publications are published by various ethnic groups in over 40 languages.

BASIC FEATURES OF ETHNIC PUBLICATIONS

Language Pattern

Ethnic publications generally appear in three linguistic patterns: a) non-English languages; b) bi-lingual; c) English. The first two categories are tailored mainly to the requirements of different social strata within the ethnic groups and reveal strong tendencies to preserve and promote their language and cultural heritage. Ethnic press publications in English serve two major purposes: 1) to reach those members of an ethnic group who have little or no knowledge of their native tongue, in order to preserve their identity; b) to acquaint the American English-speaking community with the culture, history, and social life of individual ethnic groups. In many instances they serve as communication vehicles for the dissemination and promotion of their political, social, and religious values with the American community.

Data from our survey of the ethnic press (1970-1971) reveal that from a total of 903 ethnic publications, 410 titles were published in non-English, 207 were bi-lingual, and 286 were in English.[4]

Types of Publication and Circulation

The ethnic press reflects the same bibliographical pattern as the regular English language press with emphasis placed on weekly and monthly publications. Table 1 presents a distribution of the ethnic press by type.

TABLE 1

	NATIVE LANGUAGE	BI-LINGUAL	ENGLISH
Daily	43	13	5
Semi-weekly	13	4	2
Weekly	104	55	84
Semi-monthly	34	20	22
Monthly	105	61	88
Quarterly	42	23	44
Other	69	31	41
TOTAL	**410**	**207**	**286**
Circulation	2,638,258	1,745,878	4,301,986

TOTAL CIRCULATION: **8,786,122**

The numerical strength of individual ethnic presses is presented in Table 2, on page 11.

The determination of the circulation for individual ethnic publications presents a rather difficult task. A majority of ethnic press publishers do not submit their circulation figures to the Audit Bureau of Circulation, Business Publications Audit Circulation, Verified Audit Circulation Company, and other agencies dealing with circulation. Only well-established ethnic publications with strong advertising sections list circulation. Circulation of the ethnic press fluctuates from year to year, thus making it difficult to obtain reliable data.

In this Directory, circulation figures are based mainly on editors' statements in the questionnaire and on annual publishers' statements in the publications themselves. The total circulation of individual ethnic presses is indicated in Table 3.

TABLE 2

	Daily	Semi-weekly	Weekly	Semi-monthly	Monthly	Quarterly	Other	Total
Albanian	0	0	2	0	1	3	0	6
Arabic	0	2	11	2	3	1	0	19
Armenian	2	3	6	0	9	7	3	30
Assyrian	0	0	0	0	0	0	1	1
Belgian-Flemish	0	0	1	0	0	0	0	1
Bulgarian	0	0	1	1	1	0	1	4
Byelorussian	0	0	1	0	2	3	8	14
Carpatho-Ruthenian	0	0	3	3	5	0	2	13
Chinese	11	1	7	1	3	0	2	25
Cossack	0	0	0	0	0	1	0	1
Croatian	0	0	4	0	1	1	4	10
Czech	2	1	10	1	13	4	2	33
Danish	0	0	1	1	3	0	1	6
Dutch	0	0	2	1	2	1	0	6
Estonian	0	0	1	0	1	0	1	3
Filipino	0	0	0	1	5	0	0	6
Finnish	0	4	1	0	1	1	2	9
French	0	0	5	1	1	2	3	12
Georgian	0	0	0	0	0	0	1	1
German	3	1	29	2	25	3	3	66
Greek	2	0	7	4	8	0	6	27
Hungarian	2	0	9	4	8	1	1	25
Italian	1	0	20	6	11	4	7	49
Japanese	7	1	4	0	3	0	1	16
Jewish	4	0	55	11	48	27	25	170
Korean	1	0	1	2	0	1	1	6
Latvian	0	1	0	1	0	0	0	2
Lithuanian	3	3	3	3	13	6	11	42
Luxembourg	0	0	0	0	1	0	0	1
Norwegian	0	0	4	2	4	1	2	13
Polish	3	0	18	10	12	8	7	58
Portuguese	1	0	2	2	2	0	1	8
Romanian	0	0	0	3	3	0	1	7
Russian	2	1	2	1	9	5	11	31
Serbian	0	0	1	1	1	0	3	6
Slovak	0	0	7	1	12	2	2	24
Slovenian	2	0	1	2	4	1	0	10
Spanish	7	1	15	3	11	1	1	39
Swedish	0	0	6	4	9	3	1	23
Swiss	0	0	2	0	1	0	0	3
Turkish	0	0	0	0	0	1	0	1
Ukrainian	2	0	7	2	18	20	26	75
Welsh	0	0	0	0	1	0	0	1

TABLE 3

ETHNIC GROUP	CIRCULATION	NUMBER OF PUBLICATIONS
1. Jewish	3,694,419	170
2. Spanish	1,142,630	39
3. Polish	626,014	58
4. German	449,666	66
5. Italian	437,801	50
6. Greek	184,184	27
7. Swedish	183,131	23
8. Ukrainian	172,261	73
9. Czech	169,191	33
10. Slovak	168,046	24
11. Lithuanian	139,239	42
12. Chinese	138,253	25
13. French	134,327	12
14. Hungarian	122,181	25
15. Norwegian	109,922	13
16. Japanese	96,694	16
17. Arabic	96,540	19
18. Slovenian	78,192	10
19. Carpatho-Ruthenian	74,940	13
20. Croatian	73,110	10
21. Armenian	66,757	30
22. Russian	65,128	31
23. Dutch	60,990	6
24. Portuguese	49,333	8
25. Filipino	48,750	6
26. Korean	40,068	6
27. Serbian	32,460	6
28. Danish	28,700	6
29. Finnish	25,014	9
30. Latvian	13,150	2
31. Romanian	12,320	7
32. Bulgarian	10,143	4
33. Byelorussian	10,000	14
34. Swiss	8,600	3
35. Albanian	6,650	6
36. Estonian	5,826	3
37. Turkish	4,697	1
38. Belgian-Flemish	2,855	1
39. Assyrian	1,600	1
40. Georgian	1,000	1
41. Cossack	690	1
42. Luxembourg	650	1
43. Welsh		1
TOTALS	**8,786,122**	**903**

Affiliation and the Content of Ethnic Press

The content of the ethnic publications in the major part relates to its affiliation and sponsoring organization. Historical data indicate that many early ethnic publications were sponsored by various churches, or by religious and fraternal organizations. Later, ethnic political, scholarly, literary, sport, professional, and other organizations became noticeably involved as sponsors or publishers of such publications. In his article on the role of the ethnic press, Jerzy Zubrzycki states that a typical "foreign language newspaper" allots its space to five major divisions: "news of the country of settlement, world news, home country news, group life and interest, editorial features."[5] Our content analysis of publications basically supports these findings. However, the content of periodicals (especially monthlies and quarterlies) varies and in-depth coverage of such areas as literature, politics, economics, religion, ideology and other subjects of direct interest to individual ethnic groups is included. With respect to ethnic publications in English, it was found that coverage included topics which appeal to the general American reader. To a certain extent the degree and role of assimilation and acculturation may be determined on the basis of content analysis of individual ethnic presses. Unfortunately, there remains a need for fundamental studies dealing with the content analysis of ethnic publications in the United States.

BIBLIOGRAPHICAL CONTROL

Bibliographical control of the ethnic press constitutes a serious, neglected area. It may be measured in terms of conducted and published surveys of the ethnic press and published directories which list ethnic newspapers and periodicals. The significant study by Park today has only historical value. The last comprehensive survey was conducted by J. A. Fishman and his associates and was published in 1966.[6] His study presents a statistical analysis of the ethnic press and to a certain respect continues Park's work through 1960. However, the survey does not include all detailed statistical analysis of all individual ethnic presses. The most recent survey of the ethnic press was conducted by the compiler of this Directory, and the results are presented in statistical tables which may be found in this article and the appendix.

One of the oldest reference tools, which has been listing ethnic periodicals since 1884, is *Ayer Directory*. At the present time it maintains a separate section, "Foreign language publications," which includes some ethnic periodicals and newspapers *mixed together* with trade and professional publications in various languages. Included titles are arranged not by individual ethnic presses but by foreign languages. *Ayer Directory* can not be considered as a dependable reference tool for the ethnic press, since its information is incomplete and often outdated. Its major handicap is the omission of many ethnic titles. The following comparative table of ethnic titles selected at random will support this statement.

NUMBER OF TITLES

Ethnic Press	Ayer 1970	Ayer 1971	*Encyclopedic Directory*
Albanian	2	2	6
Arabic	5	5	19
Byelorussian	0	0	14
Italian	29	29	43
Lithuanian	21	21	42
Polish	29	29	59
Ukrainian	13	13	72
Yiddish	14	14	30

The recent *Ayer Directory* lists 366 ethnic publications, which does not even constitute 50 percent of the ethnic press in the United States. It should also be pointed out that the "foreign language" criterion adopted by Ayer is not adequate for the bibliographical control of ethnic publications. The same language may be used by several ethnic groups.

Another directory listing ethnic publications is *The Standard Periodicals Directory* (last edition published in 1970). It includes more titles than the *Ayer Directory*. However, *SPD* has many serious handicaps. Ethnic titles are included under a special "Ethnic" section and are listed in straight alphabetical order. Bibliographical descriptions of the entries are too brief and access to the publications is difficult. There is no information on the language of listed titles and no designation of any ethnic affilications. The index does not assist the user in this respect, thus making the reference value of *SPD* highly questionable. In many instances information in *SPD* is out-dated and unreliable.

Foreign Language and Nationality Press is yet another source for ethnic publications. This mimeographed listing is prepared by the American Council for Nationality Service in very limited numbers. The 1970 listing included 606 titles. Many of those entries are not updated; information is incomplete and several ethnic groups are omitted.

Considering the shortcomings of the above-mentioned publications and the poor bibliographical control of the ethnic press in the United States, it becomes obvious that there was a great need for the new comprehensive survey of ethnic publications which resulted in the compilation of this Directory. Since about 90 percent of ethnic newspapers and periodicals are included, even this Directory is not fully complete. However, as compared to other publications, the *Encyclopedic Directory of Ethnic Newspapers and Periodicals in the United States* has the most complete listing of currently published ethnic publications.

The establishment of the Center for the Study of Ethnic Publications at Kent State University is a good start toward providing adequate bibliographical control of the ethnic press in the United States.

REFERENCES

1. *Die Philadelphische Zeitung,* initiated by Benjamin Franklin in 1732, is considered the first non-English periodical in the United States. A good historical chronology of the ethnic press is to be found in Yaroslav Chyz, *225 Years of the U.S. Foreign Language Press.* New York, 1952 (mimeographed report), pp. 4-5.

2. Robert E. Park, *The Immigrant Press and Its Control.* New York, Harper & Brothers, 1922.

3. Park stated that "as the older immigrants learn the language of the country their foreign language press will be replaced by the English press." *Ibid.,* p. 326.

4. In comparison, Joshua A. Fishman's findings for 1960 listed 377 publications in the native language, 107 bi-lingual, and 214 in English. Joshua Fishman, Robert G. Hayden, and Mary E. Warshauer, "The Non English and Ethnic Group Press, 1910-1960," *Language Loyalty in the United States.* The Hague, Mouton, 1966, p. 69. There is clear evidence of an increase in all three groups for 1970.

5. Jerzy Zubrzycki, "The Role of Foreign Language Press in Migrant Integration," *Population Studies,* XII, 76 (1959).

6. Fishman *et al., op. cit.,* pp. 51-74. This study was conducted in conjunction with the Language Resources Project under the directorship of Professor J. A. Fishman.

ALBANIAN PRESS

Albanian and Albanian-English Publications

1.   DIELLI.   The Sun.   1909— .
25 Huntington Ave., Rm. 412A, Boston, Massachusetts 03116
      Editor: Dr. Athanas Gegaj   Language: Albanian and English
      Sponsor: Pan Albanian Federation of America, "Vatra."
      Circulation: 1,650   Frequency: Weekly   Subscription: $15.00

Articles on ethnic, social, cultural, and political issues of special interest
to Albanians.

2.   DRITA E VERTETE.   The True Light.   1958— .
54 Burroughs Street, Jamaica Plain, Massachusetts 02130
      Editor: Rt. Rev. Bishop Mark (Lipa)   Language: Albanian and English
      Sponsor: Albanian Orthodox Diocese of America
      Circulation: 1,200   Frequency: Monthly   Subscription: $10.00

This publication is the official organ of the Canonical Orthodox Church for
the Albanian Faithful. Articles focus primarily on the Orthodox faith and
coverage of the activities of the Bishop of the Albanian Orthodox Church,
along with informative notes on the developments within various church
communities. At times, articles dealing with Albanian culture, history,
ethnic traditions, and religious practices are included. Current problems
within Albanian communities in the United States are also explored.

3.   JETA KATHOLIKE SHQIPTARE.   Catholic Albanian Life.   1966— .
4221 Park Ave. & E. Tremont Ave., Bronx, New York 10457
      Editor: Rev. Joseph J. Oroshi, S.T.D.   Language: Albanian
      Sponsor: Albanian American Catholic League, Inc.
      Circulation: 600   Frequency: Quarterly   Subscription: $12.00

Features articles dealing with religious, social, cultural, and political issues
relevant to Albanians in the United States. Includes Bible translations.
Special section devoted to the activities of the Albanian Catholic Church.

4.   LIRIA.   Liberty.   1942— .
1085 Tremont St., Boston, Massachusetts 02120
      Editor: Dhimitri R. Nikolla   Language: Albanian and English
      Sponsor: Free Albania Organization
      Circulation: 1,200   Frequency: Weekly   Subscription: Unknown

5.   SHQIPTARI I LIRË.   The Free Albanian.   1957— .
150 Fifth Avenue, Rm. 1103, New York, New York 10011
    Editor: Vasil Germenji   Language: Albanian
    Sponsor: Free Albania Committee
    Circulation: 2,000   Frequency: Quarterly
    Subscription: Voluntary contribution

This publication is principally concerned with various developments in
Communist Albania for the purpose of "exposing before the United
Nations, the Assembly of Captive European Nations and other similar
organizations in the Western world, the denial of human, political, and
other rights of the Albanian people by the Communist regime" [editor's
statement]. Attention is also given to the resettlement problems of the
Albanian political refugees in the United States. Sections are devoted to
political, cultural, religious, and social activities both in the United States
and abroad.

6.   ZERI I BALLIT.   The Voice   1950— .
158-23 84 Drive, Jamaica, New York 11432
    Editor: Dr. Begeja Halim   Language: Albanian
    Sponsor: Balli Kombetar Organization
    Circulation: Unknown Frequency: Quarterly Subscription: Unknown

ARABIC PRESS

Editor's note: The section on the Arabic press in the United States
includes newspapers and journals representing various Arab nations
(e.g., Lebanese, Iraqi, Syrian, etc.) published in Arabic and English.

Arabic and Arabic-English Publications

7.   AL-ALAM AL-JADID.   The New World.   1962— .
25720 York Road, Royal Oak, Michigan 48067
    Editor: Yusuf Antone   Language: Arabic
    Circulation: 1,000   Frequency: Weekly Subscription: $12.00

Features news and articles on political, cultural, social, and religious life
of Arabs in Arab countries and in the United States. Illustrated.

8.   AL-BAYAN.   The Statement.   1910— .
126 La Belle, Detroit, Michigan 48214
    Editor: Raji Daher   Language: Arabic
    Circulation: 1,000   Frequency: Weekly   Subscription: $20.00

9.   AL-HODA.   The Guidance.   1898— .
      16 West 30th Street, New York, New York 10001
          Editor: Fred G. Koury   Language: Arabic
          Circulation: 5,400   Frequency: Semi-weekly   Subscription: $25.00

This paper, the oldest Lebanese newspaper in the United States, covers
general and local news. Emphasis is on politics, culture, and economy, but
news is also included on Lebanese activities in the United States, Canada, and
other countries.

10.   AL-ISLAAH.   The Reform.   1931— .
      260 West Broadway, New York, New York 10013
          Editor: Alphonse Chaurize   Language: Arabic and English
          Circulation: 1,000   Frequency: Weekly   Subscription: $10.00

Contains general news of special interest to Arabs. Most of the content of
this weekly is devoted to editorials, rather than to news articles.

11.   AL-MASHRIQ.   The Orient.   1949— .
      56 Chandler, Highland Park, Michigan 48203
          Editor: Hanna Yatooma   Language: Arabic
          Circulation: 1,010   Frequency: Weekly   Subscription: $12.00

Reports and reviews on current events of the Arab people throughout the
world, plus editorial comments and opinions pertaining to major issues in
the countries of the Middle East. It has an Iraqi-oriented philosophy.
Includes coverage of cultural and social activities of Iraqis and other Arabic
communities in the United States.

12.   AL-RISALA.   The Message.
      9 John F. Kennedy Highland Park, Detroit, Michigan 48203
          Editor: Rev. "Imam" Hussein Karoub   Language: Arabic and English
          Circulation: 600   Frequency: Weekly   Subscription: $12.00

Contains general and local news of interest to the Arab-Moslem community.

13.   LEESAN AL-ADL.   Voice of Justice.   1952— .
      10214 Charlevoix Ave., Detroit, Michigan 48214
          Editor: Checri Kana'am   Language: Arabic
          Circulation: 500   Frequency: Weekly   Subscription: $10.00

14. NAHDAT-AL-ARAB.   Arab Progress.   1947—1970.
     126 La Belle, Detroit, Mich. 48203
          Editor: Said D. Fayad   Language: Arabic
          Circulation: 430   Frequency: Semi-weekly   Subscription: $15.00

     Oriented toward the Catholic community, it contains news of general and
     local interest. In February, 1970, it merged with *Al-Bayan* (The Statement).

Arabic Publications in English

15. ACTION.   1969— .
     135 East 44th Street, New York, New York 10017
          Editor: Dr. M. T. Mehdi   Language: English
          Sponsor: Action, Arabic English Newspaper, Inc.
          Circulation: 9,500   Frequency: Weekly   Subscription: $20.00

     The main objective of this weekly is the "liberation of Palestine" [edi-
     tor's statement]. It covers the Middle East and the United States. Focus
     is primarily on Palestine. Besides the news articles, there is a section of
     the newspaper that is devoted to editorials and letters to the editor.

16. AMERICAN-ARAB MESSAGE.   1950— .
     17530 Woodward, Highland Park, Detroit, Michigan 48203
          Editor: Rev. Hussein Karoub   Language: English
          Circulation: 1,000   Frequency: Weekly   Subscription: $12.00

     Articles in this publication are primarily devoted to religious issues.

17. ARAB JOURNAL.   1953— .
     2929 Broadway, New York, New York 10025
          Editor: Maan Ziyadah   Language: English
          Sponsor: Organization of Arab Students in the United States and
                   Canada
          Circulation: 7,000   Frequency: Quarterly   Subscription: $3.00

     This publication features articles on political, cultural, and economic life
     of the various Arab countries.

18. ARAB NEWS AND VIEWS.   1954— .
     405 Lexington Avenue, New York, New York 10017
          Editor: Mrs. Hanan Watson   Language: English
          Sponsor: Arab Information Center
          Circulation: 14,500   Frequency: Semi-monthly   Subscription: $2.00

Contains articles on political, cultural, economic, and religious life in the Arab countries, as well as information on international organizations—especially the United Nations and its stand on Palestine. Includes illustrations.

19. THE ARAB WORLD.   1954— .
     405 Lexington Avenue, Suite 3711, New York, New York 10017
          Editor: Randa Khaldi El-Fattal   Language: English
          Sponsor: League of Arab States
          Circulation: 22,000   Frequency: Monthly   Subscription: $2.00

Articles and commentaries focus primarily on political, economic, and social issues, and on developments in the Middle East and North Africa. Sections are also devoted to artistic contributions, travel, and the people. Information and reports directly dealing with current conflicts in the Middle East are emphasized. Includes illustrations.

20. FREE PALESTINE.   1969— .
     P.O. Box 21096 Kalorama Station, Washington, D.C. 20009
          Editor: Aldeen Jabara   Language: English
          Sponsor: Friends of Free Palestine
          Circulation: Unknown   Frequency: Monthly   Subscription: $5.00

Dedicated to the liberation of Palestine, it features political articles on the Palestinian struggle against Israel. Special coverage of Al-Fatah, the Palestinian national liberation movement.

21. THE HERITAGE.   1963— .
     30 East 40th Street, New York, New York 10016
          Editor: Lou Sahadi   Language: English
          Sponsor: Heritage Press
          Circulation: 4,200   Frequency: Weekly   Subscription: $15.00

Oriented toward the Lebanese community, this weekly includes international, national, and local news. The emphasis is on the Middle East; editorials and opinions are included.

22. LEBANESE AMERICAN JOURNAL.   1952— .
     16 West 30th Street, New York, New York 10001
          Editor: Mary Mokarzel   Language: English
          Circulation: 10,000   Frequency: Weekly   Subscription: $15.00

A Lebanese-oriented publication, it covers various events occurring in Lebanon and in Lebanese communities in the United States.

23. PALESTINE DIGEST.   1971— .
    1608 New Hampshire Ave., N.W., Washington, D.C. 20009
       Editor: Not given   Language: English
       Sponsor: League of Arab States, Arab Information Center
       Circulation: Unknown   Frequency: Weekly   Subscription: Unknown

    A digest of the American and European press dealing with Palestine and
    Palestinians under Israeli occupation. Cites direct quotations.

24. SYRIAN-AMERICAN NEWS.   1932— .
    811 South Sierra Bonita Ave., Los Angeles, California 90036
       Editor: S. S. Mamey   Language: English
       Circulation: 7,400   Frequency: Semi-monthly
       Subscription: $5.00

    News coverage of international affairs as well as events in Syria and the
    United States. Community oriented.

25. THE WORD.   1905— .
    239 85th Street, New York, New York 11209
       Editor: Rev. Stephen Upson   Language: English
       Sponsor: Syrian Antiochian Orthodox Archdiocese
       Circulation: 10,000   Frequency: Monthly   Subscription: $5.00

    Features religious articles as well as information concerning the Syrian
    Orthodox Church and its membership.

ARMENIAN PRESS

Armenian and Armenian-English Publications

26. ARMENIAN-AMERICAN OUTLOOK.   1962— .
    156 Fifth Avenue, New York, New York 10010
       Editor: Rev. Dicran Y. Kassouny   Language: English, Armenian
       Sponsor: Armenian Evangelical Association of North America
       Circulation: 5,200   Frequency: Quarterly   Subscription: $3.00

    This is a religious quarterly.

27. ASBAREZ.   Arena Stage.   1908— .
    1501 Venice Boulevard, Los Angeles, California 90006
       Editor: Jirair Libaridian   Language: Armenian and English
       Sponsor: Armenian Revolutionary Federation Central Committee of
                 California
       Circulation: 1,046   Frequency: Semi-weekly   Subscription: $10.00

This publication covers international, national, cultural, and scientific affairs; political commentaries; and topics relating to Armenian communities, such as educational, cultural, and religious affairs. The goals of this publication are "to propagate the Armenian culture, inform the Armenian community of the state of Armenians worldwide, help achieve the goal of creating an independent, free and united Republic of Armenia, and to relate the Armenian community to the affairs of the world" [editor's statement].

28. BAIKAR.   Struggle.   1922— .
    755 Mount Auburn Street, Watertown, Massachusetts 02172
       Editor: Dr. Nuba Berberian   Language: Armenian
       Sponsor: Baikar Association, Inc.
       Circulation: 2,140   Frequency: Daily   Subscription: $20.00

Official publication of the Armenian Democratic Liberal Party. Contents include news of international, national, and local events which are of special interest to Armenians.

29. BARI LOUR.   Good News.   1958— .
    17231 Sherman Way, Van Nuys, California 91406
       Editor: Rev. Shahe Semerdjyan   Language: Armenian and English
       Sponsor: St. Peter Armenian Apostolic Church
       Circulation: 1,250   Frequency: Monthly   Subscription: Free

30. GERMANIK.   1930— .
    36-33 169th Street, Flushing, New York 11358
       Editor: Andraniu L. P'olatyan   Language: Armenian and English
       Sponsor: Union of Marash Armenians
       Circulation: 1,000   Frequency: Quarterly   Subscription: $3.00

31. HAIRENIK.   Fatherland.   1899— .
    212 Stuart Street, Boston, Massachusetts 02116
       Editor: James H. Tashjian   Language: Armenian
       Sponsor: Armenian Revolutionary Federation of America
       Circulation: 3,400   Frequency: Daily   Subscription: $16.00

Oldest Armenian daily in the United States. National, international, local, and group news of interest to the Armenian population. Organ of the Armenian Revolutionary Federation of America. An Armenian weekly in English is published under the same title (1933—) and edited by the same editor.

32. HAI SIRD.   Armenian Heart.   1938— .
    212 Stuart Street, Boston, Massachusetts 02116
        Editor: Mrs. Siranoush K. Mekhitarian   Language: Armenian and English
        Sponsor: Armenian Relief Society, Inc.
        Circulation: 1,520   Frequency: Quarterly   Subscription: $2.00

    This periodical is intended largely as informative propaganda and is addressed
    primarily to members of the Armenian Relief Society as well as to its
    sympathizers and contributors. Articles cover the history of the organiza-
    tion, the purposes of the organization, and reports on meetings and functions.
    Occasionally fiction or poetry in either language is published.

33. HAYASTANYAITZ YEGEGHETZY.   The Armenian Church.   1938— .
    630 Second Avenue, New York, New York 10016
        Editor: Rev. Carnig Hallajian   Language: Armenian and English
        Sponsor: Diocese of the Armenian Church of America
        Circulation: 6,225   Frequency: Monthly   Subscription: $3.00

    Until 1958 this publication was strictly in Armenian. In 1958 an English
    edition was introduced. Centers principally on news concerning Armenian
    churches in the United States. Also includes articles on Armenian literature
    and history.

34. HOOSHARAR.   The Prompter.   1915— .
    109 East 40th Street, New York, New York 10016
        Editors: Antranig Poladian (Armenian) and Bedros Horehad (English)
        Language: Armenian and English
        Sponsor: Armenian General Benevolent Union of America
        Circulation: 10,000   Frequency: Monthly   Subscriptions: $3.00

    First published in Armenian in 1915. English edition introduced in 1929.
    Primarily a fraternal, welfare magazine. Official organ of the Armenian
    General Benevolent Union of America.

35. KILIKIA.   Cilicia.   1963— .
    777 United Nations Plaza, New York, New York 10017
        Editor: Yervand Vardapet Abelyan   Language: Armenian and English
        Sponsor: Prelacy of the Armenian Apostolic Church of America
        Circulation: 4,300   Frequency: Quarterly   Subscription: Unknown

36. KIR-OU-KIRK.   Letter and Book.   1956— .
    114 First Street, Yonkers, New York 10704
        Editor: K. N. Magarian   Language: Armenian and English
        Sponsor: Armenian Literary Society, New York, Inc.
        Circulation: 2,500   Frequency: Semi-annually Subscription: Free

Covers "the world of Armenian literature, past and contemporary. . . .
As the publication of the A.L.S., it reports on the meetings, programs,
and activities of the organization" [editor's statement].

37. LOUSAVORICH.   Illuminator.   1938— .
     630 Second Avenue, New York, New York 10016
          Editor: Rev. Garen Gdanian   Language: Armenian and English
          Sponsor: St. Gregory Illuminator Church of Armenia
          Circulation: 1,150   Frequency: Weekly   Subscription: Donation

This pamphlet covers news related to church and parish affairs. It also
includes religious and spiritual passages.

38. LRAPER.   The Armenian Herald.   1937— .
     151 West 25th Street, New York, New York 10001
          Editor: V. Ghazarian   Language: Armenian and English
          Sponsor: Armenian Progressive League of America
          Circulation: 2,426   Frequency: Semi-weekly   Subscription: $12.00

International, national, local, and group news, with emphasis on issues of
special interest to Armenians.

39. MAIR YEGEGHETZI.   Mother Church.   1940— .
     221 East 27th Street, New York, New York 10016
          Editor: Rev. Moushegh Der Kaloustian   Language: Armenian and English
          Sponsor: St. Illuminator's Armenian Apostolic Cathedral
          Circulation: 1,200   Frequency: Monthly   Subscription: Free

Objectives of the publication are to inform Armenians of church affairs,
special services, and the activities of various church-affiliated groups. Information on donations, weddings, baptisms, and funerals is published. News
is primarily of a local nature.

40. THE MONTHLY BULLETIN.   Amsat'ert'ik.   1912— .
     152 East 34th Street, New York, New York 10016
          Editor: Rev. S. K. Sulahian   Language: English and Armenian
          Sponsor: The Armenian Evangelical Church of New York
          Circulation: 1,200   Frequency: Monthly   Subscription: $2.00

41. NOR ASHKAR WEEKLY.   The New World Weekly.   1947— .
     151 West 25th Street, New York, New York 10001
         Editor: Samuel H. Toumayan   Language: Armenian and English
         Sponsor: Samuel H. Toumayan—individually owned
         Circulation: 900   Frequency: Weekly   Subscription: $5.00

42. NOR OR.   New Day.   1921— .
     5076 West Pico Boulevard, Los Angeles, California 90019
         Editor: Antnanig Antreassian   Language: Armenian
         Sponsor: Nor Or Publishing Association
         Circulation: 1,500   Frequency: Semi-weekly   Subscription: $15.00

43. PAP OUKHTI.   1935— .
     12813 Gay Avenue, Cleveland, Ohio 44105
         Editor: Gevorg Melitinetsi   Language: Armenian
         Sponsor: Educational Association of Malatia, Central Executive Board
         Circulation: 500   Frequency: Quarterly   Subscription: $5.00

44. P'AROS.   Lighthouse.   1958— .
     70 Jefferson Street, Providence, Rhode Island 02908
         Editor: Hayk Quaha Tonikyan   Language: Armenian and English
         Sponsor: S. Sahak and S. Mesrop Armenian Apostolic Church
         Circulation: 900   Frequency: Monthly   Subscription: Free

45. SHOGHAKAT'.   Radiance.   1955— .
     2215 East Colorado Boulevard, Pasadena, California 91107
         Editor: Unknown   Language: Armenian
         Sponsor: S. Grigor Lousavoritch Armenian Apostolic Church
         Circulation: Unknown   Frequency: Quarterly   Subscription: Free

46. SHOGHAKAT'.   Radiance.   1962— .
     42nd Avenue and 213th Street, Bayside, New York 11361
         Editor: Asoghik Geletjyan   Language: English, Armenian
         Sponsor: St. Sargis Armenian Apostolic Church
         Circulation: 400   Frequency: Bi-monthly   Subscription: Free

47.   YERITASARD HAYASTAN.   Young Armenia.   1903— .
       P.O. Box 9, Madison Square Street, New York, New York 10010
          Editor: Unknown   Language: Armenian
          Sponsor: Hunchakian Party of America
          Circulation: Unknown   Frequency: Weekly Subscription: Unknown

       General news and political articles. This is a publication of the Social
       Democratic Armenian Party.

Armenian Publications in English

48.   ARARAT.   1960— .
       109 East 40th Street, New York, New York 10016
          Editor: Harold Bond   Language: English
          Sponsor: Armenian General Benevolent Union of America, Inc.
          Circulation: 700   Frequency: Quarterly   Subscription: $6.00

       Editorial objectives are to provide a vehicle for writers of Armenian
       ancestry, although authorship is not limited to only Armenian writers.
       Contents include articles, short stories, poetry, plays, book reviews, and
       illustrations. Topics include various facets of Armenian history and cul-
       ture as well as problems of assimilation and acculturation of the
       Armenian ethnic community in the United States, with special issues
       on such topics as religion, contemporary fiction, education, and social
       sciences.

49.   ARMENIAN CHURCH.   1958— .
       630 Second Avenue, New York, New York 10016
          Editor: Bedros Norehad   Language: English
          Sponsor: Diocese of the Armenian Church of America
          Circulation: 6,000   Frequency: Monthly   Subscription: $3.00

50.   ARMENIAN GUARDIAN.   1946— .
       630 Second Avenue, New York, New York 10016
          Editor: Miss Louise Yeghissian   Language: English
          Sponsor: Armenian Church Youth Organization of America
          Circulation: 1,500   Frequency: Monthly   Subscription: $3.00

       This periodical, religious in nature, is directed toward the youthful member-
       ship of the Armenian Church Youth Organization of America. News of groups
       affiliated with the organization and announcements of forthcoming events
       sponsored by the ACYOA are included.

51. THE ARMENIAN MIRROR-SPECTATOR.   1934— .
    755 Mount Auburn Street, Watertown, Massachusetts 02172
       Editor: Jack Antreassian   Language: English
       Sponsor: Baikar Association, Inc.
       Circulation: 2,700   Frequency: Weekly   Subscription: $7.00

This publication covers Armenian cultural and religious activities.
General news is also included. The prime objective is to keep alive "the
consciousness of the Armenian cultural heritage in the process of integration" [editor's statement].

52. THE ARMENIAN REPORTER.   1967— .
    42-60 Main Street, Flushing, New York 11355
       Editor: Edward K. Boghosian   Language: English
       Sponsor: The Armenian Reporter, Inc.
       Circulation: 3,300   Frequency: Weekly   Subscription: $9.00

This newspaper focuses primarily on reporting various social, cultural,
religious and other activities of Armenian communities both in the
United States and abroad. Special features include such sections as
Views and Opinions, Letters to the Editor, Calendar of Coming Events,
and Obituaries. Profiles of successful Armenian personalities are also
printed.

53. THE ARMENIAN REVIEW.   1947— .
    212 Stuart Street, Boston, Massachusetts 02116
       Editor: James H. Tashjian   Language: English
       Sponsor: Hairenik Association
       Circulation: 900   Frequency: Quarterly   Subscription: $6.00

Literary-historical journal of Armeniaca. Its contents include historical
articles, memoirs, political studies, commentaries, short stories, poetry,
book reviews, editorials, and translations from Armenian language
materials. The editorial objective is "support of the Armenian quest for
an independent, free, united democratic Armenian State" [editor's
statement].

54. THE ARMENIAN WEEKLY.   1933— .
    212 Stuart Street, Boston, Massachusetts 02116
       Editor: James H. Tashjian   Language: English
       Sponsor: Hairenik Association
       Circulation: 2,600   Frequency: Weekly   Subscription: $7.00

This newspaper presents materials of a social, cultural, political, and historical nature which are of interest to the people of Armenian background. Its objectives are "to encourage the concept of an independent Armenian State, to urge the retention of the Armenian identity abroad, and to encourage the practice of citizenship in the United States and Canada" [editor's statement]. Features include sections on national and international news, items of special interest to Armenians, editorials, columns, sports page, youth page, obituaries, letter forum, and translations from the Armenian language press.

55.   BULLETIN OF THE ARMENIAN SCIENTIFIC ASSOCIATION OF
        AMERICA.   1968— .
      30 Half Moon Lane, Irvington, New York 10533
        Editor: Editorial Committee   Language: English
        Sponsor: Armenian Scientific Association of America
        Circulation: 500   Frequency: Semi-annual   Subscription: Free

      This bulletin contains news on the activities of the Association.

56.   THE CALIFORNIA COURIER.   1959— .
      P.O. Box 966, Fresno, California 93714
        Editor: George Mason   Language: English
        Circulation: 3,000   Frequency: Weekly   Subscription: $8.00

ASSYRIAN PRESS

Assyrian and Assyrian-English Publications

57.   KOECHVA ATURAYA.   The Assyrian Star.   1933— .
      104 Coolidge Hill Road, Watertown, Massachusetts 02172
        Editor: Malcolm L. Karam   Language: English and Assyrian
        Sponsor: The Assyrian-American Federation
        Circulation: 1,600   Frequency: Bi-monthly   Subscription: $5.00

      A cultural and educational magazine aimed at the Assyrian community. Its chief objectives are to preserve unity among the Assyrian people, to retain Assyrian identity, and to preserve the Assyrian language.

BALTIC PRESS

see ESTONIAN, LATVIAN, and LITHUANIAN PRESS

BELGIAN-FLEMISH PRESS

Flemish Publications

58.   GAZETTE VAN DETROIT.   Detroit Gazette.   1914— .
      11243 Mack Avenue, Detroit, Michigan 48214
           Editor: Mrs. Godelieve B. Van Reybrouck   Language: Flemish
           Sponsor: Belgian Press Company
           Circulation: 2,855   Frequency: Weekly   Subscription: $4.00

      General news. Reports on the activities of Flemish groups and individuals.

BULGARIAN PRESS

Bulgarian and Bulgarian-English Publications

59.   MAKEDONSKA TRIBUNA.   Macedonian Tribune.   1927— .
      542 South Meridian Street, Indianapolis, Indiana 46225
           Editor: Christo N. Nizamoff   Language: Bulgarian and English
           Sponsor: Macedonian Patriotic Organizations of the U.S.A. and Canada
           Circulation: 3,860   Frequency: Weekly   Subscriptions: $8.00

      This newspaper deals primarily with news of various affairs in the
      Balkans. It also includes editorial comments on both national and inter-
      national issues. A section of the publication is devoted to social and
      cultural activities of Bulgarians on the American continent. The main
      objective of the newspaper is to "preserve the cultural and religious
      heritage of the Macedono-Bulgarians on this continent and to work for
      the creation of a united and independent state of Macedonia" [editor's
      statement].

60.   NARODNA VOLYA.   People's Will.   1937— .
      5856 Chene Street, Detroit, Michigan 48211
           Editor: Bocho Mircheff   Language: Bulgarian and English
           Sponsor: People's Will Co-operative Publishing Company
           Circulation: 818   Frequency: Semi-monthly   Subscription: $5.00

      General news of special interest to Bulgarians. Also includes news items
      on various Bulgarian group and individual activities in the United States.

61. RABOTNICHESKA PROSVETA.   Labor Education.   1911— .
5406 Russell Street, Detroit, Michigan 48211
    Editor: Christo Oundjieff   Language: Bulgarian
    Sponsor: Bulgarian Socialist Labor Federation
    Circulation: 465   Frequency: Monthly   Subscription: $2.00

This official organ of the Bulgarian Socialist Labor Federation features
articles on Bulgaria and Bulgarians in the United States. Covers labor,
politics, socioeconomic topics and other subjects of interest to the
Bulgarian community in America.

62. SVOBODNA I NEZAVISIMA BOLGARIA.   Free and Independent
    Bulgaria.   1949— .
200 West 57th Street, New York, New York 10019
    Editor: Dr. G. M. Dimitrov   Language: Bulgarian
    Sponsor: Bulgarian National Committee
    Circulation: 5,000   Frequency: Bi-monthly   Subscription: $5.00

Features political and educational articles dealing with the independence
of Bulgaria.

BYELORUSSIAN PRESS

Byelorussian and Byelorussian-English Publications

63. ABIEZNIK.   News Letter.   1955— .
344 Tibbett Avenue, Bronx, New York 10463
    Editor: Dr. J. Zaprudnik   Language: Byelorussian
    Sponsor: Byelorussian Institute of Arts and Sciences
    Circulation: 200   Frequency: Semi-annual, irregular
    Subscription: Free

This newsletter, the house organ of the Byelorussian Institute of Arts
and Sciences, summarizes the activities of its membership and provides
references and short annotations of publications pertaining to Byelorussian studies. Listings of the most important forthcoming events are
published regularly. Occasionally exchange lists of materials available
in the Institute's library are included, plus necrologies and short biographical data of deceased Institute members.

64. BARACBA.   Struggle.
5610 Luelda Avenue, Cleveland, Ohio 44129
    Editor: Not given.   Language: Byelorussian
    Sponsor: Byelorussian Liberation Front
    Circulation: Unknown Frequency: Unknown Subscription: Unknown

65.   BIELARUS.   Byelorussian.   1950— .
166-34 Gothic Drive, Jamaica, New York 11432
    Editor: Dr. Stanislau Stankevich   Language: Byelorussian
    Sponsor: Byelorussian-American Association, Inc.
    Circulation: 2,100   Frequency: Monthly   Subscription: $6.00

Discusses Byelorussian national problems in the USSR; Beylorussian
problems abroad, especially in the United States; American policy toward
the USSR; and Byelorussian social, cultural, and economic life in the
United States.

66.   BIELARUSKAJA DUMKA.   Byelorussian Thought.   1959— .
34 Richler Avenue, Milltown, New Jersey 08850
    Editor: Antony Danilovich   Language: English and Byelorussian
    Sponsor: Byelorussian-American Relief Committee
    Circulation: 1,500   Frequency: Semi-annually   Subscription: $1.00

This journal surveys Byelorussian political life in the United States and
in the free world; critically analyzes political events in the Byelorussian
SSR; publishes political documents pertaining to the activities of Byelorussian organizations in the United States; and gives critical literary reviews
and works of Byelorussian writers in the United States. It provides
bibliographical listings of Byelorussian publications outside the Soviet
Bloc countries and gives obituaries of Byelorussian political leaders.

67.   BYELORUSSIAN YOUTH.
Route 1, Box 281B, Matawan, New Jersey 07747
    Editors: J. Zaprudnik and G. Stankevich   Language: Byelorussian
    Sponsor: Byelorussian Youth Association of America
    Circulation: Unknown   Frequency: Quarterly   Subscription: Unknown

68.   CARKOUNY SVIETAC.   The Church's Light.   1951— .
192 Old Turnpike Road, South River, New Jersey 08882
    Editor: Rev. M. Lapitzki   Language: English and Byelorussian
    Sponsor: Byelorussian Orthodox Church in South River, New Jersey
    Circulation: 2,000   Frequency: Semi-annually   Subscription: $1.00

This paper surveys developments in the religious and cultural life of the
Byelorussian community in the United States and outside the BSSR. It
publishes research materials on the history of the Byelorussian Church,
occasional papers of literary and theological content, and obituary and
biographical notes on prominent Byelorussian church and civic leaders.

69. HOLAS CARKVY.   Voice of the Church.   1954– .
401 Atlantic Avenue, Brooklyn, New York 11217
    Editor: M. Mickievich   Language: Byelorussian
    Sponsor: Byelorussian Autocephalic Orthodox Church in America
          and Canada
    Circulation: 1,000   Frequency: Semi-annually   Subscription: $2.00

This publication of the Byelorussian Autocephalic Church prints research materials on the history of the Byelorussian Church, philosophical works, and literary reviews of religious interest. Also included are reading materials for Byelorussian Sunday Schools and surveys of activities of Byelorussian Autocephalic Orthodox Churches and affiliated organizations.

70. KAMUNIKATY.   News of the Council of BNR.   1970– .
30 East 42nd Street, New York, New York
    Editor: Dr. J. Zaprudnik   Language: Byelorussian
    Sponsor: Council of Byelorussian Democratic Republic
    Circulation: Unknown   Frequency: Irregular
    Subscription: Free to institutions

This is a newsletter of Byelorussian political parties centered around the Council of the Byelorussian Democratic Republic; it provides biographical information on Byelorussian political leaders.

71. KONADNI.   Vigils.   1955– .
3441 Tibbett Avenue, Bronx, New York 10463
    Editor: Dr. V. Tumash   Language: Byelorussian
    Sponsor: Byelorussian Institute of Arts and Sciences
    Circulation: 300   Frequency: Irregular   Subscription: $3.00

This is a paper devoted to Byelorussian literature, arts, and social sciences, which publishes new materials in literature and provides reproductions of art works. It includes extensive annotated critical bibliographies. A new volume is scheduled to be published in October-December 1971.

72. LITARATURNA-MASTACKI ZBORNIK.   Literary-Art Review.   1969– .
P.O. Box 1944, Trenton, New Jersey
    Editor: Michael Sienko   Language: Byelorussian
    Sponsor: Publishing Company, "Rodny Krai "
    Circulation: 500   Frequency: Quarterly   Subscription: $2.00

This review is devoted to an analysis of developments in the Byelorussian community in the United States. It also publishes new literary works and reprints of literary works.

73. SIAUBIT.   The Sower.   1957— .
164 Broadway, Fort Edward, New York 12828
   Editor: Rev. Francis Cherniawski   Language: Byelorussian
   Circulation: 400 Frequency: Bi-monthly   Subscription: $5.00

This magazine publishes literary works, religious articles, and documents
pertaining to the history of the Byelorussian Catholic Church. There are
also book reviews and church events.

74. VIEČA.   The Council.   1970— .
204 State Highway 18, East Brunswick, New Jersey 08816
   Editor: Dr. P. Markowski   Language: Byelorussian and English
   Sponsor: The Whiteruthenian Press
   Circulation: 1,000   Frequency: Monthly   Subscription: .50/copy

Designed primarily for young Americans of Byelorussian descent.
Analyzes Byelorussian political activities and expresses needs of the
Byelorussian community in the United States.

75. ZAPISY.   Annals (of the Byelorussian Institute of Arts and Sciences).
   1965— .
166-34 Gothic Drive, Jamaica, New York 11432
   Editor: Dr. Stanislau Stankevich   Language: Byelorussian
   Sponsor: Byelorussian Institute of Arts and Sciences
   Circulation: 500   Frequency: Annually   Subscription: $5.00

A scholarly publication dealing with new research materials on Byelorussian culture, history, social studies, arts, economics, and sciences. The
emphasis is on recent research investigations being performed outside
the Soviet Bloc countries. It provides critical reviews and analyses of
recent events in Byelorussian cultural life as well as critical bibliographical
surveys of publications pertaining to Byelorussian studies. It occasionally
publishes special volumes in conjunction with affiliated institutions in
Germany and Canada.

76. ZMAHAR.   Soldier.   1970— .
9 River Road, Highland Park, New Jersey 08904
   Editor: Dr. V. Wasilewski   Language: Byelorussian
   Sponsor: Byelorussian Veterans Association in U.S.A.
   Circulation: 500   Frequency: Weekly   Subscription: $5.00

Bulletin of the Byelorussian-American Veterans. It analyzes military
achievements throughout the world and publishes documents and materials
pertaining to the history of the Byelorussian army and various military
units in Byelorussia.

CARPATHO-RUTHENIAN PRESS

Editor's note: The Carpatho-Ruthenian community in the United States asserts itself as constituting a separate ethnic group which embraces immigrants from Carpatho-Ukraine and the Lemkian region. Presently "Carpatho-Ruthenia" or "Carpatian Rus" constitutes an integral part of the Soviet Ukraine.

The Carpatho-Ruthenian press usually is published in a special jargon (Iyazychiie) based on a mixture of Ukrainian, Russian, and Slovak dialects, and is printed in Cyrillic or Latin characters. The editors of these publications, in designating their language, use such terms as "Carpatho-Ruthenian," "Carpatho-Russian," "Ruthenian," and "Russian."

For a detailed discussion see Wasyl Halich's *Ukrainians in the United States* (Chicago, University of Chicago Press, 1937), pp. 115-117, reprinted by Arno Press in 1970.

Carpatho-Ruthenian and Carpatho-Ruthenian-English Publications

77.   CERKOVNYJ VISTNIK.   Church Messenger.   1944— .
      145 Broad Street, Perth Amboy, New Jersey 08861
         Editor: Very Rev. Stephen Sedor   Language: Carpatho-Ruthenian
                                                       and English
         Sponsor: American Carpatho-Russian Orthodox Greek-Catholic Diocese
         Circulation: Unknown   Frequency: Semi-monthly   Subscription: $4.00

   Religious topics, church news, articles on religious education. The "Carpatho" section is published in Carpatho-Ruthenian dialect and in the Latin alphabet.

78.   KARPATSKA RUS'.   Carpathian Rus'.   1927— .
      556 Yonkers Avenue, Yonkers, New York 10704
         Editor: Stephen Kitchura   Language: Carpatho-Ruthenian
         Sponsor: Lemko Association of U.S. and Canada
         Circulation: 2,488   Frequency: Semi-monthly   Subscription: $7.00

   Official organ of the Lemko-Soiuz, a fraternal organization. Features articles on Lemkos history, culture, and religion. Publishes materials on Lemko-Soiuz. Contains illustrations.

79.   LEMKOVINA.   Lemko Land.   1971– .
      18 Moresemere Place, Yonkers, New York 10701
          Editors: Teodor Dokla and Stephen M. Kitchura   Language: Lemko dialect
          Sponsor: Lemkovina Press
          Circulation: 1,000   Frequency: Monthly   Subscription: $4.00

Unofficial organ of the World Federation of Lemkos which aims at
cooperation between the Ukrainian organization "Organization for
Defense of Lemkivshchyna" and the pro-Russian Lemkos. Features
political, social, and other articles dealing with Lemkos in Ukraine,
Poland, and the United States.

80.   PRAVDA.   The Truth.   1900– .
      1733 Spring Garden Street, Philadelphia, Pennsylvania 19130
          Editor: Stephen Kopestonsky   Language: Russian and English
          Sponsor: Russian Brotherhood Organization of the U.S.A.
          Circulation: 4,962   Frequency: Monthly   Subscription: $3.50

This newspaper serves as the official organ of the Russian Brotherhood
Organization. Its contents include reports and orders of the Board of
Supreme Officers, the Executive Committee and subordinate lodges;
articles dealing with the development of the Organization; general news
items; and correspondence of particular interest ot the members of the
Organization.

81.   PROSVITA.   Enlightenment.   1917– .
      613 Sinclair Street, McKeesport, Pennsylvania 15132
          Editor: Rev. Basil Shereghy   Language: English and Ruthenian
          Sponsor: United Societies of U.S.A. (Sobranie)
          Circulation: 4,500   Frequency: Monthly   Subscription: Not listed

Promotion of the Fraternal Benefit Society interests. Emphasis on
church news and religious articles.

82.   RUSSKIJ VISTNIK.   Russian Messenger.   1916– .
      333 Boulevard of Allies, Pittsburgh, Pennsylvania 15222
          Editor: Rev. John J. Miller   Language: English and Carpatho-Russian
          Sponsor: United Russian Orthodox Brotherhood of America
          Circulation: 2,000   Frequency: Bi-monthly   Subscription: $1.00

Primarily deals with news pertaining to important religious and social
events and activities sponsored by Carpatho-Ruthenian parishes in the
United States. Religious passages are also included.

83. SVIT.   The Light.   1897—.
Russian Building, 84 East Market Street, Wilkes-Barre, Pennsylvania 18701
Editor: Rt. Rev. Peter Kohanik   Language: Carpatho-Russian and English
Sponsor: Russian Orthodox Catholic Mutual Aid Society of U.S.A.
Circulation: 1,915   Frequency: Semi-monthly   Subscription: $4.00

Contains articles on Lemko history, local news of Lemko communities,
religious articles. Most of the material was published in Carpatho-
Ruthenian dialect at first, then later in English.

84. SVOBODNOYE SLOVO KARPATSKOI RUSY.   Free Word of
Carpathian Rus'.   1959—.
P.O. Box 509, Mount Vernon, New York 10550
Editor: Michael Turjanica   Language: Russian
Circulation: 1,000   Frequency: Bi-monthly   Subscription: $3.00

Material is primarily of a political and spiritual nature.

85. VIESTNIK GREKO KAFT. SOJEDINENIJA.   Greek Catholic Union
Messenger.   1892—.
502 8th Avenue, Munhall, Pennsylvania 15121
Editor: Michael Roman   Language: Carpatho-Ruthenian
Sponsor: Greek Catholic Union of the U.S.A.
Circulation: 18,000 Frequency: Weekly   Subscription: $2.00

This publication covers the religious, social, cultural, nationalistic,
educational, political, and sports activities of members of the Greek
Catholic Union of the United States. The first title of the weekly was
Amerikansky Ruskyi Viestnik (The American Ruthenian Messenger).

Carpatho-Ruthenian Publications in English

86. BYZANTINE CATHOLIC WORLD.   1956—.
P.O. Box 7668, Pittsburgh, Pennsylvania 15214
Editor: Very Rev. Msg. Edward V. Rosack   Language: English
Sponsor: Carpatho-Ruthenian Catholic Munhall Archdiocese
Circulation: 19,875 Frequency: Weekly Subscription: $4.00

Official organ of the Byzantine Catholic Archidocese of Munhall.
Features religious articles and news. Illustrated.

87. EASTERN CATHOLIC LIFE.   1956– .
     101 Market Street, Passaic, New Jersey 07055
          Editor: Very Rev. Msg. Thomas Dolinay   Language: English
          Sponsor: Byzantine Rite Eparchy of Passaic
          Circulation: 14,000   Frequency: Weekly   Subscription: $4.00

Features religious articles and news of interest to the Catholic parishioners
of the Eparchy of Passaic. Also publishes general, national, and international news.

88. THE ORTHODOX CHURCH.   1964– .
     30 Shubert Lane, Bethpage, New York 11714
          Editor: Rev. John Meyendorf   Language: English
          Sponsor: Metropolitan Council of the Orthodox Church of America
          Circulation: Unknown   Frequency: Monthly   Subscription: $3.00

Includes articles and news on the Orthodox Church in America and
international church news.

89. THE RUSSIAN ORTHODOX JOURNAL.   1927– .
     84 East Market Street, Wilkes-Barre, Pennsylvania 18701
          Editor: Peter Melnik   Language: English
          Sponsor: Federated Russian Orthodox Clubs
          Circulation: 5,200   Frequency: Monthly   Subscription: $5.50

Covers theology of the Eastern Orthodox Church, and the history and
contemporary conditions of the church. Also relates activities of church
clubs and members.

CHINESE PRESS

Chinese and Chinese-English Publications

90. THE CHINA TIMES.   1963– .
     103-105 Mott Street, New York, New York 10013
          Editor: Kwei-sang Wang   Language: Chinese
          Sponsor: The Mei Kuo Publishing Company
          Circulation: 11,687   Frequency: Daily   Subscription: $27.00

This newspaper provides coverage of international, national, local, and
group affairs and events. A Chicago edition of this publication is also
printed.

91. CHINESE AMERICAN PROGRESS.   1951— .
2249 Wentworth Avenue, Chicago, Illinois 60619
    Editor: G. H. Wang   Language: Chinese and English
    Sponsor: Chinese American Civic Council
    Circulation: 1,500   Frequency: Irregular   Subscription: $3.00

Published for members of the Chinese American Civic Council. The
publication aims at "citizenship, betterment, and intergroup understanding" [editor's statement].

92. CHINESE PACIFIC WEEKLY.   1946— .
815 Stockton Street, San Francisco, California 94108
    Editor: Gilbert Woo   Language: Chinese
    Sponsor: Chinese Pacific Publishing Company, Inc.
    Circulation: 5,600   Frequency: Weekly   Subscription: $5.00

This newspaper is "devoted to the improvement and progress of the
Chinese community" [editor's statement]. It contains commentaries
and special news reports as well as feature articles dealing with the
ethnic situation, events in China, and national and local affairs.

93. CHINESE TIMES.   Jin Shan Shyr Pao. 1924— .
117-119 Waverly Place, San Francisco, California 94108
    Editor: Kwai Fong Chan   Language: Chinese
    Sponsor: The Chinese Times Publishing Company, Inc.
    Circulation: 10,000 Frequency: Daily except Sundays
    Subscription: $30.00

Contents include news items on domestic, foreign, and Chinese group
affairs and events. Information on medical problems, editorials on
various topics, stories, and poetry are also printed.

94. EAST/WEST. Tung Hsi Pao.   1967— .
758 Commercial Street, San Francisco, California
    Editor: Kenneth Wong   Language: English and Chinese
    Sponsor: East/West Publishing Company
    Circulation: 4,985   Frequency: Weekly   Subscription: $7.50

Topics covered include civil rights, youth movements, welfare, housing
problems, working conditions, etc. The objective of the publication is
to "serve the Chinese community in this country and to serve as a
link between Chinese and English speaking worlds" [editor's statement].

95. GETTING TOGETHER.   1970— .
      24 Maricet Street, New York, New York 10002
          Editor: I Wor Kuen staff   Language: English and Chinese
          Sponsor: I Wor Kuen
          Circulation: Unknown   Frequency: Monthly   Subscription: $5.00

      "The objective of the paper is to educate through past and current news,
      people, especially Asian people, as to the nature of fascism in the U.S.
      and the revolutionary alternatives" [editor's statement]. The publication
      is political in nature and contains articles on Chinese-American and Chinese
      history, community news, the war, and liberation struggles.

96. NEW CHINA DAILY PRESS.   Hsin Chung Kuo Jih Pao.   1900— .
      P.O. Box 1656, Honolulu, Hawaii 96817
          Editor: Yick Kam Leong   Language: Chinese
          Sponsor: Chinese Democratic Constitutional Party
          Circulation: 1,150   Frequency: Daily   Subscription: $27.00

      News items on internation, national, local, and group affairs. Feature
      items often included on Chinese personalities.

97. SAN MIN YAT PO.   San Min Morning Paper.   1932— .
      2127 Archer Avenue, Chicago, Illinois 60616
          Editor: Henry Pan   Language: Chinese
          Sponsor: Kuo Min Publishing Company
          Circulation: 2,300   Frequency: Daily   Subscription: Unknown

98. SING TAO JIH PAO.   Star Island Daily.   1910— .
      766 Sacramento Street, San Francisco, California 94108
          Editor: Aw Sian, c/o Robert Chang   Language: Chinese
          Circulation: 9,500   Frequency: Daily   Subscription: $32.00

      World and national news, news from Asia in general. Special material
      concerning Chinese community in Hong Kong. "The objective of our
      U.S. edition is to serve the general public of Chinese in U.S. and Canada"
      [editor's statement].

99. SING TAO WEEKLY.   Star Island Weekly.   1910— .
      766 Sacramento Street, San Francisco, California 94108
          Editor: Aw Sian, c/o Robert Chang   Language: Chinese
          Circulation: 9,500   Frequency: Weekly   Subscription: Unknown

100. TRUTH SEMI-WEEKLY.   Chêng Yen Pao.   1967— .
    809 Sacramento Street, San Francisco, California 94108
        Editor: Frank Y. S. Wong   Language: Chinese
        Sponsor: Truth Semi-Weekly Publishing Company
        Circulation: 9,000   Frequency: Bi-weekly   Subscription: $14.00

    Covers all topics which are of special interest to Chinese in the United
    States. Includes general news on world, national, and group events.
    Activities within Chinatown are also covered.

101. TSU KUO I CHOU.   Fatherland Weekly.
    100 West 32nd Street, 3rd floor, New York, New York 10001
        Editor: James Wei   Language: Chinese
        Sponsor: China Publishing Company, c/o Chinese Information Service
        Circulation: 1,200   Frequency: Weekly   Subscription: Gift

    Condenses the most important news which has appeared in local Chinese
    newspapers in Taiwan.

102. THE YOUNG CHINA DAILY.   Shao Nien Chung Kuo Ch'ên Pao.   1910— .
    51 Hang Ah Street, San Francisco, California 94108
        Editor: George Hsu   Language: Chinese
        Sponsor: Young China Daily Publishing Company
        Circulation: 8,500   Frequency: Daily   Subscription: $30.00

    Covers national, international, and group news. Its prime objective is to
    keep the Chinese reader both here and abroad up to date on activities
    and events occurring in the nation.

Chinese Publications in English

103. AMERICAN CHINESE NEWS.
    763 North Hill Street, Los Angeles, California 90012
        Editor: Yin Po Lin   Language: English
        Sponsor: American Chinese News Company
        Circulation: 2,450   Frequency: Weekly   Subscription: Unknown

104. BULLETIN OF THE CHINESE HISTORICAL SOCIETY OF AMERICA. 1966— .
    17 Adler Place, San Francisco, California 94133
        Editor: Thomas W. Chinn   Language: English
        Sponsor: Chinese Historical Society of America
        Circulation: Unknown   Frequency: Monthly   Subscription: Members only

This publication is restricted to members of the Chinese Historical Society of America, as well as to other historical organizations on an exchange basis. Its contents are devoted primarily to topics dealing with the history of the Chinese in America and related subjects.

105. CHINA DAILY NEWS.
20 Elizabeth Street, New York, New York 10013
    Editor: James Lee   Language: English
    Sponsor: China Daily News, Inc.
    Circulation: 3,100   Frequency: Semi-weekly   Subscription: Unknown

106. CHINA TRIBUNE.   1943– .
210 Canal Street, New York, New York 10013
    Editor: Y. Y. Pan   Language: English
    Sponsor: Chinese American Cultural Corporation
    Circulation: 8,920   Frequency: Daily   Subscription: Unknown

107. CHINESE-AMERICAN WEEKLY.   1942– .
199 Canal Street, New York, New York 10013
    Editor: Chin Fu Woo   Language: English
    Sponsor: Chinese-American Press
    Circulation: 9,000   Frequency: Weekly   Subscription: Unknown

108. THE CHINESE JOURNAL.   1928– .
7 East Broadway, New York, New York 10038
    Editor: Hsoung Wu Kung   Language: English
    Sponsor: Chinese American World Publishing Corporation
    Circulation: 15,520   Frequency: Daily   Subscription: Unknown

General, national, and local news of interest to the Chinese community.

109. THE CHINESE WORLD.   1891– .
736 Grant Avenue, San Francisco, California 94108
    Editor: John S. C. Ong   Language: English
    Sponsor: Chinese World, Ltd.
    Circulation: 7,500   Frequency: Daily   Subscription: Unknown

110. FREE CHINA REVIEW.
    100 West 32nd Street, 3rd floor, New York, New York 10001
        Editor: James Wei   Language: English
        Sponsor: China Publishing Company, c/o Chinese Information Service
        Circulation: 221   Frequency: Monthly   Subscription: $3.00

111. FREE CHINA WEEKLY.
    100 West 32nd Street, New York, New York 10001
        Editor: James Wei   Language: English
        Sponsor: China Publishing Company, c/o Chinese Information Service
        Circulation: 5,900   Frequency: Weekly   Subscription: $2.50

112. UNITED CHINESE PRESS.   1951— .
    P.O. Box 1519, Honolulu, Hawaii 96817
        Editor: Kam Fui   Language: English
        Sponsor: United Chinese Press, Ltd.
        Circulation: 3,225   Frequency: Daily   Subscription: Unknown

    General, international, and national news of Chinese interest

113. THE UNITED JOURNAL.   1952— .
    199 Canal Street, New York, New York 10013
        Editor: Chin Fu Woo   Language: English
        Sponsor: Chinese-American Press, Inc.
        Circulation: 7,300   Frequency: Daily   Subscription: Unknown

114. VISTA.
    100 West 32nd Street, 3rd floor, New York, New York 10001
        Editor: James Wei   Language: English
        Sponsor: China Publishing Company, c/o Chinese Information Service
        Circulation: 195   Frequency: Bi-monthly   Subscription: $1.80

COSSACK PRESS

Cossack Publications

115. KOZACHE ZYTTIA.   Cossacks' Life.   1953— .
602 Public Street, Providence, Rhode Island 02907
    Editor: Theo Bihday   Language: Ukrainian, Russian, English
    Sponsor: Kossacks American National Alliance, Inc.
    Circulation: 690   Frequency: Quarterly   Subscription: $11.00

Until 1970 this periodical was published monthly. In January 1971 it
became a quarterly. The journal is of a literary-political nature, dealing
with the cultural and educational life of Cossacks in connection with
their historical role.

CROATIAN PRESS

Croatian and Croatian-English Publications

116. BULLETIN OF THE AMERICAN CROATIAN ACADEMIC CLUB. 1960— .
P.O. Box 18081, Cleveland Heights, Ohio 44118
    Editor: Tefko Saracevic   Language: English and Croatian
    Sponsor: American Croatian Academic Club
    Circulation: 500   Frequency: Irregular   Subscription: Free

The purpose of this publication is to report on the events and activities
of the American Croatian Academic Club. Reports on the various cultural
activities of Croatians in the United States are also included.

117. CROATIA PRESS. A REVIEW AND NEWS BULLETIN.   1947— .
P.O. Box 1767, New York, New York 10017
    Editor: Karlo Mirth   Language: Croatian and English
    Circulation: 500   Frequency: Quarterly   Subscription: $6.00

This quarterly deals with current affairs in Yugoslavia, but emphasis is
placed on Croatia. The news covers activities of a political, economic, and
cultural nature. Items on various activities of Croatian-Americans are
also published. Sections of the periodical are devoted to bibliographies of
Croatian publications world-wide. Between 1947 and 1952 the journal
was published only in Croatian. In 1952 English language articles were
introduced.

118. DANICA.   The Morning Star.   1921— .
4851 Drexel Boulevard, Chicago, Illinois 60615
    Editor: Rev. Ljubo Cuvalo   Language: Croatian
    Sponsor: Croatian Center Association
    Circulation: 4,500   Frequency: Weekly   Subscription: Unknown

This is the oldest Croatian newspaper in the United States. It provides coverage of news of Croatian interest and promotes the cause of Croatian independence. Until 1945 this weekly was called *Hrvatski List i Danica Hrvatska.*

119. HRVATSKI KATOLICKI GLASNIK.   Croatian Catholic Messenger. 1941— .
4851 Drexel Boulevard, Chicago, Illinois 60615
    Editor: Fr. Gracijan Raspudic   Language: Croatian
    Sponsor: Croatian Franciscan Fathers
    Circulation: 2,000   Frequency: Monthly   Subscription: Unknown

Monthly magazine published by the Croatian Franciscans. Features religious articles. Illustrated.

120. JUNIOR MAGAZINE.   1940— .
100 Delaney Drive, Pittsburgh, Pennsylvania 15235
    Editor: Michael Grasha   Language: English and Croatian
    Sponsor: Croatian Fraternal Union of America
    Circulation: 15,500   Frequency: Bi-monthly   Subscription: Free to members

Provides coverage of social, cultural, athletic, and fraternal activities of the Croatian Fraternal Union throughout the United States and Canada. The objectives are to deal with issues most pertinent to junior members of the Union. The publication also strives to "inculcate in those members an appreciation of the fraternal benefit system and an awareness of their ethnic background" [editor's statement].

121. NARODNI GLASNIK.   People's Herald.   1907— .
2122 South Ashland Avenue, Chicago, Illinois 60608
    Editor: Leo Fisher   Language: Croatian
    Sponsor: Narodni Glasnik Publishing Company, Inc.
    Circulation: 910   Frequency: Weekly   Subscription: $6.00

Contents include news of social and political events, achievements in science, and interpretation of events and international relationships in order to promote "the understanding of American (and other) Croats and Yugoslavs in general of the conditions, customs, institutions, history, etc., of the United States" [editor's statement]. This publication also includes items on the achievements of American Croats and other Yugoslavs in the fields of politics, science, sports, and labor.

122. NAŠA NADA.   Our Hope.   1921— .
     710 Pierce Street, Gary, Indiana 46402
        Editor: Stanley Boric   Language: Croatian
        Sponsor: Croatian Catholic Union
        Circulation: 6,000   Frequency: Weekly   Subscription: Unknown

123. VJESNIK UJEDINJENIH AMERICKIH HRVATA.   Bulletin of
     United American Croats.   1960— .
     550 West 50th Street, New York, New York
        Editor: Krunoslav Masina   Language: Croatian
        Sponsor: United American Croats
        Circulation: 2,000   Frequency: Bi-monthly   Subscription: $4.00

The major focus of this bulletin is on political events which affect
Croatians and Croatia. Sections of the journal are devoted to coverage of
news dealing with Croatia, editorials, comments, opinions, sports, education, cultural news, organizational news, and survey of the world press.
The editorial policies and goals are "against Communism and for a free
and independent Croatia" [editor's statement].

124. ZAJEDNICAR.   The Fraternalist.   1894— .
     100 Delaney Drive, Pittsburgh, Pennsylvania 15235
        Editor: John Herak, Jr.   Language: English and Croatian
        Sponsor: Croatian Fraternal Union of America
        Circulation: 40,200   Frequency: Weekly   Subscription: Members only

The primary purpose of this publication is to cover events and activities
of approximately 600 senior lodges and 400 junior groups ("Nests")
affiliated with the Croatian Fraternal Union of America throughout the
United States and Canada. News coverage deals with athletic, cultural,
and educational activities. The publication also promotes the organization's insurance portfolio and disability, surgical, and hospitalization
coverage.

Croatian Publications in English

125. JOURNAL OF CROATIAN STUDIES.   1960— .
     P.O. Box 1767 Grand Central Station, New York, New York 10017
        Editors: Jerome Jareb and Karlo Mirth   Language: English
        Sponsor: The Croatian Academy of America, Inc.
        Circulation: 1,000   Frequency: Annually   Subscription: $5.00

This is primarily a scholarly review which publishes articles pertinent to
Croatian history and culture (literature, fine arts, music, sociology,

economics, government and law, sciences, philology, and religion).
Creative translations of Croatian short stories and poems, reviews of
recent books relevant to Croatian matters, and unpublished documents
of Croatian historical and cultural significance (letters, diaries, and
records) are also published.

CZECH PRESS

Czech and Czech-English Publications

126. AMERICAN SOKOL.   American Falcon.   1879— .
     6426 West Cermak Road, Berwyn, Illinois 60402
         Editor: Charles M. Prchal   Language: Czech
         Sponsor: American Sokol Organization
         Circulation: 5,675   Frequency: Monthly
         Subscription: $3.00; Free to members

Features materials on physical education. A fraternal publication.

127. AMERICKE LISTY.   American Letters.   1962— .
     283 Oak Street, Perth Amboy, New Jersey 08861
         Editor: Josef Martinek   Language: Czech
         Sponsor: Universum Press Company
         Circulation: 1,600   Frequency: Weekly   Subscription: Unknown

Covers political, cultural, social topics of interest to the Czech
community.

128. BESIDKA SOKOLSKA.   Sokol News.   1892— .
     29-19 24th Avenue, Long Island City, New York 11105
         Editor: Bohuslav Zavorka   Language: Czech and English
         Sponsor: Czechoslovak Workingmen's Gymnastic Association
         Circulation: 420   Frequency: Monthly   Subscription: $1.20

Focuses primarily on current events within the Czechoslovak Workingmen's Gymnastic Association (SOKOL). Most of the news items deal
with sports and physical fitness.

129. BRATRSKÉ-LISTY.   The Brethren Journal.   1902— .
     5905 Carleen Drive, Austin, Texas 78731
         Editor: Rev. Jesse E. Skrivanek   Language: English and Czech
         Sponsor: Unity of the Brethren in Texas
         Circulation: 1,850   Frequency: Monthly   Subscription: $2.00

This journal publishes information concerning the activities of the Unity of the Brethren Organization. Most of the articles deal with general religious interests and activities. Spiritual passages are numerous. A section of the publication also deals with vital statistics of members (births, deaths, baptisms, and weddings).

130. BRATRSKY VESTNIK.   Fraternal Herald.   1898— .
    1402 B Street, Omaha, Nebraska 68108
        Editors: Anton Piskac, Sr. (Czech) and Henrietta Shutt (English)
        Language: English and Czech
        Sponsor: Western Bohemian Fraternal Association
        Circulation: 25,000   Frequency: Monthly
        Subscription: $1.20; Free to members

This journal publishes reports on various activities of affiliated lodges and meetings of the Board of Directors and officers. Much of the material centers on covering accomplishments of members of the Association. Biographies of deceased members are also printed. At times instructive and entertaining articles are included, especially when pertaining to Czech or Slovak history. Although the magazine is non-partisan in political matters, it does admit discussions of relevant issues.

131. CSA JOURNAL.   1892— .
    2138 South 61 Court, Cicero, Illinois 60650
        Editor: William R. Cicovsky   Language: English and Czech
        Sponsor: Czechoslovak Society of America
        Circulation: 19,000   Frequency: Monthly   Subscription: Unknown

132. DENNI HLASATEL.   The Daily Herald. 1891— .
    1545 West 18th Street, Chicago, Illinois 60608
        Editor: Dr. Anton Hrebik   Language: Czech
        Sponsor: Denni Hlasatel Printing and Publishing Company
        Circulation: 17,587   Frequency: Daily   Subscription: $20.00

General, international, and national news of interest to the Czech community.

133. HLASATEL.   The Herald.   1892— .
    1545 West 18th Street, Chicago, Illinois 60608
        Editor: Dr. Anton Hrebik   Language: Czech
        Sponsor: Denni Hlasatel Printing and Publishing Company
        Circulation: 4,622   Frequency: Semi-weekly   Subscription: Unknown

134. HLAS JEDNOTY.   Voice of the Unity.   1894—.
6907 Cermak Road, Berwyn, Illinois 60402
    Editor: R. J. Heukal   Language: Czech and English
    Sponsor: Unity of Czech Ladies and Men
    Circulation: 6,000   Frequency: Quarterly   Subscription: $1.50

This publication focuses primarily on matters pertaining to Fraternal
Life Insurance. Most of the space is devoted to letters from lodge officers
reporting on fraternal activities. Short articles on various subjects and
editorials are also occasionally included.

135. HOSPODAR.   The Farmer.   1889—.
P.O. Box 38, West, Texas 76691
    Editor: Joseph F. Holasek   Language: Czech
    Sponsor: Czechoslovak Publishing Company
    Circulation: 12,050   Frequency: Semi-monthly   Subscription: $6.00

This farmers' magazine features articles on agricultural topics, general
news, and other subjects of interest to the Czech community.

136. KATOLIK.   The Catholic.   1893—.
1637 South Allport Street, Chicago, Illinois 60608
    Editor: Very Rev. Alex Machacek   Language: Czech
    Sponsor: Bohemian Benedictine Order
    Circulation: 2,250   Frequency: Weekly   Subscription: $7.00

Contains articles which pertain to international, national, regional, and
local news. Emphasis is on the Catholic Church and related topics.
Historical and cultural themes pertaining to the origin of the Czechs,
their American setting, and their contributions to the United States
are also included.

137. KATOLICKY DELNIK.   Catholic Workman.   1907—.
Box 277, Dodge, Nebraska 68633
    Editor: Rev. Francis J. Oborny   Language: English and Czech
    Sponsor: Catholic Workmen's Fraternal Association
    Circulation: 15,584   Frequency: Monthly   Subscription: $.50

Regular monthly features include decisions of the Supreme Executive
Council; a list of new members; a list of mortuary claims; the Supreme
Treasurer's Report of Receipts; disbursements and up-to-date assets;
reports of State Executive Councils; news from branches; religious
instructions for the Supreme Spiritual Directory; editor's comments and
articles reprinted from other fraternal magazines.

138. KJZT NEWS.   1955– .
P.O. Box 1884, Austin, Texas
    Editor: Mrs. Benita Pavlu   Language: English and Czech
    Sponsor: Catholic Women's Fraternal of Texas
    Circulation: 10,600 Frequency: Monthly   Subscription: Free to members

This journal functions as a means of communication between members
of the Fraternal Benefit Society, the KJZT. Its contents include primarily
items on events and activities of the society.

139. LEADER-NEWS.   1885– .
P.O. Box 907, El Campo, Texas 77437
    Editor: Herschiel L. Hunt   Language: Czech and English
    Circulation: 5,000   Frequency: Weekly   Subscription: $4.50

140. NÁROD.   The Nation.   1893– .
1637 South Allport Street, Chicago, Illinois 60608
    Editor: Very Rev. Alex Machacek   Language: Czech
    Sponsor: Bohemian Benedictine Order
    Circulation: 2,060   Frequency: Weekly   Subscription: $8.00

This publication, like *Katolik*, is published by the Bohemian
Benedictine Order. Its contents are similar to those of *Katolik*.
However, it consists of two parts: Part one is published in the
Czech language, as a Saturday edition, while Part two is published
in English as a Sunday edition. *Narod* was a daily until 1956.

141. NASINEC.   Fellow Countryman.   1914– .
East Davila Street, P.O. Box 158, Granger, Texas 76530
    Editor: Joe Maresh, Sr.   Language: Czech
    Sponsor: Czech Catholic Union of Texas
    Circulation: 2,010   Frequency: Weekly Subscription: Free to members

142. NOVA DOBA.   New Era.   1937– .
1610 West 18th Street, Chicago, Illinois 60608
    Editor: Charles Musil   Language: Czech
    Sponsor: Nova Doba Publishing Company, Inc.
    Circulation: 1,198   Frequency: Weekly   Subscription: $6.00

143. NOVÝ DOMOV.   New Home.   1894— .
Davilla Street, Granger, Texas 76530
Editor: Walter Malec   Language: Czech
Sponsor: Union of Czech Catholic Women of Texas
Circulation: 3,067   Frequency: Weekly   Subscription: $4.00

144. NOVÝ SVET.   The New World.   1950— .
4732 Broadway, Cleveland, Ohio 44127
Editors: Miloslava Hyvnar, Frank Novotny   Language: Czech
Sponsor: Novy Svet Printing and Publishing Company
Circulation: 3,360   Frequency: Daily   Subscription: Unknown

General, international, national, and local news.

145. POSEL.   The Messenger.   1926— .
1637 South Allport Street, Chicago, Illinois 60608
Editor: Ernest Zizka   Language: Czech
Sponsor: The Czech Catholic Union
Circulation: 6,000   Frequency: Quarterly   Subscription: Free to members

146. PRAVDA A SLAVNA NADEJE.   Truth and Glorious Hope.   1919— .
316 South Park Street, Westmont, Illinois 60559
Editor: Rev. J. P. Piroch   Language: Czech and Slovak
Sponsor: Czechoslovak Baptist Convention of U.S. and Canada
Circulation: 1,027   Frequency: Monthly   Subscription: Unknown

147. PROMĚNY.   Metamorphoses.   1964— .
Room 1121, 381 Park Avenue South, New York, New York 10016
Editor: Dr. Vratislav Bušek, New York representative on Editorial Board
Language: Czech and Slovak
Sponsor: Czechoslovak Society of Arts and Sciences in America
Circulation: 750   Frequency: Quarterly   Subscription: $7.50

This is a literary quarterly whose sections are devoted to poetry; scholarly
articles on philosophy, economics, political science, history, and art; short
stories; critical book reviews and other fields in the humanities and the
social sciences. The articles in *Promeny* are indexed in the *MLA International Bibliography.*

148. SOKOL TYRS NEWSLETTER.
3689 East 131st Street, Cleveland, Ohio 44120
Editor: Elsie V. Suster   Language: Czech and English
Sponsor: American Sokol Gymnastic Organization
Circulation: Unknown   Frequency: Bi-monthly   Subscription: Unknown

This is a fraternal magazine featuring sports news.

149. SPJST VESTNIK.   SPJST Herald.   1897— .
Oak Street, West, Texas 76691
Editor: Rudy J. Sefcik   Language: English and Czech
Sponsor: Slavonic Benevolent Order of the State of Texas
Circulation: 11,760   Frequency: Weekly   Subscription: $4.50

This weekly is strictly fraternal in nature. It contains two parts; Part
one is in English and Part two is in Czech. The contents of the publication include newsbriefs and features on members; letters and reports
from the various lodges concerning their social, cultural, and financial
matters; and a section devoted to youth activities which includes
reports and letters from district youth directors, lodge youth leaders,
and youth members.

150. SVOBODNA ŠKOLA.   Free Thinking School.   1893— .
1904 South 61st Avenue, Cicero, Illinois 60650
Editor: Frances Hrdlicka   Language: Czech
Sponsor: Bohemian Free Thinking School Society
Circulation: 600   Frequency: Bi-monthly   Subscription: Unknown

151. SVOBODNE ČESKOSLOVENSKO.   Free Czechoslovakia.   1943— .
4029 West 25th Place, Chicago, Illinois 60623
Editor: Mrs. Bela Kotrsal   Language: Czech
Sponsor: Czech American National Alliance
Circulation: 800   Frequency: Monthly   Subscription: $2.00

This monthly is political in nature.

152. TEXASKY ROLNIK.   Texas Farmer.   1930— .
P.O. Box 426, Granger, Texas 76530
Editor: Joseph Maresh, Sr.   Language: Czech
Sponsor: Farmers Mutual Protection Association of Texas
Circulation: Unknown   Frequency: Quarterly
Subscription: Free to members

153. VEK ROSUMU.   The Age of Reason.   1910— .
4124 West 26th Street, Chicago, Illinois 60623
    Editor: Victor Cejka   Language: Czech
    Circulation: 514   Frequency: Weekly   Subscription: Unknown

154. VĚSTNIK.   Herald.   1954— .
2137 South Lombard Avenue, Cicero, Illinois 60650
    Editor: Vlasta Vraz   Language: Czech
    Sponsor: Czechoslovak National Council of America
    Circulation: 3,030   Frequency: Monthly   Subscription: $2.00

This magazine serves as a forum of expression mainly for members of the
Czechoslovak National Council of America. Contents include reports on
the activities of the Czech and Slovak communities in the United States,
articles on latest events in Czechoslovakia and in the United States from
the standpoint of the Czech-Slovak American citizens, and articles
devoted to the Czechoslovak culture. The journal is an "anti-communist
organ which stresses the importance of the struggle against Communist
and other totalitarian domination" [editor's statement].

155. VĚSTNIK.   Herald.   1916— .
P.O. Box 85, West, Texas 76691
    Editor: R. J. Sefcik   Language: Czech and English
    Sponsor: Slavonic Benevolent Order of Texas
    Circulation: 10,587   Frequency: Weekly   Subscription: Unknown

156. ZPRAVODAJ.   Reporter.   1969— .
2619 South Lawndale Avenue, Chicago, Illinois 60623
    Editor: Unknown   Language: Czech
    Sponsor: Alliance of Czechoslovak Exiles in Chicago
    Circulation: Unknown   Frequency: Monthly   Subscription: Unknown

157. ZPRÁVY SVU.   Bulletin of the Czechoslovak Society of Arts and
    Sciences in America.   1959— .
Room 1121, 381 Park Avenue South, New York, New York 10016
    Editor: Dr. Vratislav Bušek   Language: Czech and Slovak
    Sponsor: Czechoslovak Society of Arts and Sciences in America
    Circulation: 1,190   Frequency: Monthly   Subscription: $3.00

This bulletin includes announcements of its sponsoring organization; reports
on activities of local chapters and individual members, news items of
interest in the arts and sciences; book reviews; and biographic and
bibliographic items.

Czech Publications in English

158. AMERICAN BULLETIN.   1957— .
    4125 West 26th Street, Chicago, Illinois 60623
        Editor: Vlasta Vraz   Language: English
        Sponsor: Czechoslovak National Council of America
        Circulation: Unknown   Frequency: Monthly   Subscription: Unknown

DANISH PRESS

Danish and Danish-English Publications

159. BIEN.   The Bee.   1882— .
    435 Duboce Avenue, San Francisco, California 94117
        Editor: Sven Stribolt   Language: Danish
        Sponsor: Bien Publishing Company
        Circulation: 3,500   Frequency: Weekly   Subscription: $7.00

This newspaper is the only Danish weekly in the United States. Its
contents include national, international, and local news, plus coverage
of group activities and events. The main objective of this publication is
to "maintain and support the Danish language and customs" [editor's
statement].

160. DER DANSKE PIONEER.   The Danish Pioneer.   1872— .
    35 Elmwood Parkway, Elmwood Park, Illinois 60635
        Editor: Hjalmar Bertelsen   Language: Danish and English
        Sponsor: Bertelsen Publishing Company
        Circulation: 4,700   Frequency: Bi-weekly   Subscription: $7.00

This paper provides news coverage of events in Denmark and the United
States. Activities by Danish groups throughout the United States and
feature items on individuals and their accomplishments are also included.

Danish Publications in English

161. THE DANA REVIEW.   1945— .
    2848 College Drive, Dana College, Blair, Nebraska 68008
        Editor: Kenneth Anderson   Language: English
        Sponsor: Dana College and Trinity Seminary
        Circulation: 6,000   Frequency: Monthly   Subscription: Free to alumni

162. DANISH BROTHERHOOD MAGAZINE.   1926— .
P.O. Box 155, Askov, Minnesota 55704
    Editor: Einar Danielsen   Language: English
    Sponsor: Danish Brotherhood in America
    Circulation: 10,000   Frequency: Monthly   Subscription: $.50

163. DANISH SISTERHOOD NEWS.   1947— .
3438 North Opal Avenue, Chicago, Illinois 60634
    Editor: Mrs. Virginia Christensen   Language: English
    Sponsor: Danish Sisterhood of America
    Circulation: 4,500   Frequency: Monthly   Subscription: $.50

The purpose of this publication is to provide information concerning the
activities of lodges in the various states. Contents also include funeral
benefit notices, listings of new members, and general information pertaining to the members' duties and rights within the organization.

164. PHOEBE.   1905— .
P.O. Box B, Brush, Colorado 80723
    Editor: Rev. Raymond M. Paulsen   Language: English
    Sponsor: Eben-Ezer Lutheran Institute
    Circulation: Unknown   Frequency: Bi-monthly Subscription: Unknown

DUTCH PRESS

Dutch and Dutch-English Publications

165. THE HOLLAND HOME NEWS.   1912— .
1450 East Fulton Street, Grand Rapids, Michigan 49503
    Editor: Thomas A. DeGroot   Language: English and Dutch
    Sponsor: The Holland Union Benevolent Association
    Circulation: 4,000   Frequency: Monthly   Subscription: $1.00 donation

This publication serves primarily as a public relations instrument to keep
the Association members informed of activities and current events which
relate to the Association and its members. The paper includes articles on
a variety of topics of special interest to members and their families.

166. DE WACHTER.   The Watchman.   1868– .
2850 Kalamazoo Avenue, S.E., Grand Rapids, Michigan 49508
  Editor: Rev. William Haverkamp   Language: Dutch
  Sponsor: Christian Reformed Church
  Circulation: 2,850   Frequency: Bi-weekly Subscription: $4.00

Serves as an organ of the Christian Reformed Church. Content is
religious in nature. Articles on various aspects of the Church's activities
and affairs are included.

Dutch Publications in English

167. ATLANTIC OBSERVER–KNICKERBOCKER INTERNATIONAL.   1938–
P.O. Box 554, Lenox Hill Station, New York, New York
  Editor: Albert C. Balink   Language: English
  Sponsor: Atlantic Observer, Inc.
  Circulation: Unknown   Frequency: Monthly   Subscription: $6.00

This journal is primarily devoted to analyzing the economic policies and
situations in Holland. Various types of economic cooperation between
Holland and other countries, particularly the United States, are stressed.
The purpose of this publication is to "promote better relationships between
the United States and the Netherlands in business" [editor's statement] .

168. THE BANNER.   1866– .
2850 Kalamazoo Avenue, S.E., Grand Rapids, Michigan 49508
  Editor: Rev. John Vander Ploeg   Language: English
  Sponsor: Christian Reformed Publishing House
  Circulation: 45,000   Frequency: Weekly   Subscription: $5.00

This journal is the official organ of the Christian Reformed Church. Its
chief objectives are "to promote denominational activity and to provide
families with religious reading relevant to today's needs" [editor's state-
ment] . Although the contents reflect the spiritual aspects of life, articles
dealing with relevant topics in today's world are also included.

169. DE HALVE MAEN.   The Half Moon.   1922– .
122 East 58th Street, New York, New York 10022
  Editor: Richard H. Amerman   Language: English
  Sponsor: Holland Society of New York
  Circulation: 1,500 Frequency: Quarterly Subscription: Free to member

Historical in nature. Contents include articles on the history of the early
Dutch settlers in America (1609-1675), their contribution to American
life, and the genealogy of Dutch families from the earliest times to

date. Items on the activities of the Society and its members are also printed. In order to qualify for membership the applicant must show proof of being a descendent of a colonist who lived in New Netherland during or before 1675.

170. THE HOLLAND REPORTER.   1960— .
3680 Division Street, Los Angeles, California 90065
     Editor: Marinus W. M. Van Der Steen   Language: English
     Circulation: 7,640   Frequency: Weekly   Subscription: $6.00

Family Dutch-American weekly. Includes news from Holland and from the Dutch community in the United States.

ESTONIAN PRESS

Estonian Publications

171. MEIE TEE.   Our Path.   1941—.
243 East 43rd Street, New York, New York 10016
     Editor: Harald Raudsepp   Language: Estonian
     Sponsor: World Association of Estonians
     Circulation: 1,026   Frequency: Bi-monthly   Subscription: $4.00

This monthly is highly political in tone. Questions of a cultural and political nature of interest to Estonians are discussed. Ideologically it presents a strong anti-communist view, with a pro-American leaning.

172. UUS ILM.   The New World.   1909— .
77 Park Avenue, New York, New York 10016
     Editor: Michael Nukk   Language: Estonian
     Sponsor: Uus Ilm Publishing Company, Inc.
     Circulation: 800   Frequency: Monthly   Subscription: $4.00

Official organ of the Estonian Progressive Society "Kiir." Contains items on group activities and events. Also includes articles on labor problems.

173. VABA EESTI SONA.   Free Estonian Word.   1949— .
243 East 34th Street, New York, New York 10016
     Editor: Erich Ernits and Harald Raudsepp   Language: Estonian
     Sponsor: Nordic Press, Inc.
     Circulation: 4,000   Frequency: Weekly   Subscription: $13.50

General, international, and national news coverage.

FILIPINO PRESS

Filipino Publications in English

174. FILIPINO AMERICAN WORLD.   1968— .
    800 Southern Avenue, S.E., Room 408, Washington, D.C. 20032
        Editor: Dr. Elias J. Umali   Language: English
        Sponsor: Filipino International Community Newsletter, Inc.
        Circulation: 10,000   Frequency: Monthly   Subscription: $3.00

    This is primarily a publication for Filipino-Americans in the United
    States and Canada. Special features include Personality of the month;
    Regional headlines; a pictorial page; Philippine news; Speaking out;
    poetry corner; directory; etc. This publication aims at presenting social,
    educational, cultural, and political activities of the Filipino-American
    communities both here and abroad.

175. FILIPINO FORUM.   1928— .
    4627 43rd Avenue South, Seattle, Washington 98119
        Editor: Martin J. Sibonga   Language: English
        Circulation: 2,000   Frequency: Monthly   Subscription: $5.00

    Contains news and articles on the Filipino-American community.
    "We believe, also, each minority can—and should—retain its ethnic
    heritage as each maintains its share in the quest for civil rights, for
    everyone" [editor's statement] .

176. LAGING UNA.   Always First.   1949— .
    3003 Future Place, Los Angeles, California 90065
        Editor: Martires M. Monosco   Language: English
        Circulation: 5,000   Frequency: Monthly   Subscription: $2.50

    Provides expatriate Filipinos in the United States with news of the
    Philippines. Contains editorial analyses of the socioeconomic and
    political problems of the Philippines, Southeast Asia, Africa, Europe, and
    the Americas. Ideologically, this publication is of a leftist leaning.

177. THE MABUHAY REPUBLIC.   1969— .
    833 Market Street, Room 502, San Francisco, California 94103
        Editor: J. T. Esteva   Language: English
        Sponsor: Philippine Service Company
        Circulation: 3,450   Frequency: Monthly   Subscription: $2.00

This publication serves as the "voice" of the Filipino community in California. Prime objective is to report on the social and cultural life of the Filipino community. Items on the contribution of individual Filipinos are also included.

178. PHILIPPINE AMERICAN.   1960— .
     395 Broadway (Suite 1209), New York, New York 10013
         Editor: Teddy de Nolasco   Language: English
         Circulation: 25,000   Frequency: Semi-monthly   Subscription: $3.00

This newspaper contains news on international, national, and local affairs. Items about the Philippines and Filipinos in the United States are frequent. Sections are also devoted to commentaries, letters to the editor, and social events.

179. THE PHILIPPINES MAIL.   1930— .
     P.O. Box 1783, Salinas, California 93901
         Editor: Delfin F. Cruz   Language: English
         Circulation: 3,300   Frequency: Monthly   Subscription: $3.00

News on international, national, and local affairs and events, with emphasis on the Philippines and Filipino groups in the United States. Also included are commentaries and articles on various issues and topics of special interest to the Filipino communities in this country.

FINNISH PRESS

Finnish and Finnish-English Publications

180. AMERIKAN UUTISET.   American News.   1932— .
     P.O. Box 125, New York Mills, Minnesota 56567
         Editor: Toivo Halonen   Language: Finnish
         Sponsor: Northwestern Publishing Company
         Circulation: 5,390   Frequency: Semi-weekly   Subscription: $11.00

General, international, national, and local news of interest to the Finnish community.

181. INDUSTRIALISTI.   Industrialist.   1917— .
     106 East First Street, Duluth, Minnesota 55802
         Editor: Ivar Vapaa   Language: Finnish and English
         Sponsor: Workers Publishing Company
         Circulation: 2,548   Frequency: Semi-weekly   Subscription: $8.00

182. NAISTEN VIIRI.   Women's Banner.   1910— .
601 Tower Avenue, Superior, Wisconsin 54880
    Editor: Mary Kolehmainen   Language: Finnish
    Sponsor: Tyomies Society
    Circulation: 2,586   Frequency: Weekly   Subscription: $5.00

This publication features news and articles of interest to Finnish
women.

183. NEW YORKIN UUTISET.   The Finnish New York News.   1906— .
4418-22 Eighth Avenue, Brooklyn, New York 11220
    Editor: Esa Arra   Language: Finnish
    Sponsor: Finnish Newspaper Company, Inc.
    Circulation: 2,580   Frequency: Semi-weekly   Subscription: $15.00

Contains news of a general nature. Also includes items on various
cultural and social activities and events among the Finnish people.

184. RAIVAAJA.   The Pioneer.   1905— .
48 Wallace Avenue, Fitchburg, Massachusetts 01420
    Editor: Savele Syrjala   Language: Finnish
    Sponsor: Finnish American League for Democracy
    Circulation: 2,680   Frequency: Semi-weekly   Subscription: $12.00

185. RAUHAN TERVEHDYS.   Peace Greetings.   1920— .
120 Amygdaloid Street, Laurium, Michigan 49913
    Editors: Walter Torola and P. A. Heidman   Language: Finnish
    Sponsor: Finnish Apostolic Lutheran Church of America
    Circulation: 750   Frequency: Monthly   Subscription: $1.50

Contains religious news and articles on the Finnish Lutheran Church,
its parishes and parishioners.

186. SUOMI-OPISTON VIESTI.   Message.   1958— .
Hancock, Michigan. 49930
    Editor: E. Olaf Rankinen   Language: Finnish
    Sponsor: Suomi College
    Circulation: 6,000   Frequency: Quarterly   Subscription: Free

This publication is a college quarterly. All items are related to the
activities, events, and affairs of Suomi College.

187. TYOMIES-ETEENPAIN.   Workingman-Forward.   1903— .
     601-3 Tower Avenue, Superior, Wisconsin 54880
          Editor: Frank Walli   Language: Finnish
          Sponsor: Tyomies Society
          Circulation: 2,080   Frequency: 3 times/week   Subscription: $10.00

     This publication serves the interests of American-Finns in cultural,
     political, and trade union fields.

Finnish Publications in English

188. FINAM NEWS LETTER.   1962— .
     P.O. Box 3515, Portland, Oregon 97208
          Editor: Walter Mattila   Language: English
          Sponsor: Finnish American Historical Society of the West
          Circulation: 400   Frequency: Irregular   Subscription: $1.50; members only

     Includes promotional literature on Finns in the West, as well as research
     into the various achievements of Finnish pioneers.

FLEMISH PRESS

see BELGIAN-FLEMISH PRESS

FRENCH PRESS

French and French-English Publications

189. L'ACTION.   Action.   1950— .
     136 Middle Street, Manchester, New Hampshire 03101
          Editor: Paul Giugras   Language: French
          Sponsor: Franco-American Publishing Corporation
          Circulation: 4,500   Frequency: Weekly   Subscription: $5.00

     The principal objective of this publication is to "preserve the French
     language among French descendants in the U.S." [editor's statement].
     The newspaper is also distributed to both teachers and students of French
     in the United States. It contains news of a general and group nature.

190. LE CALIFORNIEN.   The Californian.   1963— .
1603 Hyde Street, San Francisco, California 94109
    Editor: Pierre Idiart   Language: French
    Sponsor: Le Californien Publishing Company
    Circulation: 1,900   Frequency: Weekly   Subscription: $8.50

Contains news items on world affairs, political and cultural events in France, and social and cultural activities among the French-Americans in California and other states. Also included are editorials; excerpts from *Le Monde, Le Figaro, Paris Match,* etc.; and a page for women.

191. LE CANADO-AMÉRICAIN.   The American Canadian.   1900— .
52 Concord Street, Manchester, New Hampshire 03101
    Editor: Gérald Robert   Language: French
    Sponsor: Association Canado-Américaine
    Circulation: 16,500   Frequency: Quarterly   Subscription: $2.00

This is the official publication of the Association Canado-Américaine, a fraternal insurance society. It includes reports on fraternal activities in its courts and villas, as well as at the home office.

192. FRANCE-AMÉRIQUE—LE COURRIER FRANÇAIS DES ÉTATS-UNIS.
    The French Newspaper in the United States.   1827— .
1111 Lexington Avenue, New York, New York 10021
    Editor: Jacques Habert   Language: French
    Sponsor: Tricolor Publications Inc.
    Circulation: 35,000   Frequency: Weekly   Subscription: $8.00

This is the oldest French language newspaper in the United States. Principal emphasis is placed on news from France and news about the French in the United States. Also included are international news, comments on world events, a literary page, feature articles, interviews, movies, art, theater, music, fashion, sports, short stories, etc. Well illustrated.

193. LA LIBERTÉ NEWS.   Liberty.   1909— .
872 Main Street, Fitchburg, Massachusetts 01421
    Editor: Jerome R. Rand   Language: French
    Sponsor: La Liberté Publishing Company
    Circulation: 3,500   Frequency: Bi-weekly   Subscription: $4.25

194. LE MESSAGER.   The Messenger.   1879— .
225 Lisbon Street, Lewiston, Maine 04240
    Editor: Roger P. Saucier   Language: French
    Sponsor: Le Messager Publishing Company
    Circulation: 1,227   Frequency: Weekly   Subscription: Unknown

195. MIEUX VIVRE.   Better Living.   1917— .
1350 Villa Street, Mountain View, California 94040
    Editor: Serve V. Collins   Language: French
    Sponsor: Seventh Day Adventist Church
    Circulation: 5,000   Frequency: Monthly   Subscription: $4.00

Published by the Seventh Day Adventist Church for the French-speaking
public. Primarily includes articles on religious teachings.

196. LA SALETTE.   1969— .
Enfield, New Hampshire 03748
    Editor: Rev. Donald Jeffrey, M.S.
    Language: French and English (alternate months)
    Sponsor: La Salette Center of Light
    Circulation: 15,100   Frequency: Bi-monthly   Subscription: $2.00

A bi-monthly newsletter published in French and English editions by the
La Salette Center of Light. Materials of an informative nature are
limited to the activities of the La Salette Fathers.

197. LE TRAVAILLEUR.   The Hustler.   1931— .
P.O. Box 314, Linwood, Massachusetts 01525
    Editor: Wilfrid Beaulieu   Language: French
    Sponsor: Le Travailleur
    Circulation: 5,000   Frequency: Weekly   Subscription: $5.00

A weekly devoted to the recording and promotion of Franco-American
activities. Articles are devoted to literary, cultural, educational, historical,
and other topics.

198. L'UNION.   The Union.   1902— .
1 Social Street, Woonsocket, Rhode Island 02895
    Editor: Gabriel Crevier   Language: French
    Sponsor: Union Saint-Jean-Baptiste
    Circulation: 45,100   Frequency: Quarterly   Subscription: Free to members

Official organ of the Union Saint-Jean-Baptiste, a mutual benefit fraternal
society. Informs members of activities of home office and 225 lodges.

French Publications in English

199. AMERICAN SOCIETY LEGION OF HONOR MAGAZINE.   1930– .
22 East 60th Street, New York, New York 10022
Editor: Sylviane Glad   Language: English
Sponsor: American Society of the French Legion of Honor
Circulation: Unknown   Frequency: 3 times/year
Subscription: Free to members of the Society, selected universities,
and public libraries in the United States and abroad

The objective of this journal is to promote appreciation in the United
States of French culture and to strengthen the friendship between the
people of the United States and France. Articles are devoted to history,
art, literature, music, and other subjects related to French and American
culture.

GEORGIAN PRESS

Georgian Publications

200. GEORGIAN OPINION.   1951– .
149 Avenue A, New York, New York 10009
Editor: M. Sindikeli   Language: Georgian
Sponsor: Georgian National Alliance
Circulation: 1,000   Frequency: Bi-monthly   Subscription: $10.00

Provides "the opinion of immigrees of Georgian origin on historical and
current events. Its purpose is to keep the hope that some day the men
and women within Georgia will be able to express and enjoy individual
freedom" [editor's statement].

GERMAN PRESS

German and German-English Publications

201. ABENDPOST.   Eveningpost.   1878– .
223 West Washington Street, Chicago, Illinois 60606
Editor: Werner Baroni   Language: German
Sponsor: The Abendpost Company
Circulation: 17,000   Frequency: Daily   Subscription: $13.50

News coverage of international and national events. Also includes news items of activities and developments in Germany and reports on events occurring within German communities in the United States.

202. AMERICA HEROLD—LINCOLN FREIE PRESSE.   America Herald
     & Lincoln Free Press.   1873— .
     2002 North 16th Street, Omaha, Nebraska 68110
         Editor: William Peter   Language: German
         Sponsor: Tribune Publishing Company
         Circulation: 5,223   Frequency: Weekly   Subscription: $6.50

International, national, and local news coverage of interest to the German community.

203. AMERIKANISCHE SCHWEIZER ZEITUNG.   American Swiss
     Gazette.   1868— .
     1 Union Square West, Room 410, New York, New York 10003
         Editor: Franz X. Amrein   Language: German and English
         Sponsor: Swiss Publishing Company
         Circulation: 2,400   Frequency: Weekly   Subscription: $8.00

See also SWISS PRESS.

204. AUFBAU.   Reconstruction.   1934— .
     2121 Broadway, New York, New York 10023
         Editor: Dr. Hans Steinitz   Language: German and English
         Sponsor: New World Club, Inc.
         Circulation: 31,000   Frequency: Weekly   Subscription: $10.50

This newspaper was first created to represent the interests and viewpoints of German, mostly Jewish, refugees from Hitler's Germany. Editorially it represents several major themes: the cultural German background, Jewish faith and traditions, and a loyalty to the United States. Contents include special correspondents, reports on life in Germany and Israel, coverage of cultural life, literature, theater, music, etc. Special sections and supplements are devoted to such topics as life on the West Coast, the German restitution issues, book reviews, vacation and travel, etc.

205. BAHN FREI.   Clear Track.   1883— .
     Lexington Avenue & 85th Street, New York, New York 10028
         Editor: Walter Pfister   Language: German
         Sponsor: New York Turn Verein
         Circulation: 800   Frequency: Monthly   Subscription: $2.00

206. BALTIMORE CORRESPONDENT.   1841– .
2002 North 16th Street, Omaha, Nebraska 68101
    Editor: Mrs. B. C. Snider   Language: German
    Sponsor: Tribune Publishing Company
    Circulation: Unknown   Frequency: Weekly   Subscription: $7.50

This paper presents news of general interest to the German-speaking community.

207. BUFFALO VOLKSFREUND.   Buffalo People's Friend.   1868– .
3614 South Creek Road, Hamburg, New Jersey 14075
    Editor: Burt Erickson Nelson   Language: German
    Sponsor: Tribune Publishing Company
    Circulation: 1,500   Frequency: Weekly   Subscription: $7.50

This publication provides coverage of western New York State's German-American communities, and includes articles of state, national, and international news, with an emphasis on German-speaking countries. Ads for this family newspaper are translated into German and are also accepted in English.

208. CALIFORNIA FREIE PRESSE. California Free Press. 1949– .
149 California Street, Room 224, San Francisco, California 94111
    Editor: Mrs. Liselotte Siou   Language: German
    Sponsor: Tribune Publishing Company
    Circulation: 2,640   Frequency: Weekly   Subscription: $6.50

209. CALIFORNIA STAATS-ZEITUNG.   California State Journal.   1890– .
221 East Pico Boulevard, Los Angeles, California 90015
    Editor: Albert Ebert   Language: German
    Sponsor: Raymond E. Stuetz, Publisher
    Circulation: 10,100 Frequency: Weekly   Subscription: $3.00

210. CINCINNATI KURIER.   Cincinnati Courier.   1964– .
432 Walnut Street, Cincinnati, Ohio 45202
    Editor: Marie Lamers-Engel   Language: German
    Sponsor: Peter Publications
    Circulation: 2,700   Frequency: Weekly   Subscription: $7.50

International and national news, sports features, and women's page. Literary materials. Illustrations included.

211. DETROITER ABEND-POST.   Detroiter Evening-Post.   1854— .
1436 Brush Street, Detroit, Michigan 48226
   Editor: Knuth Beth   Language: German
   Sponsor: Detroit Abend-Post Publishing Company
   Circulation: 8,800   Frequency: Semi-weekly   Subscription: $14.95

This newspaper provides political, social, cultural, sports and other news
for German-Americans. Special features include a women's page and a
finance page.

212. DER DEUTSCHAMERIKANER.   The German-American.   1960— .
4740 North Western Avenue, Chicago, Illinois 60625
   Editor: Walter A. Kollacks   Language: German and English
   Sponsor: German American National Congress, Inc.
   Circulation: 12,200   Frequency: Monthly   Subscription: $4.00

This is the official organ of the German American National Congress,
presenting organizational news.

213. DEUTSCHE WOCHENSCHRIFT.   German Weekly.   1939— .
2507 South Jefferson Avenue, St. Louis, Missouri 63104
   Editor: Eugene Geissler   Language: German
   Sponsor: Marie Geissler, owner and publisher
   Circulation: 1,450   Frequency: Weekly   Subscription: $5.00

214. EINTRACHT.   Harmony.   1923— .
9456 North Lawler Street, Skokie, Illinois 60076
   Editor: Gottlieb Juengling   Language: German
   Circulation: 4,250   Frequency: Weekly   Subscription: $7.00

Official organ of the German-Austro-Hungarian Societies. Includes news
from Germany, Austria, and German organizations in Chicago. A special
feature is the permanent sports section with emphasis on soccer-football.
Illustrated.

215. EVANGELISCH-LUTHERISCHES GEMEINDEBLATT.   Evangelical-
   Lutheran Church Letter for Congregations.   1865—1969.
3616-1632 West North Avenue, Milwaukee, Wisconsin 53208
   Editor: Professor Heinrich J. Vogel   Language: German
   Sponsor: Wisconsin Evangelical-Lutheran Synod
   Frequency: Monthly

This weekly, published primarily in Gothic script, promoted teaching of
the Bible as interpreted by the Church of God. Suspended publication
with the December 1969 issue.

216. EVANGELIUMS POSAUNE.   Gospel Trumpet.   1895— .
4912 Northwestern Avenue, Racine, Wisconsin 53406
    Editor: Rev. Fritz Lenk   Language: German
    Sponsor: Christian Unity Press
    Circulation: 2,300   Frequency: Weekly   Subscription: $5.00

217. FLORIDA STAATS-ZEITUNG UND HEROLD.   Florida State Journal
and Herald.   1965— .
60-20 Broadway, Woodside, New York 11377
    Editor: Gerhard Hirseland   Langauge: German
    Sponsor: Staats-Herold Corporation
    Circulation: 2,000   Frequency: Weekly   Subscription: $10.40

Special Florida edition of *New Yorker Staats Zeitung und Herold.*
International, national and regional news. Special coverage of the
activities of German-Americans.

218. DAS FREIE WORT.   Voice of Freedom.
2617 West Fond du Lac Avenue, Milwaukee, Wisconsin 53206
    Editor: Paul A. Kaufmann   Language: German
    Sponsor: Freie Gemeinde
    Circulation: Unknown   Frequency: Unknown   Subscription: Unknown

219. DIE HAUSFRAU.   The Housewife.   1904— .
1517 West Fullerton Avenue, Chicago, Illinois 60614
    Editor: J. Edelman   Language: German
    Sponsor: Die Hausfrau, Inc.
    Circulation: 42,000   Frequency: Monthly   Subscription: $4.00

General interest magazine for the whole family.

220. HEROLD DER WAHRHEIT.   Herald of Truth.   1912— .
Route 2, Kalona, Iowa 52247
    Editors: Lester B. Miller and Jonas J. Beachy
    Language: German and English
    Sponsor: Amish-Mennonite Publishing Association
    Circulation: 1,325   Frequency: Monthly   Subscription: $2.50

This is a religious monthly published in the interest of the Amish
Mennonite Churches. The German section is published in Gothic script.

221. INTERNATIONAL MONTHLY.   1959– .
P.O. Box 8522, San Jose, California 95125
    Editor: Ute Lorenz   Language: German and English
    Sponsor: International Monthly
    Circulation: 6,000   Frequency: Monthly   Subscription: $4.00

Includes a review of the German press and world affairs, cultural and
historical articles, and commentaries on numerous facets of German
life. Special feature: trade and travel news.

222. INTERNATIONALE BIBELLEKTIONEN.   International Bible
    Lessons.   1920– .
4912 Northwestern Avenue, Racine, Wisconsin 53406
    Editor: Rev. Fritz Lenk   Language: German
    Sponsor: Christian Unity Press
    Circulation: 1,200   Frequency: Quarterly   Subscription: $1.00

Promotes the teachings of the Bible as understood by the Church of
God. Gothic script.

223. KATHOLISCHER JUGENFREUND.   Catholic Young People's
    Friend.   1877– .
2001 Devon Avenue, Chicago, Illinois 60645
    Editor: John S. West   Language: German
    Sponsor: Angel Guardian Orphanage
    Circulation: Unknown   Frequency: Monthly   Subscription: Unknown

224. KATHOLISCHES WOCHENBLATT UND DER LANDMANN.   Catholic
    Weekly and the Farmer.   1902– .
P.O. Box 1071, Omaha, Nebraska 68101
    Editor: William Peter   Language: German
    Sponsor: Tribune Publishing Company
    Circulation: 430   Frequency: Weekly   Subscription: Unknown

This weekly presents Catholic and agricultural news.

225. KIRCHLICHES MONATSBLATT FUER DAS EVANGELISCH-
    LUTHERISCHE HAUS.   Church Monthly for the Evangelical
    Lutheran Homes.   1943– .
584 East Geneva Avenue, Philadelphia, Pennsylvania 19120
    Editor: Pastor Karl Schild, S.T.M.   Language: German
    Sponsor: German Interest Conference of the Lutheran Church in America
    Circulation: 3,000   Frequency: Monthly   Subscription: $2.00

Official organ of the German Interest Conference of the Lutheran Church
in America. Features church news of special interest for the German-
speaking congregations. Missionary news, religious poetry, and devotional
material.

226. LOS ANGELES KURIER.   Los Angeles Courier.   1964— .
5858 Hollywood Boulevard, Los Angeles, California 90028
    Editor: Theodore Val Peter   Language: German
    Sponsor: Tribune Publishing Company
    Circulation: 1,390   Frequency: Weekly   Subscription: Unknown

227. DER LUTHERANER.   The Lutheran.   1845— .
3440 Tedmar, St. Louis, Missouri 63139
    Editor: Rev. Herman A. Mayer, D.D.   Language: German
    Sponsor: Concordia Publishing House
    Circulation: 4,675   Frequency: Monthly   Subscription: $2.25

Official organ of the Lutheran Church—Missouri Synod. Contains news
of the activities of the church, plus doctrinal and devotional materials.
Annual subscription includes the bi-weekly *Lutheran Witness Reporter.*
Illustrated.

228. MILWAUKEE DEUTSCHE ZEITUNG.   Milwaukee German Journal. 1890—
223 West Washington Street, Chicago, Illinois 60606
    Editor: William Schnabel   Language: German
    Sponsor: Elmer Relnords, Jr., Publisher
    Circulation: Unknown   Frequency: Daily   Subscription: $21.00

229. MILWAUKEE HEROLD.   Milwaukee Herald.   1854— .
2002 North 16th Street, Omaha, Nebraska 68101
    Editor: William A. Peter   Language: German
    Sponsor: Peter Publications
    Circulation: 1,965   Frequency: Weekly   Subscription: $7.50

This weekly includes general and local news of interest to the German-
speaking community.

230. NACHRICHTEN DER DONAUSCHWABEN IN AMERIKA.   News of
the Danube Swabians in America.   1955— .
4219 North Lincoln Avenue, Chicago, Illinois 60618
Editor: Dr. Jacob Awender   Language: German
Sponsor: Society of the Danube Swabians of the United States
Circulation: 3,200   Frequency: Monthly   Subscription: $2.00

The main objective of this monthly is "to promote the social life, culture, economy and progress of Danube Swabians" [editorial statement]. Contains information on various activities of the Danube Swabians in the United States.

231. NEUE ZEITUNG.   American European Weekly.   1966— .
9471 Hidden Valley Place, Beverly Hills, California 90210
Editor: Heinz Jurisch   Language: German
Sponsor: German American League, Inc.
Circulation: 12,050   Frequency: Weekly   Subscription: $5.00

This weekly covers the highlights of European politics, and presents articles on commerce and travel. Also includes a women's page and reports on sports and local club activities.

232. NEW JERSEY FREIE ZEITUNG.   New Jersey Free Newspaper.   1856— .
P.O. Box 167, Irvington, New Jersey 07111
Editor: Helmut Heimsch   Language: German
Sponsor: New Jersey Freie Zeitung, Inc.
Circulation: 2,175   Frequency: Weekly   Subscription: $4.00

233. NEW YORKER STAATS-ZEITUNG UND HEROLD.   New York
State Journal and Herald.   1834— .
60-20 Broadway, Woodside, New York 11377
Editor: Gerhard Hirseland   Language: German
Sponsor: Staats-Herold Corporation
Circulation: 38,000   Frequency: Daily   Subscription: $32.00

This is one of the most influential German dailies in the United States. International, national, and regional news is presented, with the emphasis on German events. Special coverage is given to the German-American community. Special Florida and Philadelphia editions.

234. OSTFRIESEN ZEITUNG.   East Frisia News.   1881— .
Wall Lake, Iowa 51466
    Editor: D. B. Aden   Language: German
    Circulation: 1,275   Frequency: Monthly   Subscription: $3.00

235. PHILADELPHIA GAZETTE-DEMOCRAT.   1838— .
Reading Terminal Arcade, Room 217, 12th and Market Streets,
    Philadelphia, Pennsylavnia 19107
    Editor: Erwin Single   Language: German
    Sponsor: Staats-Herold Corporation
    Circulation: 8,000   Frequency: Weekly   Subscription: $10.40

News, commentary, and analysis of domestic, world-wide, and German
events with special emphasis on Germany and German-Americans.
Illustrated. Major German weekly in Pennsylvania.

236. PLATTDEUTSCHE POST.   Platt-German Post.   1934— .
91 New Dorp Plaza, Staten Island, New York 10306
    Editor: Herbert Stein   Language: German
    Sponsor: Plattdeutsche Post, Inc.
    Circulation: 2,257   Frequency: Weekly   Subscription: $4.00

General and local news published in German dialect.

237. SAENGER ZEITUNG.   Journal for Singers.   1924— .
1832 Hillsdale Avenue, Dayton, Ohio 45414
    Editor: Walter Hoops   Language: German and English
    Sponsor: Federation of Workers' Singing Societies of America
    Circulation: 700   Frequency: Monthly   Subscription: Members

Official organ of the Federation of Workers' Singing Societies of the
United States. Publishes reports of the affiliated singing societies and
promotes various song festivals.

238. DER SENDBOTE.   The Messenger.   1853— .
7308 Madison Street, Forest Park, Illinois 60130
    Editor: Rev. Reinhold J. Kerstan   Language: German
    Sponsor: North American Baptist General Conference (Roger Williams Press
    Circulation: 3,000   Frequency: Monthly   Subscription: $3.50

Monthly magazine of North American Baptists. Contains religious materials
and denominational news. Subjects covered include race relations, war and
peace, poverty, pornography, etc. Illustrated.

239. SIEBENBUERGISCH-AMERIKANISCHES VOLKSBLATT.
Transylvanian-American People's Letter.   1905— .
1436 Brush Street, Detroit, Michigan 48226
　　Editor: Berthold Vogt　　　Language: German
　　Sponsor: Central Verband der Siebenbuerger Sachsen of the U.S.
　　Circulation: 3,850　　Frequency: Weekly　　Subscription: $3.25

240. SONNTAGSPOST.   Sunday Post.   1873— .
2002 North 16th Street, Omaha, Nebraska 68110
　　Editor: William Peter　　　Language: German
　　Sponsor: Tribune Publishing Company
　　Circulation: 5,219　　Frequency: Weekly　　Subscription: $6.50

This is an independent weekly featuring general and local news.

241. DER STAATS-ANZEIGER.   State Advertiser.   1906— .
622 12th Street, Bismarck, North Dakota 58501
　　Editor: Phillip Wall　　　Language: German
　　Sponsor: Tribune Publishing Company
　　Circulation: 789　　Frequency: Weekly　　Subscription: $6.50

242. ST. JOSEPH'S BLATT.   St. Joseph's Page.   1888— .
Mount Angel Abbey, St. Benedict, Oregon 97373
　　Editor: Manfred Ellenberger　　　Language: German
　　Sponsor: Benedictine Press
　　Circulation: 4,874　　Frequency: Semi-monthly　　Subscription: $5.00

This is a Catholic religious magazine.

243. THE SWISS AMERICAN
603 Forest Avenue, Paramus, New Jersey 07652
　　Editor: Anton Haemmerle　　　Language: German
　　Sponsor: North American Swiss Alliance
　　Circulation: Unknown　　Frequency: Monthly　　Subscription: Unknown

See also SWISS PRESS

244. TÄGLICHE ANDACHTEN.   Daily Devotions.   1937— .
3558 South Jefferson Avenue, St. Louis, Missouri 63118
　　Editor: Rudolph F. Norden　　　Language: German
　　Sponsor: The Lutheran Church—Missouri Synod
　　Circulation: 28,880　　Frequency: Bi-monthly　　Subscription: $1.25

This bi-monthly publication contains daily devotions consisting of
Biblical text. The authors are mostly retired pastors.

245. VOLKSZEITUNG TRIBUNE.   People's Journal and Tribune.   1875— .
P.O. Box 1071, Omaha, Nebraska 68101
    Editor: William Peter   Language: German
    Sponsor: Tribune Publishing Company
    Circulation: 1,770   Frequency: Weekly   Subscription: $6.50

This independent weekly contains general news of interest to the
German community.

246. WAECHTER UND ANZEIGER.   Observer and Announcer.   1852— .
4164 Lorain Avenue, Cleveland, Ohio 44113
    Editor: Stefan Deubel   Language: German
    Sponsor: Waechter und Anzeiger Publishing Company
    Circulation: 3,550   Frequency: Weekly   Subscription: $6.00

This weekly publishes mostly international, society, and local news.

247. WASHINGTON JOURNAL.   1859— .
3132 M Street N.W., Washington, D.C. 20007
    Editor: Gerald R. Kainz   Language: German
    Sponsor: Washington Journal, Inc.
    Circulation: Unknown   Frequency: Weekly   Subscription: $9.50

International, national, and local news. Includes feature articles on
Germany and news items on the activities of German-Americans.
Illustrated.

248. DIE WELT POST.   The World Post.   1916— .
P.O. Box 1071, Omaha, Nebraska 68110
    Editor: William Peter   Language: German
    Circulation: 527   Frequency: Weekly   Subscription: $6.50

249. ZEICHEN DER ZEIT.   Signs of the Times.   1879— .
1350 Villa Street, Mountain View, California 94040
    Editor: Gustav G. Tobler   Language: German
    Sponsor: Pacific Press Publishing Association
    Circulation: 10,000   Frequency: Weekly   Subscription: $4.00

Contains religious materials, interpretation of Biblical texts, and Bible
history.

German Publications in English

250. AMERICAN TURNER TOPICS.   1885– .
   1550 Clinton Avenue North, Rochester, New York 14621
      Editor: Dr. E. A. Eklund   Language: English
      Sponsor: American Turners
      Circulation: 15,298   Frequency: Bi-monthly
      Subscription: Included in membership dues

   Features recreational and sports articles and general news.

251. BAY AREA INTERNATIONAL MONTHLY.   1959– .
   P.O. Box 322, San Jose, California 94133
      Editor: S. Scott Lee   Language: English
      Sponsor: Scott Lee Services
      Circulation: Unknown   Frequency: Monthly   Subscription: Unknown

252. THE BLACK AND RED.   1897– .
   Northwestern College, Watertown, Wisconsin 53094
      Editor: Lloyd H. Lemke   Language: English
      Sponsor: Students of Northwestern College
      Circulation: 850   Frequency: Monthly   Subscription: $2.50

   This is a student paper whose objective is "to encourage students in
   preparation for the Lutheran ministry in the Wisconsin Evangelical
   Lutheran Synod (WELS)" [editor's statement].

253. THE BULLETIN OF THE HOME FOR AGED LUTHERANS.   1959– .
   7500 West North Avenue, Wauwatosa, Wisconsin 53213
      Editor: Rev. William T. Baaess   Language: English
      Sponsor: Home for Aged Lutherans
      Circulation: 10,000   Frequency: Quarterly   Subscription: Unknown
   Contains news items concerning the Home of Aged Lutherans. Illustrated.

254. CATHOLIC WOMEN'S JOURNAL.   1921– .
   3835 Westminster Place, St. Louis, Missouri 63108
      Editor: Harvey Johnson   Language: English
      Sponsor: National Catholic Women's Union
      Circulation: 1,446   Frequency: Monthly   Subscription: $1.50

255. G.B.U. REPORTER.   1892— .
   4254 Clairton Boulevard, Pittsburgh, Pennsylvania 15227
       Editor: Karl Filsinger   Language: English
       Sponsor: Greater Beneficial Union of Pittsburgh
       Circulation: 20,150   Frequency: Monthly   Subscription: Unknown
   A fraternal magazine.

256. GERMAN AMERICAN TRADE NEWS.   1946— .
   666 Fifth Avenue, New York, New York 10019
       Editor: Peter F. Kerr   Language: English
       Sponsor: German American Chamber of Commerce
       Circulation: Unknown   Frequency: Monthly   Subscription: $5.00
   This monthly is dedicated to economic and financial information. Special
   section covers United States—German business.

257. KOLPING BANNER.   1929— .
   125 North Stratton Lane, Mt. Prospect, Illinois
       Editor: Herbert Bauer   Language: English
       Sponsor: Catholic Kolping Society of America
       Circulation: 2,148   Frequency: Monthly   Subscription: $1.00
   A fraternal monthly.

258. LUXEMBOURG NEWS OF AMERICA.   1967— .
   201 Sunset Drive, Wilmette, Illinois 60091
       Editor: Victor Jacoby   Language: English
       Sponsor: Luxembourgers of America
   See LUXEMBOURG PRESS, p. 150.

259. THE MELTING POT.   1931— .
   630 North Van Buren Street, Milwaukee, Wisconsin 53202
       Editor: Claire K. Vajda   Language: English
       Sponsor: The Melting Pot News Company, Mrs. A. B. Vajda
       Circulation: 30,000   Frequency: Monthly   Subscription: $3.00

260. THE MENNONITE.   1885— .
   722 Main Street, Box 347, Newton, Kansas 67114
       Editor: Maynard Shelly   Language: English
       Sponsor: General Conference Mennonite Church
       Circulation: 15,300   Frequency: Weekly   Subscription: $4.50

"A magazine of news, comment, and discussion on church and world affairs of interest to Mennonites" [editor's statement]. Illustrated.

261. NINTH MANHATTAN MASONIC NEWS.   1937– .
220 East 15th Street, New York, New York 10003
    Editor: Marvin Goldsmith   Language: English
    Sponsor: Ninth Manhatten District, German Masonic Home Corporation
    Circulation: Unknown   Frequency: Semi-monthly   Subscription: Unknown

A fraternal magazine.

262. THE SCHWENKFELDIAN.   1903– .
1 Seminary Street, Pennsburg, Pennsylvania 18073
    Editor: Jack R. Rothenberger   Language: English
    Sponsor: Board of Publication of the Schwenkfelder Church
    Circulation: 1,510   Frequency: Quarterly   Subscription: $1.50

Contains congregational information for members of the various churches, as well as general purpose editorial material concerning contemporary church-related issues.

263. SOLIDARITY.   1906– .
714 Seneca Avenue, Ridgewood (Brooklyn), New York 11227
    Editor: Jack Hengerson   Language: English
    Sponsor: Workmen's Benefit Fund of the U.S.A.
    Circulation: 22,500   Frequency: Monthly   Subscription: Membership fee

"It shall be the policy of *Solidarity* to emphasize the democratic way of life of the American people and to disseminate the spirit of fraternalism for purposes of mutual help and protection" [editor's statement]. Articles deal with the questions of health, economic security, social problems, and international affairs. The German edition was discontinued after the December 1968 issue.

264. STEUBEN NEWS.   1929– .
369 Lexington Avenue, Suite 2003, New York, New York 10017
    Editor: Edward J. Sussmann   Language: English
    Sponsor: Steuben Society of America
    Circulation: Unknown   Frequency: Monthly   Subscription: $3.00

General, national, and local news. News of the Steuben Society. Features articles about European affairs written by European correspondents.

265. TOGETHER.   1956— .
    1661 North Northwest Highway, Park Ridge, Illinois 60068
      Editor: Curtis A. Chambers   Language: English
      Sponsor: United Methodist Church
      Circulation: Unknown   Frequency: Monthly   Subscription: $5.00

    Editorial purpose is "to provide a medium for United Methodists of
    information, interpretation, and inspiration, through the use of
    printed word and picture of the news affecting the religious life"
    [editor's statement].

266. THE WANDERER.   1867— .
    128 East 10th Street, St. Paul, Minnesota 55101
      Editor: Walter Matt   Language: English
      Sponsor: Wanderer Printing Company
      Circulation: 34,000   Frequency: Weekly   Subscription: $7.00

    This Catholic magazine features various topics of interest to the
    German Catholic community.

GREEK PRESS

Greek and Greek-English Publications

267. ATHENAI.   Detroit Athens.   1928— .
    520 Monroe Avenue, Detroit, Michigan 48226
      Editor: Basil Lukos   Language: Greek
      Sponsor: Eagle Printing and Publishing Company
      Circulation: 4,030   Frequency: Weekly   Subscription: $6.00

    Oriented toward the interests of all Greek readers in the area. International,
    national, and local news coverage.

268. ATLANTIS.   1894— .
    521 West 23rd Street, New York, New York 10011
      Editor: Panayiotis J. Gazouleas   Language: Greek
      Sponsor: Solon G. Vlasto, Publisher
      Circulation: 14,337   Frequency: Daily   Subscription: $20.00

    Daily and Sunday editions, with international, national, and local news
    coverage. Features articles on Greek-American relationships and on cul-
    tural, social, and political topics.

269. ELLENIKOS-ASTER.   The Greek Star.   1904— .
4731 North Western, Chicago, Illinois 60625
    Editor: Nicholas Philippidis   Language: English and Greek
    Sponsor: Lerner Newspapers
    Circulation: 7,500   Frequency: Weekly   Subscription: $5.00

Provides general news of interest to the Greek community. Currently
ninety percent of the newspaper is published in English.

270. ELLENIKOS TYPOS.   The Greek Press.   1911— .
509 North LaSalle Street, Chicago, Illinois 60610
    Editor: Aris Angelopoulos   Language: Greek and English
    Sponsor: The Greek Press, Inc.
    Circulation: 15,250   Frequency: Monthly   Subscription: $10.00

Covers "all aspects of the news that affect the Greek community including
news from Greece, political, social, cultural, educational" [editor's statement].

271. ELLENOAMERIKANOS.   The Greek-American.   1969— .
251 West 42nd Street, New York, New York 10036
    Editor: Michael E. Halkias   Language: English and Greek
    Sponsor: Grekam Publications, Inc.
    Circulation: 12,000   Frequency: Semi-monthly   Subscription: $5.00

Emphasis is on Greek activities in the United States; general and local
news coverage is also provided.

272. HELLAS.   1963— .
809 West Jackson Boulevard, Chicago, Illinois 60607
    Editor: E. Constantopoulos   Language: Greek
    Sponsor: Hellas Publishing Company
    Circulation: Unknown   Frequency: Monthly   Subscription: Unknown

Features articles on Greek culture, politics, and social issues.

273. HELLENIC FREE PRESS.   1957— .
809 West Jackson Boulevard, Chicago, Illinois 60607
    Editor: E. Constantopoulos   Language: Greek and English
    Sponsor: National Hellenic Free Press Publishing Corporation
    Circulation: Unknown   Frequency: Semi-monthly   Subscription: Unknown

General news coverage of interest to the Greek community.

274. ILLUSTRATED ATLANTIS.   1895– .
521 West 23rd Street, New York, New York 10011
Editor: Panayiotis J. Gazouleas   Language: Greek
Sponsor: S. G. Vlasto, Publisher
Circulation: Unknown   Frequency: Monthly   Subscription: $5.00

275. KAMPANA.   Campana.   1918– .
360 West 36th Street, New York, New York 10013
Editor: Costas Athanasiades   Language: Greek
Circulation: 8,300   Frequency: Semi-monthly   Subscription: $10.00

Features articles on Greek culture.

276. KRETE.   Crete.   1928– .
263 West 30th Street, New York, New York 10001
Editor: George H. Terezakis   Language: Greek
Sponsor: Pancretan Association of America
Circulation: 2,299   Frequency: Monthly   Subscription: $1.50

277. KYPIAKATIKA NEA.   Greek Sunday News.   1944– .
231 Harrison Avenue, Boston, Massachusetts 02111
Editor: Mary Sampos   Language: Greek and English
Sponsor: William A. Harris, Publisher
Circulation: 17,500   Frequency: Weekly   Subscription: $5.00

278. MAKEDONIA.   Macedonia.   1953– .
246 Eighth Avenue, New York, New York 10011
Editor: V. T. Daniels   Language: Greek and English
Sponsor: Pan-Macedonian Association
Circulation: 3,000   Frequency: Bi-monthly   Subscription: $5.00

Includes national and local Greek news. Its main objective is to "advance
friendly relations between Greece and the Americans, to support religious
and educational causes and to distribute information on the land and
people of Macedonia, Greece" [editor's statement] .

279. NATIONAL GREEK TRIBUNE.   1920– .
1215 Brush Street, Detroit, Michigan 48226
Editor: James Lagos   Language: Greek
Circulation: 1,260   Frequency: Weekly   Subscription: $7.00

280. NATIONAL HERALD.   Ethnikos Kerix.   1915—.
140 West 26th Street, New York, New York 10001
　　Editor: B. J. Marketos   Language: Greek and English
　　Sponsor: National Herald, Inc.
　　Circulation: 14,583   Frequency: Daily   Subscription: $20.00

International, national, and local news coverage. Special English section
in the Sunday edition.

281. THE NEW CALIFORNIA.   Nea California.   1907—.
1666 Market Street, San Francisco, California 94102
　　Editor: N. S. Dallas   Language: Greek and English
　　Sponsor: Acropolis Publishing Corporation
　　Circulation: 3,000   ,Frequency: Weekly   Subscription: $8.00

Provides general, national, and local news coverage.

282. NEW YORK HELLENIC NEWS.   Ellenika Nea.   1963—.
367 West 36th Street, New York, New York 10018
　　Editor: Spyros Triantafyllou   Language: Greek and English
　　Sponsor: Hellenic News, Inc.
　　Circulation: 5,338   Frequency: Weekly   Subscription: Unknown

Contains general news of interest to the Greek community.

283. THE ORTHODOX OBSERVER.   1934—.
777 United Nations Plaza, New York, New York 10017
　　Editor: Rev. Dr. N. D. Patrinacos   Language: English and Greek
　　Sponsor: Greek Archdiocese of North and South America
　　Circulation: 6,000   Frequency: Monthly   Subscription: Unknown

This is a religious monthly featuring news and articles on the Greek
Orthodox Church in the United States, religious education, and other
related topics.

284. ROUMELI PRESS.   1964—.
2412 Broadway, New York, New York 10011
　　Editor: Efthimios Thomopoulos   Language: Greek and English
　　Circulation: 2,500   Frequency: Monthly   Subscription: $6.00

285. THE TRIBUNE OF G.A.P.A.
    3600 Fifth Avenue, Pittsburgh, Pennsylvania 15213
        Editor: Editorial Committee   Language: Greek and English
        Sponsor: Greek-American Progressive Association
        Circulation: Unknown   Frequency: 5 times/year   Subscription: Unknc

    A fraternal publication.

286. THE VOICE OF THE GOSPEL.   I Fone Tou Evangeliou.   1941— .
    801 Broad Avenue, Ridgefield, New Jersey 07657
        Editor: Spiros Zodhiates   Language: Greek
        Sponsor: American Mission to Greeks
        Circulation: 3,000   Frequency: Monthly   Subscription: $3.00

    This is a religious monthly containing "Biblical exposition, sermons,
    missionary news—chiefly for the spiritual education of Greek Evan-
    gelicals" [editor's statement].

Greek Publications in English

287. THE AHEPA MESSENGER.   1931— .
    409 West 44th Street, New York, New York
        Editor: Angelos G. Chaoush   Language: English
        Sponsor: Metropolitan Chapter of Ahepa
        Circulation: 2,000   Frequency: Monthly
        Subscription: Membership dues

    Published by the American Hellenic Educational Progressive Association,
    this monthly is a fraternal publication.

288. AHEPAN.   1927— .
    601 Kappock Street, Riverdale, New York 10463
        Editor: Nicholas Zannetos   Language: English
        Sponsor: The Order of Ahepa
        Circulation: 27,070   Frequency: Bi-monthly   Subscription: Unknown

    This is a fraternal publication.

289. THE CHICAGO PHYX.   1939— .
    P.O. Box 67, Glenview, Illinois 60025
        Editor: Peter N. Mantzoros   Language: English
        Sponsor: PNYX Publishing Company
        Circulation: 2,000   Frequency: Semi-monthly   Subscription: $5.00

    National and local news coverage, plus informative materials on Greece.
    Special feature: news items on the Order of Ahepa.

290. THE GREEK ORTHODOX THEOLOGICAL REVIEW.   1954— .
50 Goddard Avenue, Brookline, Massachusetts 02146
   Editor: Rev. Dr. Demetrios J. Constantelos   Language: English
   Sponsor: Holy Cross Greek Orthodox Theological School, Hellenic College
   Circulation: 1,000   Frequency: Bi-annually   Subscription: $5.00

Includes scholarly papers and reviews in the field of Biblical studies,
orthodox theology, church history, and related subjects.

291. THE HELLENIC CHRONICLE.   1950— .
324 Newbury Street, Boston, Massachusetts 02115
   Editor: James Anagnostos   Language: English
   Sponsor: Hellenic Publishing Corporation
   Circulation: 32,717   Frequency: Weekly   Subscription: $5.00

Provides international, national, and local news of interest to the Greek
community.

292. LOGOS.   The Logos.   1950— .
P.O. Box 5333, St. Louis, Missouri 63115
   Editor: Rev. G. Mastrantonis   Language: English
   Sponsor: Orthodox Lore of the Gospel of Our Saviour
   Circulation: Unknown   Frequency: Bi-monthly   Subscription: $2.00

293. G.O.Y.A. BULLETIN
319 East 74th Street, New York, New York 10021
   Editor: Editorial Committee   Language: English
   Sponsor: Greek Orthodox Youth of America
   Circulation: 8,500   Frequency: Bi-monthly   Subscription: Unknown

HEBREW PRESS

see JEWISH PRESS

HUNGARIAN PRESS

Hungarian and Hungarian-English Publications

294. AMERIKAI MAGYAR SZEMLE.   The American Hungarian Review.
     1963— .
     5410 Kerth Road, St. Louis, Missouri 63128
     Editor: Leslie Konnyu   Language: English and Hungarian
     Sponsor: The American Hungarian Review
     Circulation: 1,000   Frequency: Quarterly   Subscription: $5.00

The contents of this magazine center primarily on the arts, sciences, and humanities. American-Hungarian historical and cultural relations are also explored.

295. AMERIKAI MAGYAR NEPSZAVA.   American Hungarian People's
     Voice.   1899— .
     1736 East 22nd Street, Cleveland, Ohio 44114
     Editor: Zoltan Gombos   Language: Hungarian
     Sponsor: Liberty Publishing Company
     Circulation: 10,830   Frequency: Daily   Subscription: $30.00

This newspaper prints special news and events of interest to Hungarian readers. Included are general news items on domestic and foreign affairs, sports, arts, theater, and news on local events. Sections are also devoted to reports from foreign correspondents, novels, essays, and poetry. The "publication is politically independent" [editor's statement].

296. AMERIKAI MAGYAR SZO.   Hungarian Word.   1902— .
     130 East 16th Street, New York, New York 10003
     Editor: James Lustig   Language: Hungarian
     Sponsor: Hungarian Word, Inc.
     Circulation: 3,000   Frequency: Weekly   Subscription: $10.00

Contains information of a general and group nature. Includes news on domestic and foreign affairs, editorials and comments on various societal problems, reports on international sports events, humor, and short items on various personalities.

297. CALIFORNIAI MAGYARSAG.   California Hungarians.   1922— .
648 North Western Avenue, Los Angeles, California 90004
　　Editor: Maria Fenyes　　　Language: Hungarian
　　Circulation: 7,500　　Frequency: Weekly　　Subscription: $8.00

About one third of the items in this newspaper are devoted to international and domestic events. Also included are news items on Hungarians
and their church, club, and social activities both in this country and else-
where. Critical analyses of music and drama are often printed.

298. CHICAGO ES KORNYEKE.   Chicago and Vicinity.   1906— .
1541 West Touhy Avenue, Chicago, Illinois 60626
　　Editor: Dr. Julius Hovany　　Language: Hungarian
　　Circulation: 2,301　　Frequency: Weekly　　Subscription: $8.00

This weekly provides general, international, national, and local news
coverage.

299. DETROITI UJSAG.   Detroit Hungarian News.   1911— .
7907 West Jefferson Avenue, Detroit, Michigan 48217
　　Editor: Amelia Fodor　　　Language: Hungarian
　　Circulation: 4,100　　Frequency: Weekly　　Subscription: Unknown

300. EVANGELIUMI HIRNÖK.   Gospel Messenger.   1908— .
609 Woodridge Drive, Murfreesboro, North Carolina 26855
　　Editor: Bela Udvarnoki　　　Language: Hungarian
　　Sponsor: Hungarian Baptist Union of America
　　Circulation: 600　　Frequency: Semi-monthly　Subscription: $4.00

This is the official publication of the Hungarian Baptist Union of America.
Its contents are primarily inspirational and doctrinal articles. Church
activities and events are also covered.

301. KATOLIKUS MAGYAROK VASARNAPJA.   Catholic Hungarians'
　　Sunday.   1894— .
517 Belle Vista Avenue, Youngstown, Ohio 44509
　　Editors: Fr. Nicholas Dengl and Dr. Stephen Eszterhas
　　Language: Hungarian
　　Sponsor: Commissat of St. Stephen Franciscan Province
　　Circulation: 4,300　　Frequency: Weekly　　Subscription: $9.00

This newspaper contains information regarding the state of the Church in
Hungary as well as in other countries with Hungarian populations. Also
included are news items dealing with various aspects of Hungarian

cultural, social, and political activities and events in the various countries. One major objective of this publication is to "protest against the presence of foreign troops in Hungary and the oppression of civil liberties" [editor's statement].

302. **LITERARY HERALD.**   Irodalmi Hiradó.   1955– .
323 East 79th Street, New York, New York 10021
    Editor: Samuel Weiss   Language: Hungarian and English
    Sponsor: New York First Hungarian Literary Society
    Circulation: 2,500   Frequency: Monthly   Subscription: $2.00

303. **LORAIN ES VIDEKE.**   Lorain & Vicinity.   1913– .
1826 East 28th Street, Lorain, Ohio 44055
    Editor: Louis P. Bodnar   Language: Hungarian
    Sponsor: Bodnar Printing Company
    Circulation: 648   Frequency: Semi-monthly   Subscription: $5.00

This publication is directed toward the Hungarian population in Lorain, Ohio, and its nearby communities. News items deal primarily with church, lodge, and social activities of interest to Hungarians in this area. At times, news dealing with national affairs and events in Hungary is included.

304. **MAGYAR EGYHAZ.**   Magyar Church.   1922– .
175 Pershing Avenue, Carteret, New Jersey 07008
    Editor: Rev. Dr. Andrew Harsanyi   Language: Hungarian and English
    Sponsor: Magyar Egyhaz Publishing Company
    Circulation: 4,500   Frequency: Monthly   Subscription: $3.00

This magazine is the official organ of the Hungarian Reformed Church in America. The main objective of the publication is "to inform members of the denomination about events in the ecclesiastical world—the denomination, the U.S., and the world, with special emphasis on events concerning the Reformed and Presbyterian Churches" [editor's statement]. Material includes devotional and doctrinal articles. Each issue contains a section on "News from the Congregations" in both Hungarian and English.

305. **MAGYAR HIRNÖK—MAGYAR HERALD.**   Hungarian
    Herald.   1909– .
222 Amboy Avenue, Metuchen, New Jersey 08840
    Editor: Laszlo I. Dienes   Language: Hungarian
    Sponsor: Liberty Publishing Company; Associated Hungarian Press, Inc.
    Circulation: 2,000   Frequency: Weekly   Subscription: $10.00

This weekly contains news of general interest for Hungarian groups. Its contents include items on world and domestic events, activities within Hungarian communities, and news from Hungary. Much of the space of this publication is devoted to articles by individual writers on a variety of topics.

306. MAGYARSAG.   Hungarian People.   1925— .
200 Johnston Avenue, Pittsburgh, Pennsylvania 15207
    Editor: Eugene Szebedinszky   Language: Hungarian
    Circulation: 3,840   Frequency: Weekly   Subscription: $5.00

307. MAGYAR UJSAG.   Hungarian News.   1935— .
518 Octavia Street, San Francisco, California 94102
    Editor: Unknown   Language: Hungarian
    Sponsor: Pannonia Press, Inc.
    Circulation: Unknown   Frequency: Monthly   Subscription: $5.00

308. NEMZETVEDELMI TAJEKOZTATO.   Information About Defense of Nation.   1967— .
P.O. Box 38031, Hollywood, California 90038
    Editor: Geza Gorgenyi   Language: Hungarian
    Sponsor: Hungarian World Federation of the Defense of Nation
    Circulation: Unknown   Frequency: Monthly · Subscription: $6.00

Politically and historically oriented. Ideologically, this publication takes an anti-communist stand.

309. NÖK VILAGA.   Women's World.   1932— .
130 East 16th Street, New York, New York 10003
    Editor: Rose Weinstock   Language Hungarian
    Sponsor: Nok Vilaga, Inc.
    Circulation: 1,175   Frequency: Monthly   Subscription: $3.00

This is a magazine of interest to women.

310. THE SOUTHWEST JOURNAL.   Délnyngati Ujság.   1914— .
8502 West Jefferson Avenue, Detroit, Michigan 48217
    Editor: Mrs. Ernest Palos.   Language: Hungarian and English
    Circulation: 12,505   Frequency: Weekly   Subscription: $2.00

This weekly journal provides general, national, and local news coverage.

311. ST. LOUIS ES VIDEKE.   St. Louis and Vicinity.   1913– .
5535 Alcott Avenue, St. Louis, Missouri 63120
　　Editor: Dr. Louis B. Denes   Language: Hungarian
　　Circulation: 10,000 Frequency: Bi-weekly   Subscription: $6.00

312. SZABADSAG.   Liberty.   1891– .
1736 East 22nd Street, Cleveland, Ohio 44114
　　Editor: Zoltan Gombos   Language: Hungarian
　　Sponsor: Liberty Publishing Company
　　Circulation: 10,830   Frequency: Daily   Subscription: $30.00

Covers general, foreign, and domestic news and events of interest to
Hungarian readers. Also includes literature (novels, poetry, essays).

313. A SZIV.   The Heart.   1915– .
76 Locust Hill Avenue, Yonkers, New York 10701
　　Editor: Rev. Rochus Radanyi, S.J.   Language: Hungarian
　　Sponsor: Hungarian Jesuit Fathers
　　Circulation: 2,800   Frequency: Monthly   Subscription: $3.00

This is a Roman Catholic devotional publication. Its contents deal with
various subjects which are relevant to contemporary Roman Catholic
life.

314. TESTVERISEG.   Fraternity.   1923– .
3216 New Mexico Avenue, N.W., Washington, D.C. 20016
　　Editor: Rt. Rev. Dr. Zoltan Beky   Language: English and Hungarian
　　Sponsor: Hungarian Reformed Federation of America
　　Circulation: 16,786   Frequency: Monthly   Subscription: Free to mem

315. AZ UJSAG.   The Hungarian News.   1921– .
5705 Detroit Avenue, Cleveland, Ohio 44102
　　Editor: Zoltan Kotai   Language: Hungarian
　　Sponsor: Karpat Publishing Company
　　Circulation: 1,266   Frequency: Weekly   Subscription: $5.00

316. VIRRASZTO.   Vigilant.   1970– .
45-54 41st Street, Apt. 6E, Long Island City, New York 11104
　　Editor: Erdelyi Istvan   Language: Hungarian
　　Sponsor: Virraszto Research Committee in the U.S.A.
　　Circulation: 1,000   Frequency: Unknown   Subscription: $3.00

Virraszto is the successor of the *Larmafa*, which was published and edited in Austria between 1959 and 1968. *Virraszto* publishes historical and political essays and documents dealing with the Carpathian territory. The aim of this publication is "to nullify the Trianon Peace Treaty of 1920 and to restore the political unity of the Carpathian basin" [editor's statement].

317. WILLIAM PENN LIFE.   1965— .
429 Forbes Avenue, Pittsburgh, Pennsylvania 15219
    Editor: Elmer Charles   Language: Hungarian and English
    Sponsor: William Penn Fraternal Association
    Circulation: Unknown   Frequency: Monthly   Subscription: Free to members

318. "WISCONSINI MAGYARSA'G" HUNGARIAN NEWSPAPER.   Wisconsin
    Hungarians.   1924— .
609 North Plankinton Avenue, Room 508, Milwaukee, Wisconsin 53203
    Editor: Charles Klein   Language: Hungarian
    Circulation: 18,700   Frequency: Semi-monthly   Subscription: $5.00

This publication was established for the Hungarians residing in the state of Wisconsin. Its contents primarily concern news items on various group activities and events as well as articles dealing with topics of special interest to Hungarian groups.

ITALIAN PRESS

Editor's note: For additions to this section see pages 219 and 220, entries 897 through 903.

Italian and Italian-English Publications

319. L'ADUNTA DEI REFRATTARI.   The Call of the 'Refractaires.'   1922— .
216 West 18th Street, New York, New York 10011
    Editor: Owen Agostinelli   Language: Italian
    Circulation: 3,990   Frequency: Bi-weekly   Subscription: $3.00

This publication features general and political articles.

320. THE AMERICAN CITIZEN.   1923— .
P.O. Box 944, Omaha, Nebraska
    Editor: Victor Failla   Language: Italian
    Circulation: 541   Frequency: Semi-monthly   Subscription: $3.00

Provides coverage of international, national, and local news of special interest to Italian-Americans.

321. BOLLETTINO DELLA FEDERAZIONE CATTOLICA ITALIANA.
Bulletin of the Italian Catholic Federation.   1924— .
678 Green Street, San Francisco, California 94133
   Editor: Mario J. Cugia   Language: English and Italian
   Sponsor: Central Council of the Italian Catholic Federation
   Circulation: 20,825   Frequency: Monthly   Subscription: $1.00

This is the official organ of the Italian Catholic Federation. It contains news items on activities of the various branches composing the Federation. Also included are articles on travel, comments on religious matters, and book reviews.

322. THE BULLETIN OF ITALIAN CHAMBER OF COMMERCE OF CHICAGO.
1907— .
712 Rosedale, Glenview, Illinois 60025
   Editor: Dr. Benny G. Zucchini, P.R.   Language: English and Italian
   Sponsor: Italian Chamber of Commerce of Chicago
   Circulation: 1,600   Frequency: Bi-monthly   Subscription: Unknown

The aim of this publication is to "strengthen and increase relations between members" [Italian Chamber of Commerce] by providing information on firms in the United States. It also provides information on customs regulations, foreign trade rules, and governmental controls.

323. CONNECTICUT ITALIAN BULLETIN.   1950— .
P.O. Box 1264, Hartford, Connecticut 06105
   Editor: Unknown   Language: Italian and English
   Sponsor: Connecticut Italian Publishing Company, Inc.
   Circulation: 5,000   Frequency: Bi-weekly Subscription: Free

324. IL CORRIERE DEL BERKSHIRE.   The Berkshire Courier.   1930— .
45 Thomson Place, Pittsfield, Massachusetts 01202
   Editor: Enzo Marinare   Language: Italian
   Sponsor: Courier Printing Company
   Circulation: 3,600   Frequency: Weekly   Subscription: $1.00

This is a political magazine.

325. IL CORCIATO.   The Crusader.   1933— .
One Hanson Place, Brooklyn, New York 11217
   Editors: Very Rev. Msgr. Santi J. Privitera and Rev. Nicholas Russo
   Language: Italian and English
   Sponsor: Roman Catholic Diocese of Brooklyn
   Circulation: 5,620   Frequency: Weekly   Subscription: Unknown

326. THE ECHO.   1896– .
236 Broadway, Providence, Rhode Island
    Editor: Harold A. Pace   Language: English and Italian
    Circulation: 2,500   Frequency: Weekly   Subscription: $4.00

This publication contains primarily local and group news of interest to the Italian-American community.

327. L'ECO D'ITALIA.   Italian Echo.   1966– .
1441 Stockton Street, San Francisco, California 94133
    Editor: Pierino Mori   Language: Italian
    Circulation: 2,933   Frequency: Weekly   Subscription: Unknown

328. LA FOLLIA DI NEW YORK.   Folly.   1893– .
125 East 95th Street, New York, New York 10028
    Editor: Luigi Sola   Language: Italian
    Sponsor: Italian National Magazine Company
    Circulation: 4,150   Frequency: Monthly   Subscription: $7.00

This monthly publication features articles on Italian culture, literature, etc.

329. FORUM ITALICUM.   Italian Forum.   1967– .
221 Crosby Hall, Buffalo, New York 14214
    Editor: M. Ricciardelli   Language: English and Italian
    Sponsor: State University of New York at Buffalo
    Circulation: 600   Frequency: Quarterly   Subscription: $4.00

This publication serves as a forum for the expression of views by scholars and teachers on the language, culture, and literature of Italy and of other countries in relation to Italy. Contains sections on poetry, creative essays, reviews, and news.

330. GIUSTIZIA.   Justice.   1918– .
1710 Broadway, New York, New York 10019
    Editor: Lino Manocchia   Language: Italian
    Sponsor: International Ladies Garment Workers Union
    Circulation: 51,000   Frequency: Monthly   Subscription: $2.00

This is the official organ of the Ladies Garment Workers Union. It is primarily devoted to news of Union activities and politics, although it also contains general news on women's fashions.

331. ITALAMERICAN MAGAZINE.   1935— .
14 Centre, Edgeworth Park, Bronx, New York 10465
     Editor: Louis Angelino   Language: English and Italian
     Sponsor: Angelino Enterprises
     Circulation: 25,000   Frequency: Weekly   Subscription: Unknown

332. THE ITALIAN BULLETIN.   1949— .
P.O. Box 1264, Hartford, Connecticut 06105
     Editor: Ven Sequenzia   Language: Italian and English
     Sponsor: Connecticut Publishing Company—European Cultural Bureau
     Circulation: 3,500   Frequency: Bi-weekly   Subscription: Unknown

333. ITALIAN NEWS.   1921— .
Box 94, Hanover Station, Boston, Massachusetts 02113
     Editor: Varoujan Samuelian   Language: Italian
     Sponsor: Italian News Publishing Company, Inc.
     Circulation: 2,705   Frequency: Weekly   Subscription: $3.00

334. ITALICA.   1924— .
Dept. of Italian, Columbia University, New York, New York 10027
     Editor: Olga Ragusa   Language: Italian and English
     Sponsor: American Association of Teachers of Italian
     Circulation: 1,820   Frequency: Quarterly   Subscription: $6.00

The principal objective of this publication is to promote the study of
the Italian language and literature in both the United States and Canada.

335. L'ITALO AMERICANO DI LOS ANGELES.   Los Angeles Italian
American.   1908— .
1035 North Broadway, Los Angeles, California 90012
     Editor: Cleto M. Baroni   Language: Italian
     Circulation: 4,400   Frequency: Weekly   Subscription: $2.00

336. IL LEONE.   The Lion.   1931— .
5051 Mission Street, San Francisco, California 94112
     Editor: Roland G. DeRocili   Language: Italian
     Sponsor: Grand Lodge of California, Order of Sons of Italy in America
     Circulation: 12,007   Frequency: Monthly   Subscription: $3.00

A fraternal magazine.

337. LA LIBERA PAROLA.   Free Speech.   1918— .
1505 South 15th Street, Philadelphia, Pennsylvania 19146
    Editor: Joseph Colucci   Language: Italian
    Circulation: 560   Frequency: Weekly   Subscription: Unknown

338. IL MESSAGGERO.   The Messenger.   1921— .
544 Wabash, Kansas City, Missouri 64124
    Editor: Dr. J. B. Bisceglia   Language: Italian and English
    Sponsor: The Italian Mission
    Circulation: 800   Frequency: Monthly   Subscription: $1.00

The contents of this publication are religious and educational in nature.
It is intended primarily for Italian-Americans residing in Kansas City.

339. MIDDLETOWN BULLETIN.   1948— .
790 Ridge Road, Middletown, Connecticut 06457
    Editor: Max B. Corvo   Language: English and Italian
    Sponsor: Middletown Bulletin, Inc.
    Circulation: 1,335   Frequency: Weekly   Subscription: $2.00

Provides general, national, and local news coverage.

340. IL MONDO LIBERO.   The Free World.   1956— .
2844 Syracuse Street, Dearborn, Michigan 48124
    Editor: Dr. G. Oberdam Rizzo   Language: Italian and English
    Sponsor: Free World International Academy, Inc.
    Circulation: 24,000   Frequency: Monthly Subscription: $5.00

This publication is basically cultural in nature. It includes poetry,
literature, science, the arts, commentaries, and coverage of current events.

341. THE NEW AURORA.   The New Dawn.   1903— .
314 Richfield Road, Upper Darby, Pennsylvania
    Editor: Anthony F. Vasquez   Language: English and Italian
    Sponsor: The Association of Evangelicals for Italian Missions
    Circulation: 1,300   Frequency: Monthly   Subscription: $3.00

The contents of this monthly consist of articles of an international and
informational nature in the field of religion, for Americans of Italian
background.

SEE page 219 and 220 for additions to this section (numbers 897, 898, 899).

342. IL PENSIERO.   The Thought.   1904— .
5634 South Magnolia, St. Louis, Missouri 63110
    Editor: Antonino Lombardo   Language: Italian and English
    Circulation: 6,855   Frequency: Semi-monthly   Subscription: $3.00

Provides coverage of news events in Italy as well as activities within
Italian communities in the United States.

343. IL POPOLO ITALIANO.   The Italian People.   1935— .
1228-34 Locust Street, Philadelphia, Pennsylvania 19107
    Editor: Arnold Orsatti   Language: Italian
    Sponsor: Italian Community Publishing Company
    Circulation: 2,052   Frequency: Monthly   Subscription: Unknown

344. IL PROGRESSO ITALO-AMERICANO.   Italian-American Progress.   1880-
260 Audubon Avenue, New York, New York 10033
    Editor: Fortune Pope   Language: Italian
    Sponsor: Il Progresso Italo-Americano Publishing Company, Inc.
    Circulation: 70,548   Frequency: Daily   Subscription: $28.00

The objective of this publication is "to provide Italian readers with
international, national, and local news" [editor's statement]. News
coverage of events in Italy is stressed.

345. IL RINNOVAMENTO.   The Renewal.   1933— .
117 North Broadway, Nyack, New York 10960
    Editor: Rev. J. Jerry Cardo   Language: Italian
    Sponsor: Italian Evangelical Publication Society
    Circulation: 300   Frequency: Bi-monthly   Subscription: Unknown

346. SONS OF ITALY NEWS.
69 Hauman Street, Revere, Massachusetts 02151
    Editor: Ralph Ferruzzi   Language: English and Italian
    Sponsor: Grand Lodge of Massachusetts, Order of Sons of Italy in America
    Circulation: 14,000   Frequency: Weekly   Subscription: Members only

A fraternal monthly providing news about member lodges throughout
Massachusetts, their functions, and memos.

347. SONS OF ITALY TIMES.   1936— .
Broad & Federal Streets, Philadelphia, Pennsylvania 19146
    Editor: Joseph L. Monte   Language: English and Italian
    Sponsor: Grand Lodge of Pennsylvania, Order of Sons of Italy in America
    Circulation: 29,000   Frequency: Weekly   Subscription: $2.00

Fraternal newspaper dealing with news concerning the 300 lodges throughout Pennsylvania. Also contains editorials on topics such as education, law,
pollution, politics, etc.

348. LA TRIBUNA ITALIANA.   The Italian Tribune.   1933— .
4962 North Hopkins Street, Milwaukee, Wisconsin 53209
    Editor: Filbert E. Cacchione   Language: Italian
    Circulation: Unknown   Frequency: Monthly   Subscription: $2.00

349. LA TRIBUNA ITALIANA D'AMERICA.   Italian Tribune of America.   1909— .
13517 Gratiot Avenue, Detroit, Michigan 48205
    Editor: Ferrucio Serdoz   Language: Italian
    Sponsor: Giuliano Travel, Inc.
    Circulation: 1,600   Frequency: Weekly   Subscription: $6.00

350. UNIONE.   Union.   1890— .
1719 Liberty Avenue, Pittsburgh, Pennsylvania
    Editor: Victor Frediani   Language: Italian
    Sponsor: Order of Italian Sons and Daughters of America
    Circulation: 13,287   Frequency: Weekly   Subscription: $2.50

A fraternal magazine.

351. LA VOCE ITALIANA.   The Italian Voice.   1934— .
77-79 Mill Street, Paterson, New Jersey 07501
    Editor: Emilio Augusto   Language: Italian
    Circulation: 4,764   Frequency: Weekly   Subscription: $3.50

This weekly provides general, national, and local news coverage.

352. LA VOCE DEL POPOLO.   Voice of the People.   1910— .
7050 Pinehurst, Dearborn, Michigan 48126
    Editor: Victor Viberti   Language: Italian and English
    Sponsor: Pious Society of St. Paul
    Circulation: 2,000   Frequency: Weekly   Subscription: Unknown

Italian Publications in English

353. ACIM DISPATCH.   1953— .
    5 East 35th Street, New York, New York
    Editor: Unknown   Language: English
    Sponsor: American Committee on Italian Migration
    Circulation: Unknown   Frequency: Irregular   Subscription: Unknown

354. AMERICA-ITALY NEWSLETTER.
    22 East 60th Street, New York, New York 10022
    Editor: Hedy Giusti-Lanham   Language: English
    Sponsor: America-Italy Society, Inc.
    Circulation: 1,600   Frequency: Irregular
    Subscription: $7.50 (membership dues)

    This organ of the American-Italy Society provides news on events and
    activities sponsored by the Society.

355. COLORADO.   1923— .
    3630 Osage Street, Denver, Colorado 80211
    Editor: Frank Mancini   Language: English
    Circulation: 1,866   Frequency: Weekly   Subscription: $3.00

    This weekly provides general, national, and local news coverage.

356. COLUMBUS PRESS.   1933— .
    315 Larimer Avenue, Pittsburgh, Pennsylvania 15206
    Editor: Unknown   Language: English
    Sponsor: Federation of Sons of Columbus of America
    Circulation: Unknown   Frequency: Semi-monthly   Subscription: Unkn

SEE page 220 for additions to this section (numbers 900, 901, 902, 903).

357. ITALO-AMERICAN TIMES.   1964— .
    Box 1492, Baychester Station, The Bronx, New York, New York 10469
    Editor: Rudy Damonte   Language: English
    Sponsor: Italo-American Times Publishing Company
    Circulation: 10,000   Frequency: Bi-monthly   Subscription: $1.00

    This publication provides news of special interest for the Italian-American
    community of Bronx County, plus coverage of international, national, and
    local events. It also contains reports on developments in Italy, and analyses
    of topics of special concern to Americans of Italian descent.

358. OMAHA PUBLIC LEDGER.   1932— .
304 Patterson Building, Omaha, Nebraska 68102
    Editor: Sam Klaver   Language: English
    Sponsor: Ledger Publishing Company
    Circulation: 1,076   Frequency: Weekly   Subscription: Unknown

359. OSIA NEWS.   1945— .
25 Foster Street, Worcester, Massachusetts 01608
    Editor: Albert A. Maino   Language: English
    Sponsor: Supreme Lodge of Order of Sons of Italy in America
    Circulaton: 32,300   Frequency: Monthly   Subscription: Unknown

This is a fraternal magazine.

360. POST-GAZETTE.   1896— .
5 Prince Street, Boston, Massachusetts 02113
    Editor: Caesar Donnaruma   Language: English
    Circulation: 14,900   Frequency: Weekly   Subscription: $7.50

This weekly provides general, international, national, and local news coverage.

361. STAR BULLETIN.   1959— .
77-79 Mill Street, Paterson, New Jersey 07501
    Editor: Emilio Augusto   Language: English
    Circulation: 134   Frequency: Weekly   Subscription: Unknown

JAPANESE PRESS

Japanese and Japanese-English Publications

362. THE CHICAGO SHIMPO.   Chicago News.   1945— .
3744 North Clark Street, Chicago, Illinois 60613
    Editor: Ryeichi Fujii   Language: Japanese and English
    Sponsor: The Chicago Shimpo, Inc.
    Circulation: 3,020   Frequency: Semi-weekly   Subscription: $10.00

Provides general coverage, including international, national, and local news. Also presents news concerning the Japanese community in the United States.

363. HAWAII HOCHI.   Hawaii Post.   1912— .
917 Kokea Street, Honolulu, Hawaii 96817
    Editor: Don T. Fujicawa   Language: Japanese and English
    Sponsor: Hawaii Hochi, Ltd.
    Circulation: 12,125   Frequency: Daily   Subscription: $31.50

This daily provides general, international, national, and local news coverage. Illustrated.

364. HAWAII TIMES.   1895— .
P.O. Box 1230, Honolulu, Hawaii 96817
    Editor: Ryokin Toyomira   Language: English and Japanese
    Sponsor: Hawaii Times, Ltd.
    Circulation: 12,475   Frequency: Daily   Subscription: $36.50

365. HOKUBEI HOCHI.   North American Post.
215 Fifth Avenue, Seattle, Washington 98104
    Editor: Takami Hibiya   Language: Japanese and English
    Circulation: 2,050   Frequency: Daily   Subscription: $17.00

366. HOKUBEI MAINICHI.   North American Daily.   1948— .
1737 Sutter Street, San Francisco, California 94115
    Editor: Iwao Shimizu   Language: Japanese and English
    Sponsor: Hokubei Mainichi, Inc.
    Circulation: 7,000   Frequency: Daily   Subscription: $30.00

367. JAPAN-AMERICA SOCIETY BULLETIN.   1957— .
1755 Massachusetts Avenue, N.W., No. 308, Washington, D.C. 20036
    Editor: Ann F. Rushforth   Language: English and Japanese
    Sponsor: Japan-American Society of Washington
    Circulation: 1,100   Frequency: Monthly   Subscription: $10.00

"A publication designed to help bring the peoples of the U.S. and Japan closer together in their appreciation and understanding of each other and each other's way of life" [editor's statement]. Special features include a calendar of events and information on new books on Japan.

368. KASHU MAINICHI.   California Daily News.   1931— .
346 East First Street, Los Angeles, California 90012
    Editor: Haruo Murokana   Language: English and Japanese
    Circulation: 5,610   Frequency: Daily   Subscription: $17.00

This daily presents international, national, and local news. The emphasis is on articles of general interest to Japanese Americans. Published daily except Sundays and holidays.

369. THE NEW YORK NICHIBEI.   New York Japanese American.   1945–.
260 West Broadway, New York, New York 10013
    Editor: Isaku Kida   Language: Japanese and English
    Sponsor: Japanese American News Corporation
    Circulation: 1,066   Frequency: Weekly   Subscription: $6.00

370. THE NICHI BEI TIMES.   Japanese-American Times.   1946–.
1375 Eddy Street, San Francisco, California 94115
    Editor: Yasuo W. Abiko   Language: Japanese and English
    Sponsor: Nichi Bei Times Company
    Circulation: 6,990   Frequency: Daily   Subscription: $22.00

371. RAFU SHIMPO.   Los Angeles Japanese Daily News.   1903–.
242 South San Pedro Street, Los Angeles, California 90012
    Editors: Teiho Hashida (Japanese) and Ellen Kayano (English)
    Language: Japanese and English
    Sponsor: Los Angeles News Publishing Company
    Circulation: 19,669   Frequency: Daily   Subscripton: $17.00

This daily consists of two sections: Japanese and English. It is "an ethnic-oriented newspaper specializing in news concerning or involving persons of Japanese descent with emphasis on the Japanese American community in Southern California" [editor's statement]. The Japanese section also highlights international and national news and includes a few popular serial novels.

372. ROCKY MOUNTAIN JIHO.   Rocky Mountain Times.   1962–.
28 East 20th Avenue, Denver, Colorado 80202
    Editor: Sadako Tsubokawa   Language: English and Japanese
    Sponsor: Rocky Mountain Jiho
    Circulation: 1,030   Frequency: Weekly   Subscription: $11.00

This weekly provides local news about the Japanese-American community, aiming especially at the non-English-speaking first generation of Japanese Americans.

373. THE UTAH NIPPO.
    52 North Ninth West Street, Salt Lake City, Utah 84116
        Editor: Terumasa Adachi   Language: Japanese and English
        Circulation: 910   Frequency: 3 times/week   Subscription: $7.00

Japanese Publications in English

374. THE CROSSROADS.   1949— .
    210 South San Pedro Street, Los Angeles, California 90012
        Editor: William T. Hiroto   Language: English
        Circulation: 2,450   Frequency: Weekly   Subscription: $5.00

The emphasis of this Los Angeles Japanese weekly is on local community
events of interest to Japanese American populace. "Feature materials
and columnists, while primarily edited with an eye toward ethnicity,
do not require a 'Nisei' angle to be printed" [editor's statement].

375. GIDRA.   1969— .
    P.O. Box 18046, Los Angeles, California 90018
        Editor: Unknown   Language: English
        Sponsor: Gidra, Inc.
        Circulation: 2,230   Frequency: Monthly   Subscription: $2.50

This is an Asian-American monthly which aims to inform the Asian-
American community about matters related to them both politically
and culturally.

376. NIPPON & AMERICA.
    267 16th Avenue, San Francisco, California 90012
        Editor: Suimei Azumi   Language: English
        Circulation: Unknown Frequency: Monthly   Subscription: Unknown

377. PACIFIC CITIZEN.   1930— .
    125 Weller Street, Los Angeles, California 90012
        Editor: Harry K. Honda   Language: English
        Sponsor: Japanese American Citizens League
        Circulation: 18,969   Frequency: Weekly Subscription: $6.00

Official publication of the Japanese American Citizens League. Includes
articles on achievements, contributions, problems, and issues affecting
persons of Japanese ancestry. Illustrations included.

JEWISH PRESS

Jewish Publications in Hebrew and Hebrew-English

378. BITZARON.   Fortress.   1939— .
1141 Broadway, New York, New York 10001
    Editor: Dr. Maurice E. Chernowitz   Language: Hebrew
    Sponsor: Bitzaron, Inc.
    Circulation: 18,510   Frequency: Monthly   Subscription: $7.00

Covers political, social, and cultural topics, with articles written by outstanding Jewish writers and scholars. Includes books and film reviews.

379. HADOAR HEBREW WEEKLY.   The Mail.   1921— .
120 West 16th Street, New York, New York 10011
    Editor: David Epstein   Language: Hebrew
    Sponsor: Histadruth Ivrith of America
    Circulation: 5,100   Frequency: Weekly   Subscription: $20.00

"From its earliest beginning the *Hadoar* encouraged the creative work of Hebrew writers, poets, scholars, and thinkers in this country to create in Hebrew" [editor's statement]. Includes articles, news, and book reviews of interest to Jews.

380. HADOROM.   Torah-Oriented Journal.   1957— .
220 Park Avenue South, New York, New York
    Editor: Rabbi C. B. Chavel   Language: Hebrew
    Sponsor: Rabiinical Council of America
    Circulation: 1,100   Frequency: Semi-annually   Subscription: $5.00

Covers biblical, talmudic, historic, and other subjects. Also includes bibliographical material.

381. HAPARDES.   Orchard.   1926— .
4809 14th Avenue, Brooklyn, New York 11219
    Editor: Rabbi S. Elberg   Language: Hebrew
    Circulation: 1,950   Frequency: Monthly   Subscription: Unknown

This is a religious monthly.

382. IGERET.   Newsletter.   1966— .
515 Park Avenue, New York, New York 10022
    Editor: Ram Oren   Language: Hebrew
    Sponsor: Israeli Students Organization in the United States and Canada
    Circulation: 6,000   Frequency: Monthly   Subscription: Free

Covers topics of interest to Israeli students in the United States and
Canada.

383. JEWISH HERITAGE.   1957— .
1640 Rhode Island Avenue, N.W., Washington, D.C. 20036
    Editor: Lily Edelman   Language: Hebrew and English
    Sponsor: B'nai B'rith Commission on Adult Jewish Education
    Circulation: 8,100   Frequency: Quarterly   Subscription: $3.00

This family-oriented magazine is devoted to all aspects of Jewish life.
Also published in Spanish, Portuguese, and English.

384. LAMATCHIL.   Easy Hebrew Paper.   1960— .
515 Park Avenue, New York, New York 10022
    Editor: Rachel Enver   Language: Hebrew
    Sponsor: Jewish Agency for Israel—American Section
    Circulation: 4,500   Frequency: Weekly   Subscription: $5.00   ıknown

Middle-Eastern and world news in Hebrew (made simpler by the inclu-
sion of vowel markings).

385. PANIM EL PANIM.   Face to Face.   1957— .
P.O. Box 462, New York, New York 10025
    Editor: Dr. Pinchos Peli   Language: Hebrew
    Sponsor: Jewish Orientation Fellowship
    Circulation: 22,000   Frequency: Weekly   Subscription: $18.00

Includes general news, book reviews, and entertainment news. Aimed
at teachers, rabbis, and activists in Jewish communities.

386. PIONEER WOMAN.   1926— .
315 Fifth Avenue, New York, New York 10016
    Editor: Ruth Levine   Language: Hebrew, Yiddish, and English
    Sponsor: Pioneer Women, the Women's Labor Zionist Organization of
                America, Inc.
    Circulation: 30,000   Frequency: Monthly   Subscription: $2.00

387. SHEVILEY HAHINUCH.   Paths of Education.   1939— .
101 Fifth Avenue, New York, New York 10003
    Editor: Professor Zevi Scharfstein   Language: Hebrew
    Sponsor: National Council for Jewish Education
    Circulation: Unknown   Frequency: Quarterly   Subscription: Unknown
An educational magazine.

388. TALPIOTH.   1943— .
Amsterdam Avenue & 186th Street, New York, New York 10033
    Editor: Editorial Board   Language: Hebrew
    Sponsor: Yeshiva University
    Circulation: 850   Frequency: Irregular   Subscription: $6.50/copy
This publication is dedicated to Hebrew philosophy, law, and ethics.

389. YOUNG JUDEAN.   1914— .
116 West 14th Street, New York, New York 10011
    Editor: Doris B. Gold   Language: Hebrew, Yiddish, and English
    Sponsor: Hadassah Zionist Youth Commission
    Circulation: 8,500   Frequency: Monthly   Subscription: $1.75
An Israeli-oriented Zionist youth house organ for Young Judean Clubs
in the United States. Emphasis is on cultural Judaism and Zionism.
Aimed at children aged 8 to 14.

Jewish Publications in Yiddish and Yiddish-English

390. BIALYSTOKER STIMME.   Voice of Bialystok.
228 East Broadway, New York, New York 10002
    Editor: Rabbi Azriel Weissman   Language: Yiddish and English
    Sponsor: Bialystoker Center and Home for the Aged
    Circulation: 4,000   Frequency: Semi-annually   Subscription: Free
A house organ which is aimed at aged Jewish people and which includes
news concerning the Bialystoker Center activities.

391. B'NAI YIDDISH.   1968— .
22 East 17th Street, New York, New York 10003
    Editors: Itzhok Koslovsky and Moshe Starkman
    Language: Yiddish and English
    Sponsor: B'nai Yiddish Society
    Circulation: 1,300   Frequency: Bi-monthly   Subscription: $3.50

General articles on Judaism and Jewish history, etc., plus news analyses. The main objective is "to check assimilation, to perpetuate the Yiddish language as a means or a barrier to keep assimilation out of the Jewish community" [editor's statement].

392. DAY-JEWISH JOURNAL.   Der Tog-Morgen Journal.   1914— .
183 East Broadway, New York, New York 10002
   Editor: David Meckler   Language: Yiddish
   Sponsor: Day Publishing Company
   Circulation: 43,340   Frequency: Daily   Subscription: $30.00

Includes general, international, national, and local news for the Yiddish readers.

393. FARBAND NEWS.   1912— .
575 Sixth Avenue, New York, New York 10011
   Editor: Jacob Katzman   Language: Yiddish and English
   Sponsor: Farband-Labor Zionist Order
   Circulation: 25,000   Frequency: Irregular   Subscription: Unknown

394. FREIHEIT.   Freedom.   1922— .
35 East 12th Street, New York, New York 10003
   Editor: P. Novick   Language: Yiddish
   Sponsor: Morgen Freiheit Publishing Company
   Circulation: 6,091   Frequency: Daily   Subscription: $23.00

395. JEWISH DAILY FORWARD.   1897— .
175 East Broadway, New York, New York 10002
   Editor: Morris Crystal   Language: Yiddish
   Sponsor: Forward Association
   Circulation: 50,000   Frequency: Daily   Subscription: $35.00

Contains general, national, international, and local news. The oldest Jewish daily in the United States. It "specializes in news of Jewish interest from all over the world. Supports the state of Israel and opposes communism" [editor's statement].

396. KINDER JOURNAL.   1919— .
41 Union Square, New York, New York 10003
   Editor: Saul Goodman   Language: Yiddish
   Sponsor: Sholem Aleichem Folk Institute
   Circulation: 1,200   Frequency: Bi-monthly   Subscription: $2.00

The main objective of this publication is "to acquaint children with Jewish culture—particularly Yiddish literature, poetry, and folklore" [editor's statement].

397. KINDER ZEITUNG.   Children's Newspaper.   1930— .
175 East Broadway, New York, New York 10002
   Editor: Joseph Mlotek   Language: Yiddish
   Sponsor: Workmen's Circle, Education Department
   Circulation: Unknown   Frequency: Bi-monthly   Subscription: Unknown

News, stories, songs, humor, and poetry in Yiddish for children.

398. KULTUR UN LEBEN.   Culture and Life.   1911— .
175 East Broadway, New York, New York 10002
   Editor: Joseph Mlotek   Language: Yiddish
   Sponsor: The Workmen's Circle
   Circulation: 21,800   Frequency: Bi-monthly   Subscription: $2.00

National publication of a Jewish labor fraternal organization. Features articles on "Yiddish cultural subjects, Jewish affairs, national and world affairs, intra-organizational matters, and poetry in Yiddish" [editor's statement].

399. MIZRACHI WOMAN.   1935— .
250 Park Avenue South, New York, New York 10003
   Editor: Gabriel Levenson   Language: Yiddish and English
   Sponsor: Mizrachi Women's Organization
   Circulation: 26,000   Frequency: Monthly   Subscription: Free to members

Provides general information on Jewish life in the world, especially in the United States and Israel. Special emphasis on education and social topics. Promotes Zionism.

400. MORGEN FREIHEIT.   Morning Freedom.   1922— .
35 East 12th Street, New York, New York 10003
   Editor: Paul Novick   Language: Yiddish
   Circulation: 7,000   Frequency: Daily   Subscription: $25.00

Provides general, international, national, and local news.

401. OIFN SHVEL.   On the Threshold.   1941— .
    200 West 72nd Street, New York, New York 10023
        Editor: M. Schaechter   Language: Yiddish
        Sponsor: Freeland League
        Circulation: Unknown   Frequency: Bi-monthly   Subscription: Unknown

402. SHMUESSEN MIT KINDER UN YUGNT.   Talks with Children and
    Youths.   1942— .
    770 Eastern Parkway, Brooklyn, New York 11213
        Editor: Dr. Nissan Mindel   Language: Yiddish
        Sponsor: Merkos L'Inyonei Chinuch, Inc.
        Circulation: 4,500   Frequency: Monthly   Subscription: $1.50

English and Yiddish are published in separate pamphlets, but simultaneously
each month. General articles on Jewish life and history, with a column
devoted to "do's" and "don'ts" for upcoming Jewish holidays.

403. UNZER VEG.   Our Way.   1925— .
    305 Broadway, Room 910, New York, New York 10007
        Editor: Yehuda Tyberg   Language: Yiddish
        Sponsor: United Labor Zionist Party of the U.S.A. and Canada
        Circulation: Unknown   Frequency: Monthly   Subscription: Unknown

404. UNZER WEG.   Jewish Way.   1945— .
    166 West Washington, Chicago, Illinois 60602
        Editor: Nathan Kravitz   Language: Yiddish and English
        Circulation: 5,000   Frequency: Quarterly   Subscription: Unknown

A political quarterly.

405. UNSER TSAIT.   Our Time.   1941— .
    25 East 78th Street, New York, New York 10021
        Editor: Dr. Emanuel Scherer   Language: Yiddish
        Sponsor: International Jewish Labor Bund
        Circulation: 5,500   Frequency: Monthly   Subscription: Unknown

"Covers topics of general and Jewish political, social, and cultural character, reflecting Bund's ideals of democratic internationalistic socialism. Is
against both assimilation and Zionism, but for maintaining national Jewish
identity" [editor's statement]. Critical attitude toward the state of Israel.

406. DER WECKER.   The Awakener.   1921— .
175 East Broadway, New York, New York 10002
   Editor: Dr. Elias Schulman   Language: Yiddish
   Sponsor: Jewish Socialist Verband of America
   Circulation: 3,200   Frequency: Monthly   Subscription: $7.00

A political, socialist Jewish monthly

407. YEDIES FUN YIVO.   News of the YIVO.   1925— .
1048 Fifth Avenue, New York, New York 10028
   Editor: Shmuel Lapin   Language: Yiddish and English
   Sponsor: YIVO Institute for Jewish Research
   Circulation: 5,000   Frequency: Quarterly
   Subscription: Membership dues

408. DER YID.   The Jew.   1951— .
134 Broadway, Brooklyn, New York 11211
   Editor: Sender Deutsch   Language: Yiddish
   Sponsor: Der Yid Publishing Association
   Circulation: 7,250   Frequency: Semi-monthly   Subscription: $5.00

General and local news of interest to the Jewish community in the
greater New York area. Includes book reviews and illustrations.

409. YIDDISH LINGO.   1969—1971.
33 East Minor Street, Emmaus, Pennsylvania 18049
   Editor: Lottie Robins   Language: Yiddish and English
   Sponsor: Rodale Press, Inc.
   Circulation: 9,500   Frequency: Bi-monthly   Subscription: $5.00

Publication ceased as of July 1971.

410. DI YIDDISHE HEIM.   The Jewish Home.   1959— .
770 Eastern Parkway, Brooklyn, New York 11213
   Editors: Tema Gurary (Yiddish) and Rachel Altein (English)
   Language: Yiddish and English
   Sponsor: Lubavitch Women's Organization
   Circulation: 5,000   Frequency: Quarterly   Subscription: $2.00

General articles on Judaism, essentially from the Hassidic viewpoint.
Specifically geared to the interests of the Jewish woman.

411. YIDDISHE KULTUR.   Yiddish Culture.   1938— .
1133 Broadway, Suite 1023, New York, New York 10010
   Editor: I. Goldberg   Language: Yiddish
   Sponsor: Yiddisher Kultur Farband, Inc.
   Circulation: 3,900   Frequency: Monthly   Subscription: $10.00

Middle-Eastern, American, and world news, with analyses and a few
general articles on Jewish personalities, literature, and culture.

412. DOS YIDDISHE VORT.   The Yiddish Word.
5 Beekman Street, New York, New York 10038
   Editor: Joseph Friedenson   Language: Yiddish
   Sponsor: Agudath Israel of America
   Circulation: 10,050   Frequency: Monthly   Subscription: $5.00

Features articles on Jewish culture and life in general.   Its purpose is to
"present the Orthodox Jewish viewpoint on current issues of Jewish
interest in the U.S.A." [editor's statement].

413. YIDDISHER KEMFER.   The Jewish Combatant.   1906— .
45 East 17th Street, New York, New York 10003
   Editor: Mordchai Shtrigler   Language: Yiddish
   Sponsor: Labor Zionist Letters, Inc.
   Circulation: 4,750   Frequency: Weekly   Subscription: $15.00

News about Zionism, Judaism; also includes Middle East and world news.

414. DER YIDDISHER KWAL.   Jewish Well.   1967— .
545 Bedford Avenue, Brooklyn, New York 11211
   Editor: Sender Deutsch   Language: Yiddish
   Sponsor: United Talmudical Academy
   Circulation: 3,100   Frequency: Semi-monthly   Subscription: $5.00

415. YIDISHE SHPRAKH.   Jewish Language.   1941— .
1048 Fifth Avenue, New York, New York 10028
   Editor: Mordkhe Schaechter   Language: Yiddish
   Sponsor: YIVO Institute for Jewish Research
   Circulation: 3,500   Frequency: 3 times/year
   Subscription: Membership dues

416. YIVO BLETER.   1931— .
1048 Fifth Avenue, New York, New York 10028
    Editor: Dr. Shlomo Noble   Language: Yiddish
    Sponsor: YIVO Institute for Jewish Research
    Circulation: 3,000   Frequency: Irregular
    Subscription: Membership dues

"Provides a forum for the researcher in Jewish social sciences and
humanities" [editor's statement]. Emphasis is on the Eastern European
Jewish experience, as well as on problems of acculturation, bilingualism,
etc.

417. YUGNTRUF.   Call of Youth.   1964— .
3328 Bainbridge Avenue, Bronx, New York 10467
    Editor: David Roskies   Language: Yiddish
    Sponsor: Yugntruf—Youth for Yiddish, Inc.
    Circulation: 2,500   Frequency: Quarterly   Subscription: $3.00

Contains articles on Jewish history and culture. The objective is "to
stimulate Yiddish creativity among the younger generation" [editor's
statement].

418. ZAMLUNGEN.   Gatherings.   1954— .
35 East 12th Street, New York, New York 10003
    Editor: Ber Green   Language: Yiddish
    Sponsor: Yiddish Writers Organization at the YKUF.
    Circulation: 1,100   Frequency: Quarterly   Subscription: $4.00

Dedicated to Yiddish literature and Jewish culture.

419. ZEIN.   To Be.   1954— .
144 West 73rd Street, New York, New York 10023
    Editor: L. Rosof   Language: Yiddish
    Circulation: 1,400   Frequency: Quarterly   Subscription: $5.00

Includes general articles, stories, and poetry.

420. THE ZUKUNFT.   The Future.   1892— .
25 East 78th Street, New York, New York 10021
    Editors: Morris Crysta, Hyman Bass, Eliezer Greenberg
    Sponsor: Congress for Jewish Culture   Language: Yiddish
    Circulation: 4,000   Frequency: Monthly   Subscription: $7.00

Covers all aspects of Jewish cultural and social life in the United States
as well as in the world.

Jewish Publications in English

421. AMERICAN ISRAELITE.   1854– .
906 Main Street, Cincinnati, Ohio 45202
    Editor: Henry C. Segal   Language: English
    Circulation: 8,381   Frequency: Weekly   Subscription: $6.00

This community-oriented publication provides coverage of Jewish
organizations and religious institutions in the Cincinnati area, as well as
news coverage of events in Israel and national and international issues
of special interest to Jews. Believed to be the oldest American-Jewish
newspaper in the country.

422. AMERICAN JEWISH HISTORICAL QUARTERLY.   1893– .
2 Thornton Road, Waltham, Massachusetts 02154
    Editor: Nathan M. Kaganoff   Language: English
    Sponsor: American Jewish Historical Society
    Circulation: 3,150   Frequency: Quarterly   Subscription: $15.00

Contains research articles devoted to the broad analysis of American
Jewish history (European background, immigration, assimilation, and
adjustments in the United States, and impact of the Jewish community
on the United States and aborad). Also features book reviews, bibliography notes and documents, and historical news.

423. AMERICAN-JEWISH LIFE.   1958– .
701 South Broad Street, Trenton, New Jersey 08618
    Editor: Kent H. Jacobs   Language: English
    Circulation: 18,000   Frequency: Monthly   Subscription: $3.00

Emphasis is placed on Israel and the Middle East, with coverage also of
national, local, and group affairs of importance to the Jewish people.
Includes items on the activities of community leaders, plus commentaries
and opinions.

424. AMERICAN JEWISH TIMES-OUTLOOK.   1933– .
P.O. Box 10306, Charlotte, North Carolina 28201
    Editor: George Einhart   Language: English
    Sponsor: American Jewish Times-Outlook, Inc.
    Circulation: 4,030   Frequency: Monthly Subscription: $3.00

This community-oriented monthly focuses on the activities of Jewish
organizations and families in North Carolina, South Carolina, and
Virginia.

425. AMERICAN JEWISH WORLD.   1912— .

822 Upper Midwest Building, 422 Hennepin Avenue, Minneapolis,
Minnesota 55401

Editor: L. H. Frisch   Language: English

Circulation: 15,472   Frequency: Weekly   Subscription: $5.00

International, national, and local news of special interest to the Jewish
people.

426. AMERICAN POST.   1954— .

349 East 36th Street, Paterson, New Jersey 07504

Editor: Dr. Reuben Kaufman   Language: English

Sponsor: American Post, Inc.

Circulation: 1,381   Frequency: Weekly   Subscription: $5.00

Covers local, national, and international news with emphasis on Israel
and Jewish communities. It includes editorial comments on Jewish
problems, congregational announcements, social news, biblical quota-
tions and interpretations, announcements from various Jewish organizations, book reviews, youth features, entertainment, etc.

427. AMERICAN ZIONIST.   1910— .

145 East 32nd Street, New York, New York 10016

Editor: Dr. Elias Cooper   Language: English

Sponsor: Zionist Organization of America

Circulation: 50,000   Frequency: Monthly   Subscription: $4.00

Articles on Jewish, Israeli, and Zionist issues. Emphasis is placed on the
Zionist movement. Special features include editorial commentary, book
reviews, and the American Zionist Forum.

428. ARIZONA POST.   1943— .

102 North Plumer, Tucson, Arizona 85719

Editor: Mrs. Samuel Rothman   Language: English

Sponsor: Tucson Jewish Community Council

Circulation: 3,000   Frequency: Bi-weekly   Subscription: $4.00

This publication is community oriented, although local and national
news of special interest to Jews is also included. Provides coverage of
activities by Jewish organizations and communities in Arizona, with
special features for youth.

429. BALTIMORE JEWISH TIMES.   1919— .
1800 North Charles Street, Baltimore, Maryland 21201
    Editor: Bert F. Kline   Language: English
    Circulation: 17,850 Frequency: Weekly   Subscription: $3.50

Coverage of local, national, and international news of special interest
to the Jewish population. Emphasis on Israel and Judaism. Includes
sections devoted to entertainment, youth, travel, sports, and food.

430. BEKITZUR.   In Brief.   1970— .
218 East 70th Street, New York, New York 10021
    Editor: Pesach Schindler   Language: English
    Sponsor: Solomon Schechter Day School Association, United Synagogue
           Commission on Jewish Education
    Circulation: 500   Frequency: Monthly   Subscription: Free

This newsletter provides a description of the various programs and
developments in the Solomon Schechter School Movement (forty
conservative Jewish Day Schools in North America).

BIALYSTOKER STIMME.   See Jewish Publications in Yiddish and Yiddish-
Yiddish-English.

431. B'NAI B'RITH MESSENGER.   1897— .
2510 West 7th Street, Los Angeles, California 90057
    Editor: Joseph J. Cummins   Language: English
    Circulation: 49,994   Frequency: Weekly   Subscription: $6.00

Coverage of international, national, and local news of special interest to
the Jewish population in Southern California. Includes sections on book
reviews, business, future social events, and items of interest to women.

B'NAI YIDDISH. See Jewish Publications in Yiddish and Yiddish-English.

432. BROTHERHOOD.   1967— .
838 Fifth Avenue, New York, New York 10021
    Editor: Sylvan Lebow   Language: English
    Sponsor: National Federation of Temple Brotherhoods, and Jewish
           Chautauqua Society
    Circulation: 72,000   Frequency: Bi-monthly   Subscription: $1.00

Emphasis is placed on religious and educational topics. Includes articles,
book reviews, and a youth section.

433. BUFFALO JEWISH REVIEW.   1918– .
 110 Pearl Street, Buffalo, New York 14202
   Editor: Elias R. Jacobs   Language: English
   Circulation: 13,000   Frequency: Weekly   Subscription: $5.00

Provides coverage of various activities within Jewish communities in the
Buffalo area, but also includes national and international news. Sections
cover editorials, youth items, book reviews, and future events.

434. CALIFORNIA JEWISH RECORD.   1943– .
 P.O. Box 983, San Francisco, California 94101
   Editor: David Reznek   Language: English
   Sponsor: Orot, Inc.
   Circulation: 10,000   Frequency: Unknown   Subscription: $4.00

Provides coverage of Jewish communities in northern and central
California. Includes national and international news of interest to the
Jewish people. There are sections devoted to youth features, music,
entertainment, and book reviews.

435. CALIFORNIA JEWISH VOICE.   1922– .
 406 South Main Street, Los Angeles, California 90013
   Editor: I. Lechtman   Language: English
   Circulation: 32,500   Frequency: Weekly   Subscription: $5.00

Extensive coverage of local Jewish events, religious, and organizational
activities. Also includes national and international news of special
concern to the Jewish population. Zionist-oriented.

436. CALL.   1952– .
 175 East Broadway, New York, New York 10002
   Editor: William Stern   Language: English
   Sponsor: Workmen's Circle
   Circulation: Unknown Frequency: Bi-monthly   Subscription: $1.00

Published for the benefit of the members of the Workmen's Circle, a
Jewish fraternal organization. Emphasis is placed on news concerning
various activities, events, and developments within the organization.
Also includes articles on Jewish issues.

CENTRAL VALLEY JEWISH HERITAGE. See HERITAGE-SOUTHWEST
 JEWISH PRESS (Number 450).

437. CLEVELAND JEWISH NEWS.   1964—.
2108 Payne Avenue, Cleveland, Ohio 44114
    Editor: Jerry D. Barach   Language: English
    Sponsor: Cleveland Jewish Publication Company
    Circulation: 16,894   Frequency: Weekly   Subscription: $6.00

Coverage of various Jewish events and activities in the greater Cleveland area. Also includes national and international news, with an emphasis on Israel.

438. COMMENTARY.   1945—.
165 East 56th Street, New York, New York 10022
    Editor: Norman Podhoretz   Language: English
    Sponsor: American Jewish Committee
    Circulation: 60,500   Frequency: Monthly   Subscription: $10.00

Contains analytical articles on political and social issues for the purpose of clarification and understanding. Also includes book reviews and letters to the editor.

439. CONGRESS BI-WEEKLY.   1933—.
15 East 84th Street, New York, New York 10028
    Editor: Herbert Poster   Language: English
    Sponsor: American Jewish Congress
    Circulation: 35,000   Frequency: Bi-weekly   Subscription: $5.00

Contains analytical articles and comments on political, social, and economic issues. Jewish activities are emphasized.

440. CONNECTICUT JEWISH LEDGER.   1929—.
P.O. Box 1107, Hartford, Connecticut 06101
    Editor: Rabbi A. J. Feldman   Language: English
    Circulation: 22,895   Frequency: Weekly   Subscription: $5.00

News coverage of international, national, and local events of special interest to the Jewish population, including news of financial matters and announcements of forthcoming events.

441. CONSERVATIVE JUDAISM.   1943—.
3080 Broadway, New York, New York 10027
    Editor: Rabbi Mordecai Waxman   Language: English
    Sponsor: Rabbinical Assembly and the Jewish Theological Seminary
    Circulation: 3,000   Frequency: Quarterly   Subscription: $5.00

Study of Judaica in terms of its theology, philosophy, and education. Examination of the philosophical stance of Conservative Judaism in the United States. Also includes articles on the problems of the Jewish community in the United States and abroad, Israel, and politics of the Middle East. Reviews of books with a Jewish content.

442. DAYTON JEWISH CHRONICLE.   1965— .
      118 Salem Avenue, Dayton, Ohio 45406
          Editor: Anne M. Hammerman   Language: English
          Sponsor: Dayton Jewish Chronicle, Inc.
          Circulation: 1,450   Frequency: Weekly   Subscription: $4.50

National and international news of special interest to the Jewish reader, plus coverage of local Jewish social and other events.

443. DETROIT JEWISH NEWS.   1942— .
      17515 West Nine Mile Road, Southfield, Michigan 48075
          Editor: Philip Slomovitz   Language: English
          Sponsor: Jewish News Publishing Company
          Circulation: 16,575   Frequency: Weekly   Subscription: $8.00

Coverage of Jewish communities in Michigan and Windsor, Ontario, is emphasized. International and national news of special interest to the Jewish people is also included. Sections are devoted to special features such as commentaries on important issues, business news, social affairs, club and organizational news, future events, and book reviews.

444. DIMENSIONS IN AMERICAN JUDAISM.   1966— .
      838 Fifth Avenue, New York, New York 10021
          Editor: Myrna Pollak   Language: English
          Sponsor: Union of American Hebrew Congregations
          Circulation: 10,000   Frequency: Quarterly   Subscription: $3.00

This religious publication also includes articles dealing with various social, philosophical, and political issues. Features sections on the arts and book reviews.

FARBAND NEWS. See Jewish Publications in Yiddish and Yiddish-English.

445. FREE SONS OF ISRAEL REPORTER.   1950– .
150 Fifth Avenue, New York, New York 10011
   Editor: Louis Friedman   Language: English
   Sponsor: Free Sons of Israel
   Circulation: 10,000 Frequency: Quarterly   Subscription: Unknown

A fraternal newspaper which presents news items on the various activities of the Order, as well as reports on the lodges.

446. HABONEH.   1937– .
200 Park Avenue South, New York, New YOrk 10003
   Editor: Melvin Kasinetz   Language: English
   Sponsor: Habonim Labor Zionist Youth
   Circulation: Unknown   Frequency: Quarterly   Subscription: $1.50

A publication for youth which includes items on Jewish culture and Israel, group interests, and activities. Educational in nature.

447. HADASSAH MAGAZINE.   1925– .
65 East 52nd Street, New York, New York 10022
   Editor: Miriam K. Freund   Language: English
   Sponsor: Hadassah, Women's Zionist Organization of America
   Circulation: 350,000   Frequency: Monthly   Subscription: Unknown

Articles on various social issues in the Middle East, with emphasis on cultural, educational, and philanthropic activities of Jewish groups both in the United States and in Israel. Book reviews are included.

448. HEBREW WATCHMAN.   1925– .
277 Jefferson Avenue, Memphis, Tennessee 38103
   Editor: Herman I. Goldberger   Language: English
   Circulation: 2,196   Frequency: Weekly Subscription: $6.00

Coverage of international, national, and local news of a special interest to the Jewish community in Tennessee.

449. HEIGHTS SUN PRESS.
2156 Lee Road, Cleveland Heights, Ohio 44118
   Editor: Harry Volk   Language: English
   Sponsor: Comcorp Newspapers
   Circulation: 44,000   Frequency: Weekly   Subscription: $5.00

Community-oriented newspaper covering social, organizational, and club news of the Jewish people in Cleveland. Also features book reviews, letters to the editor, and entertainment.

450. HERITAGE-SOUTHWEST JEWISH PRESS. 1954—.
2130 South Vermont Avenue, Los Angeles, California 90007
Editor: Herb Brin   Language: English
Sponsor: Heritage Publishing Company
Circulation: 10,800   Frequency: Weekly   Subscription: $7.50

Heritage-Southwest Jewish Press (Los Angeles) is one of four papers
published by the Heritage Publishing Company. In addition to this
newspaper, the Heritage Publishing Company also publishes *Southwest
Jewish Press-Heritage*, which originally began in 1914 as the *Southwest
Jewish Press* but which was taken over by Heritage in 1958 (San Diego,
weekly, circulation 4,600); *Orange County Jewish Heritage* (Orange
County, monthly, circulation 2,300); and *Central Valley Jewish Heritage*
(Fresno, monthly, circulation 1,500). All four publications are edited by
Herb Brin. Coverage includes national and international news of special
interest to the Jewish community. Heavy emphasis is placed on Jewish
local events, organizations, and individual personalities. Also featured
are book reviews.

451. HILLCREST SUN MESSENGER.
2156 Lee Road, Cleveland Heights, Ohio 44118
Editor: Harry Volk   Language: English
Sponsor: Comcorp Newspapers
Circulation: 23,000   Frequency: Weekly   Subscription: $5.00

Community-oriented publication with extensive coverage of organizations,
temple events, social activities, and clubs in the Cleveland area.

452. HISTADRUT FOTO NEWS. 1948—.
33 East 67th Street, New York, New York 10021
Editor: Nahum Guttman   Language: English
Sponsor: National Committee for Labor Israel, Inc.
Circulation: 26,000   Frequency: Monthly   Subscription: $2.00

Publishes the various activities and programs of the Committee related
to the work of Histadrut, the Israeli labor organization.

453. INDIANA JEWISH CHRONICLE. 1921—.
241 East Ohio Street, Indianapolis, Indiana 46205
Editor: Morris Strauss   Language: English
Circulation: 10,000   Frequency: Weekly   Subscription: $5.00

This community-oriented publication maintains an emphasis on various
events within the Jewish community in Indianapolis. It also includes
world and national news coverage.

454. IN JEWISH BOOKLAND.   1945– .
15 East 26th Street, New York, New York 10010
    Editor: A. Alan Steinbach   Language: English
    Sponsor: Jewish Book Council of America
    Circulation: 19,000   Frequency: 7 times/year   Subscription: $2.00

This periodical is devoted entirely to book reviews. The main objective
is "to evaluate books of Jewish interest and to stimulate their sale and
reading" [editor's statement].

455. INTERMOUNTAIN JEWISH NEWS.   1913– .
1275 Sherman Street, Denver, Colorado 80203
    Editor: Max Goldberg   Language: English
    Circulation: 4,800   Frequency: Weekly   Subscription: $8.00

Regional publication devoted to covering activities of the Jewish communities in Colorado, Wyoming, Utah, and New Mexico. Special features
include news on Israel and book reviews.

456. ISRAEL DIGEST.   1950– .
515 Park Avenue, New York, New York 10022
    Editor: Dan Leon   Language: English
    Sponsor: Jewish Agency for Israel—American Section
    Circulation: 8,000   Frequency: Semi-monthly   Subscription: $3.00

Presents items on various activities and events in Israel. Objective of the
publication is to keep the American Jewish population informed on
Israeli affairs.

457. ISRAEL INVESTOR'S REPORT.   1961– .
110 East 59th Street, New York, New York 10022
    Editor: Joseph Yoshor   Language: English
    Sponsor: Israel Communications, Ltd.
    Circulation: 5,000   Frequency: Semi-monthly   Subscription: $20.00

Although this paper is published in Israel, it is aimed at the Jewish
population primarily in the United States, and to some extent in Canada.
It includes reports and articles on all aspects of Israeli economy (economic
trends, industrial achievements, financial activities, investments, new
projects, etc.) of special interest to American and Canadian Jews holding
various investments in Israel.

458. ISRAEL MAGAZINE.   1968– .
155 West 68th Street, New York, New York 10023
    Editor: Howard Blake   Language: English
    Sponsor: Israel Publishing Company
    Circulation: 42,000   Frequency: Monthly   Subscription: $10.00

This illustrated magazine is devoted to presenting an overview of life in
Israel. Each issue usually spotlights a given theme. Regular features
include tourism, book reviews, art, and literature.

459. JEWISH ADVOCATE.   1902– .
251 Causeway Street, Boston, Massachusetts 02114
    Editor: Joseph G. Weisberg   Language: English
    Sponsor: Jewish Advocate Publishing Corporation
    Circulation: 24,300   Frequency: Weekly   Subscription: $7.50

This newspaper is "dedicated to Americanism, Judaism, and Social
Justice" [editor's statement]. It publishes comprehensive local, national,
international, and Israeli news of special interest to the Jewish people.
Also featured are heavy coverage of the Jewish community in Boston,
book reviews, political commentary, financial news, entertainment, and
society news.

460. JEWISH CHRONICLE.   1962– .
315 South Bellefield Avenue, Pittsburgh, Pennsylvania 15213
    Editor: Albert Bloom   Language: English
    Sponsor: Pittsburgh Jewish Publication and Education Foundation
    Circulation: 14,850   Frequency: Weekly   Subscription: $6.00

National, international, and Jewish community news, with an emphasis
on Israel and Jewish activities and affairs in the United States.

461. JEWISH CIVIC LEADER.   1923– .
11 Norwich Street, Worcester, Massachusetts 01608
    Editor: Conrad H. Isenberg   Language: English
    Sponsor: Worcester Leader Publishing Company
    Circulation: 16,302   Frequency: Weekly   Subscription: $5.00

The main purpose of this publication is "to disseminate news of Jewish
content on the local, national, and international scene" [editor's state-
ment]. It also includes news on current Jewish organizational and religious
activities, and special announcements, such as births, engagements,
marriages, and social events. Occasionally editorials and book reviews
are featured.

462. JEWISH CIVIC PRESS.   1965— .
P.O. Box 15500, New Orleans, Louisiana 70115
   Editor: Audrey Wulf   Language: English
   Circulation: 4,261   Frequency: Monthly   Subscription: $3.00

This is primarily a community-oriented newspaper with heavy emphasis
on the various activities within the Jewish community in New Orleans
(institutional, and organizational news, announcements of births,
marriages, Jewish charities, etc.). It also covers international and
national events and issues.

463. JEWISH COMMUNITY REPORTER.   1949— .
999 Lower Ferry Road, Trenton, New Jersey 06818
   Editor: Arnold Ropeik   Language: English
   Sponsor: Jewish Federation of Trenton
   Circulation: 2,900   Frequency: Monthly   Subscription: Free

A community-oriented publication with coverage of local and international
news.

464. JEWISH CURRENTS.   1946— .
22 East 17th Street, New York, New York 10003
   Editor: Morris Schappes   Language: English
   Sponsor: Jewish Currents, Inc.
   Circulation: 4,389   Frequency: Monthly   Subscription: $4.00

Provides coverage of various current issues such as Israeli affairs, the
black movement, black-Jewish relations, Jewish culture, Jews in Eastern
Europe, and American Jewish organizational life.

465. JEWISH DIGEST.   1955— .
P.O. Box 153, Houston, Texas 77001
   Editor: Bernard Postal   Language: English
   Sponsor: Jewish Digest, Inc.
   Circulation: 13,500   Frequency: Monthly   Subscription: $6.00

Presents condensations of materials from newspapers, magazines, books,
reports, documents, etc., on every phase of Jewish life, history, and
problems of the past and present.

466. JEWISH EXPONENT.   1887– .
1513 Walnut Street, Philadelphia, Pennsylvania 19102
    Editor: Leon E. Brown   Language: English
    Sponsor: Federation of Jewish Agencies of Greater Philadelphia
    Circulation: 68,000   Frequency: Weekly   Subscription: $4.00

Coverage of news and opinions pertaining to or of interest to the Jewish community, including local, national, and international news with heavy emphasis on organizational activity and Israel. Also featured are book reviews, a food column, sports, and financial news.

467. JEWISH FLORIDIAN.   1928– .
120 N.E. Sixth Street, Miami, Florida 33131
    Editor: Fred K. Shochet   Language: English
    Circulation: 22,000   Frequency: Weekly   Subscription: $5.00

National and international news, with emphasis on Israel and the various activities of the Jewish community in the greater Miami area.

468. JEWISH FRONTIER.   1934– .
45 East 17th Street, New York, New York 10003
    Editor: Marie Syrkin   Language: English
    Sponsor: Labor Zionist Letters, Inc.
    Circulation: 8,850   Frequency: Monthly   Subscription: $5.00

This is the official organ of the Labor Zionist Movement in the United States. It is concerned primarily with commentary, with the purpose of "interpreting Zionism and Israel from the viewpoint of Labor Zionist ideology" [editor's statement]. It presents articles on American social, political, and economic developments; the situation of world Jewry; and the Middle East. Its periodic supplement, "Israel Seen From Within," gives information about Israel's current problems and is prepared by Israelis. The publication features letters to the editor and book reviews.

469. JEWISH HERALD-VOICE.   1908– .
4410 Fannin Street, Houston, Texas 77004
    Editor: D. H. White   Language: English
    Sponsor: D. H. White and Company
    Circulation: 3,800   Frequency: Weekly   Subscription: $5.00

A community-oriented paper which stresses activities and events of the Jewish community in Houston. Also featured are national and international news coverage, and book reviews.

470. JEWISH HERITAGE.   1957— .
1640 Rhode Island Avenue, N.W., Washington, D.C. 20036
    Editor: Lily Edelman   Language: English
    Sponsor: B'nai B'rith
    Circulation: 10,000   Frequency: Quarterly   Subscription: $3.00

This quarterly publication offers articles on all aspects of Jewish life, past and present.

471. JEWISH HOMEMAKER.   1968— .
105 Hudson Street, New York, New York 10013
    Editor: Rabbi Bernard Levy   Language: English
    Sponsor: O. K. Laboratories
    Circulation: 40,000   Frequency: Bi-monthly   Subscription: $2.50

This home-oriented magazine is aimed at the Jewish housewife. Contains articles pertaining to the observance of traditional Judaism in the home, in education, in child psychology and child raising, in recipes, in decorating, and in book reviews.

472. JEWISH HORIZON.   1937— .
200 Park Avenue South, New York, New York 10003
    Editor: Rabbi William Herskowitz   Language: English
    Sponsor: Religious Zionists of America
    Circulation: 10,000   Frequency: Quarterly   Subscription: $1.50

Contains articles, editorials, short stories, and poems relating to Zionism, Israel, and Judaica. Social and religious issues in the United States are also covered.

473. JEWISH LEDGER.   1926— .
721 Monroe Avenue, Rochester, New York 14607
    Editor: Donald Wolin   Language: English
    Circulation: 8,000   Frequency: Weekly   Subscription: $4.00

National, international, and local news coverage. Emphasis is placed on the community activities of the Jewish population in the Rochester area. Features book reviews, by-lined columns on Israel, and business news.

474. JEWISH LIFE.   1946— .
84 Fifth Avenue, New York, New York
    Editor: Saul Bernstein   Language: English
    Sponsor: Union of Orthodox Jewish Congregations of America
    Circulation: 10,000   Frequency: Bi-monthly   Subscription: $2.50

475. JEWISH MONITOR.   1948— .
P.O. Box 9155, Crestline Station, Birmingham, Alabama 35213
    Editor: Dr. J. S. Gallinger   Language: English
    Sponsor: Jewish Monitor
    Circulation: 3,591   Frequency: Monthly   Subscription: $2.00

Provides coverage of a braod scope of issues affecting Judaism both in
the United States and abroad, along with news of Jewish activities in
the Mississippi and Alabama region.

476. THE JEWISH NEWS.   1947— .
32 Central Avenue, Newark, New Jersey 07102
    Editor: Harry Weingast   Language: English
    Sponsor: Jewish Community Council of Essex County
    Circulation: 26,200   Frequency: Weekly   Subscription: Unknown

Provides national and international news coverage with the emphasis on
Israel. Stresses news coverage of Jewish activities, organizations, and
affairs in Essex County.

477. JEWISH OBSERVER.   1963— .
5 Beekman Street, New York, New York 10038
    Editor: Rabbi Nisson Wolpin   Language: English
    Sponsor: Agudath Israel of America
    Circulation: 16,250   Frequency: Monthly   Subscription: $5.00

Examines national and international events, and current issues and
problems for an Orthodox Jewish perspective.

478. THE JEWISH PARENT.   1948— .
156 Fifth Avenue, New York, New York 11219
    Editor: Dr. Joseph Kaminetsky   Language: English
    Sponsor: National Association of Hebrew Day Schools PTA's
    Circulation: 8,000   Frequency: Quarterly   Subscription: $2.00

Educational orientation. Articles on the Hebrew Day School programs
and problems, religious education, psychology and child-training.
Special features include educational news, book reviews, and reader
contributions.

479. JEWISH POST AND OPINION.   1931— .
611 North Park Avenue, Indianapolis, Indiana 46204
    Editor: Gabriel Cohen   Language: English
    Sponsor: National Jewish Post, Inc.
    Circulation: 22,600   Frequency: Weekly   Subscription: $10.00

This publication provides national and international news coverage of special interest to Jews. It also features opinions, commentaries, and book reviews.

480. JEWISH PRESS.   1921— .
101 North 20th Street, Omaha, Nebraska 68102
    Editor: Mrs. Robert Gerelick   Language: English
    Sponsor: Omaha Jewish Federation
    Circulation: 4,621   Frequency: Weekly   Subscription: $5.00

Local, national, and world news of Jewish interest. Provides editorial columns on controversial issues, public forum for opinions of readers, and a book review section.

481. JEWISH PRESS.   1951— .
2427 Surf Avenue, Brooklyn, New York 11224
    Editor: Rabbi Sholom Klass   Language: English
    Sponsor: The Jewish Press
    Circulation: 162,250   Frequency: Weekly   Subscription: $7.00

Coverage of national and international news of special interest to the Jewish population. News on the Jewish community in New York as well as coverage of Israel and world Jewry. Features theological discourse on the Bible and the Talmud, book reviews, a youth section, letters to the editor, and commentaries.

482. JEWISH RECORD.   1939— .
1537 Atlantic Avenue, Atlantic City, New Jersey 08401
    Editor: Martin Korik   Language: English
    Circulation: 3,337   Frequency: Weekly   Subscription: $3.50

Local, national, and international news of significance to the Jewish communities of southern New Jersey. The objective of the publication is to "sustain a Jewish awareness" [editor's statement].

483. JEWISH SOCIAL STUDIES.   1939— .
2929 Broadway, New York, New York 10025
    Editor: Perry Goldman   Language: English
    Sponsor: Conference on Jewish Social Studies
    Circulation: 1,350   Frequency: Quarterly   Subscription: $10.00

This contemporary journal is devoted to contemporary and historical aspects of Jewish life. Publishes scholarly articles and book reviews of Jewish issues in the various social science fields.

484. JEWISH SPECTATOR.   1935— .
250 West 57th Street, New York, New York 10019
    Editor: Dr. Trude Weiss-Rosmarin   Language: English
    Sponsor: Jewish Spectator
    Circulation: 19,000   Frequency: Monthly   Subscription: $6.00

This is a journal of "Jewish opinion on Jewish affairs and letters" [editor's statement]. Israel and the American Jewish community are principal subject areas. Also features short stories and book reviews. Its objective is to "inform and bring the insights of the Jewish tradition to bear upon and illuminate current problems and issues" [editor's statement].

485. JEWISH STANDARD.   1931— .
924 Bergen Avenue, Jersey City, New Jersey 07306
    Editor: Meyer Pesin   Language: English
    Circulation: 9,500   Frequency: Weekly   Subscription: $4.00

Presents national and international news coverage of special interest to the Jewish population. Emphasis is placed on Jewish community news in Jersey City. Features include book reviews, entertainment, youth news, and a food column.

486. JEWISH STAR.   1947— .
693 Mission Street, Room 405, San Francisco, California 94105
    Editor: Alfred Berger   Language: English
    Sponsor: Language Press
    Circulation: 2,000   Frequency: Bi-monthly   Subscription: $3.00

Provides national and international news with an emphasis on Israel.

487. THE JEWISH TIMES.   1945— .
118 Cypress Street, Brookline, Massachusetts 02146
    Editor: James Kahn   Language: English
    Sponsor: Jewish Times Publishing Company
    Circulation: 10,500   Frequency: Weekly   Subscription: $3.00

This weekly publishes local, national, and international news of interest to the Jewish people, providing coverage of Jewish organizational activities on the local (Boston and New England) and national levels. It also includes youth features, book reviews, and business news.

488. JEWISH TRANSCRIPT.   1924— .
614 Securities Building, Seattle, Washington 98101
    Editor: Colin Shellshear   Language: English
    Sponsor: Jewish Federation and Council of Seattle
    Circulation: 5,500   Frequency: Semi-monthly   Subscription: $3.00

Features articles on topics of special interest to the Jewish people in the
Seattle area, including reports from Israel, national news as it relates to
Jews, and local news items of the Jewish community.

489. THE JEWISH VETERAN.   1896— .
1712 New Hampshire Avenue, N.W., Washington, D.C. 20009
    Editor: Albert Schlossberg   Language: English
    Sponsor: Jewish War Veterans of the United States
    Circulation: 100,000   Frequency: Monthly   Subscription: $2.00

This organizational journal covers the various events, activities, and
affairs of the Jewish War Veterans of the United States, on both the
national and the local level.

490. THE JEWISH VOICE.   1940— .
701 Shipley Street, Wilmington, Delaware 19801
    Editor: Morton Schlossman   Language: English
    Sponsor: Jewish Federation of Delaware
    Circulation: 3,100   Frequency: Monthly   Subscription: $3.00

Provides general news on various issues of special interest to the Jewish
people in Delaware.

491. JEWISH WEEK AND AMERICAN EXAMINER.   1857— .
3 East 40th Street, New York, New York 10016
    Editor: Philip Hochstein   Language: English
    Sponsor: American Examiner, Inc.
    Circulation: 85,000   Frequency: Weekly   Subscription: $10.00

This weekly publishes news, editorials, features, and articles about the
Jewish world, both here and abroad. A column on the United Nations
is also included.

492. JEWISH WEEKLY NEWS.   1945— .
38 Hampden Street, Springfield, Massachusetts 01103
    Editor: Leslie Bennett Kahn   Language: English
    Circulation: 8,000   Frequency: Weekly   Subscription: $4.00

Provides in-depth coverage of international, national, and local news of
special interest to the Jewish population. Jewish events are stressed.
Also includes book reviews.

493. JEWISH WORLD.   1965— .
771 State Street, Schenectady, New York 12307
    Editor: Sam Clevenson   Language: English
    Circulation: 4,500   Frequency: Weekly   Subscription: $5.00

This community-oriented weekly provides coverage of Jewish civic,
organizational, and synagogue activities in the Albany, Troy, and
Schenectady areas. It also includes articles on Judaism and Jewish
events around the world.

494. JPS BOOKMARK.   1953— .
222 North 15th Street, Philadelphia, Pennsylvania 19102
    Editor: Dr. Chaim Potok   Language: English
    Sponsor: Jewish Publication Society of America
    Circulation: 13,700   Frequency: Quarterly   Subscription: $.50

This quarterly provides members of the Society with information regarding
current and planned activities in the Jewish book field.

495. JUDAISM.   1952— .
15 East 84th Street, New York, New York 10028
    Editor: Robert Gordis   Language: English
    Sponsor: American Jewish Congress
    Circulation: 2,800   Frequency: Quarterly   Subscription: $8.00

The purpose of this publication is "to stimulate an informed awareness
of Jewish affairs, encourage Jewish scholarship and adequate opportuni-
ties for Jewish education, and generally foster the affirmation of Jewish
religious, cultural, and historic identity" [editor's statement]. It features
articles on the religious, moral, and philosophical concepts of Judaism
and their relationship to modern society. Also includes book reviews.

496. KANSAS CITY JEWISH CHRONICLE.   1920— .
P.O. Box 8709, Kansas City, Missouri 64114
    Editor: Milton Firestone   Language: English
    Sponsor: Kansas City Jewish Chronicle Company
    Circulation: 12,500   Frequency: Weekly   Subscription: $6.50

This weekly, aiming at the Jewish public of western Missouri and eastern
Kansas, covers social, religious, cultural, national, international, and local
news events.

497. KEEPING POSTED.   1955– .
838 Fifth Avenue, New York, New York 10021
   Editor: Edith Samuel   Language: English
   Sponsor: Union of American Hebrew Congregations
   Circulation: 40,603   Frequency: Monthly   Subscription: $2.25

This magazine is aimed at the Jewish youth attending grades 7 through
12 of Jewish religious schools. It is used as reading, study and discussion
material for Jewish youth groups, adult Jewish study circles, and educational camps. Each issue deals with a specific theme, value or concept.
A Teacher's Edition of each issue provides eight additional pages of
background, bibliography, ideas for class projects, discussions, and
debates. Included in the Teacher's Edition is a "Parent's Guide to K.P."

498. KEEPING POSTED WITH NCSY.   1962– .
84 Fifth Avenue, New York, New York 10011
   Editor: Rabbi Pinchas Stolpeh   Language: English
   Sponsor: National Conference of Synagogue Youth
   Circulation: 12,000   Frequency: Monthly   Subscription: $1.00

Youth-oriented publication which prints news for youth leaders and
tips on leadership.

499. KENTUCKY JEWISH POST AND OPINION.
2004 Grinstead Drive, Louisville, Kentucky 40204
   Editor: H. M. Goldman   Language: English
   Sponsor: Jewish Post and Opinion
   Circulation: Unknown   Frequency: Weekly   Subscription: $10.00

Reports on various events and activities within the Jewish community in
Louisville, also including national, international, and local news of special
interest to the Jewish population. Features editorials and a teen column.

500. LAS VEGAS ISRAELITE.   1965– .
P.O. Box 14096, Las Vegas, Nevada 89114
   Editor: Jack Tell   Language: English
   Circulation: 10,000   Frequency: Weekly   Subscription: $7.00

This is a comprehensive, in-depth weekly, reporting news of interest to
the Jewish community of Las Vegas and the Jewish tourists.

501. LONG ISLAND JEWISH PRESS.   1945— .
    95-20 63rd Road, Rego Park, New York 11374
        Editor: Rabbi Abraham Shoulson   Language: English
        Sponsor: Zionist Region in Long Island
        Circulation: 28,000   Frequency: Monthly   Subscription: $2.00

    This community-oriented monthly publishes news on events within the
    Jewish local communities. It also reports on national and international
    news of special interest to the Jewish population. Book reviews are
    included.

502. MIDSTREAM.   1955— .
    515 Park Avenue, New York, New York 10022
        Editor: Shlomo Katz   Language: English
        Sponsor: Theodor Herzl Foundation, Inc.
        Circulation: 12,000   Frequency: Monthly   Subscription: $7.00

    This Zionist publication covers topics of interest to the Jewish people,
    including by-lined articles which interpret issues such as social problems,
    ethnicity, the Middle East, and current important events. Features book
    reviews.

MIZRACHI WOMAN.   See Jewish Publications in Yiddish and Yiddish-English.

503. NASSAU HERALD.   1924— .
    379 Central Avenue, Lawrence, New York 11559
        Editor: Robert Richner   Language: English
        Sponsor: Bi-County Publishers, Inc.
        Circulation: 11,000   Frequency: Weekly   Subscription: $4.00

    Heavy coverage of Jewish local community activities such as organizations,
    clubs, charity drives, schools, and local personalities. Features a women's
    column and book reviews.

504. NATIONAL JEWISH MONTHLY.   1886— .
    315 Lexington Avenue, New York, New York 10016
        Editor: E. Grusk   Language: English
        Sponsor: B'nai B'rith
        Circulation: 216,000   Frequency: Monthly   Subscription: $1.50

    Covers activities of the B'nai B'rith chapters both here and abroad, and
    reports on activities of Jewish communities around the world. Also
    featured are articles on the Jewish culture both past and present, and
    on Israel and Soviet Jewry.

505. NEW YORK JEWISH NEWS.   1969— .
1402 St. Nicholas Avenue, New York, New York 10033
Editor: Dr. Gerald Gorin   Language: English
Circulation: 15,000   Frequency: Monthly   Subscription: Unknown

506. OHIO JEWISH CHRONICLE.   1921— .
87 North Sixth Street, Columbus, Ohio 43209
Editor: Mitchell Siegel   Language: English
Sponsor: Tri-Village Publishing
Circulation: 2,900   Frequency: Weekly   Subscription: $5.00

Main emphasis is placed on covering the various activities of Jewish groups in the Columbus area. Also included are some coverage of national and international events, book reviews, and sports.

ORANGE COUNTY JEWISH HERITAGE.   See HERITAGE-SOUTHWEST JEWISH PRESS (Number 450).

507. PARENTS' BULLETIN.   1955— .
175 East Broadway, New York, New York 10002
Editor: J. Mlotek   Language: English
Sponsor: Education Department of the Workmen's Circle
Circulation: Unknown   Frequency: Monthly   Subscription: Unknown

508. PEDAGOGIC REPORTER.   1949— .
101 Fifth Avenue, New York, New York 10003
Editor: Zalemen Slesinger   Language: English
Sponsor: American Association for Jewish Education
Circulation: 2,460   Frequency: Quarterly   Subscription: $4.50

The purpose of this publication is to provide information on the development of education in theory and practice—in terms of both general and Jewish education. Informative articles on new instructional materials and curricula are published.

509. PHILADELPHIA JEWISH TIMES.   1925— .
1530 Spruce Street, Philadelphia, Pennsylvania 19102
Editor: Arthur Klein   Language: English
Circulation: 34,220   Frequency: Weekly   Subscription: $4.00

Provides coverage of national and local news, with emphasis on the activities within the Jewish community in Philadelphia.

510. PHOENIX JEWISH NEWS.   1947– .
2928 North Seventh Avenue, Phoenix, Arizona 85013
    Editor: Pearl R. Newmark   Language: English
    Sponsor: Phoenix Jewish News, Inc.
    Circulation: 2,585   Frequency: Bi-weekly   Subscription: $4.75

Emphasis is placed on coverage of Jewish fraternal, congregational, and social activities in the Phoenix area; however, reports on national and international events are also included.

PIONEER WOMAN.   See Jewish Publications in Hebrew and Hebrew-English.

511. PORTLAND JEWISH REVIEW.   1959– .
1643 S.W. 12th Avenue, Portland, Oregon 97201
    Editor: LaNita Anderson   Language: English
    Sponsor: Jewish Welfare Federation of Portland
    Circulation: 2,900   Frequency: Monthly   Subscription: None

This monthly reports on the activities of the Jewish Welfare Federation and its agencies, along with covering news of local Jewish activities in Portland and national and international events. Book reviews are included.

512. RECONSTRUCTIONIST.   1935– .
15 West 86th Street, New York, New York 10024
    Editor: Rabbi Ira Eisenstein   Language: English
    Sponsor: Jewish Reconstructionist Foundation
    Circulation: 6,000   Frequency: 3 times/week   Subscription: $10.00

This publication presents articles and editorials dealing with religious, ethical, and philosophical questions; events in the Jewish communities in the United States and abroad; cultural developments among the Jewish people; and editorial comments on national and international events. Book reviews are also included.

513. RHODE ISLAND JEWISH HERALD.   1929– .
99 Webster Street, Pawtucket, Rhode Island 02861
    Editor: Celia Zuckerberg   Language: English
    Sponsor: Jewish Press Publishing Company
    Circulation: 13,100   Frequency: Weekly   Subscription: $6.00

Emphasis is on Jewish activities in Rhode Island, but general news is also published.

514. RHODE ISLAND JEWISH HISTORICAL NOTES.   1954– .
209 Angell Street, Providence, Rhode Island 02906
    Editor: Seebert J. Goldowsky   Language: English
    Sponsor: Rhode Island Jewish Historical Association
    Circulation: 400   Frequency: Annually   Subscription: $5.00

The main objective of this publication is to "record materials relating to
the history of Jews in Rhode Island" [editor's statement]. It includes
historical narratives, reprints of records, bibliographical material, research
reports, and pictures.

515. ROCKAWAY JOURNAL.   1883– .
379 Central Avenue, Lawrence, New York 11559
    Editor: Robert Richner   Language: English
    Sponsor: Bi-County Publishers
    Circulation: 7,000   Frequency: Weekly   Subscription: $4.00

This community-oriented weekly places emphasis on coverage of all types
of Jewish activities—individual, group, and organizational—in the Rockaway
community. Features society news and book reviews.

516. SAN FRANCISCO JEWISH BULLETIN.   1946– .
40 First Street, San Francisco, California 94105
    Editor: Geoffrey Fisher   Language: English
    Sponsor: San Francisco Jewish Publications, Inc.
    Circulation: 15,500   Frequency: Weekly   Subscription: $6.00

This publication, which was established in 1946, merged with *Emanu-el*,
which was first published in 1895. It provides comprehensive coverage of
news pertaining to the Jewish people locally, nationally, and inter-
nationally. Includes columns, editorials, opinions, vital statistics, and
book reviews.

517. SAVANNAH JEWISH NEWS.   1949– .
P.O. Box 6546, Savannah, Georgia 31405
    Editor: Irwin B. Giffen   Language: English
    Sponsor: Savannah Jewish Council
    Circulation: 1,350   Frequency: Monthly   Subscription: $2.50

This monthly provides coverage of local Jewish organizational activities
in Savannah, news of the Savannah Jewish Council, and Jewish affairs
on the national and international forum.

518. THE SENTINEL.   1911— .
216 West Jackson, Chicago, Illinois 60606
    Editor: J. I. Fishbein   Language: English
    Circulation: 41,683   Frequency: Weekly   Subscription: $8.50

This weekly publishes news articles and commentaries on all aspects of Jewish life on the local, national, and international levels, plus news on Israel. Other features are news of social activities, book reviews, and articles on culture, art, and travel.

519. SOUTH SHORE RECORD.   1953— .
Station Plaza, Hewlett, New York 11557
    Editor: Florence Schwartzberg   Language: English
    Circulation: 9,128   Frequency: Weekly   Subscription: $4.00

Coverage of general news, with the emphasis on local activities. Includes book reviews, educational news, youth features, and entertainment.

520. SOUTHERN ISRAELITE.   1925— .
1031 Juniper Lane, Atlanta, Georgia 30303
    Editor: Adolph Rosenberg   Language: English
    Sponsor: Southern Newspapers Enterprise, Inc.
    Circulation: 6,550   Frequency: Weekly   Subscription: $7.50

Provides some coverage of national and international news, but emphasis is placed on news of Jewish communities in Georgia.

521. SOUTHERN JEWISH WEEKLY.   1924— .
P.O. Box 3297, Jacksonville, Florida 32206
    Editor: Isadore Moscovitz   Language: English
    Circulation: 28,500   Frequency: Weekly   Subscription: $3.00

This weekly emphasizes activities with the Jewish communities in Florida, but also includes general news of special interest to the Jewish population.

522. SOUTHWEST JEWISH CHRONICLE.   1929— .
822 Oklahoma Mortgage Building, Oklahoma City, Oklahoma 73102
    Editor: Emma Friedman   Language: English
    Sponsor: Southwest Publishing Company
    Circulation: Unknown   Frequency: Quarterly   Subscription: $2.00

Emphasis is placed on covering the various Jewish individual and organizational activities, events, and affairs in the Southwest.

SOUTHWEST JEWISH PRESS-HERITAGE.   See HERITAGE-SOUTHWEST
JEWISH PRESS (Number 450).

523. STARK JEWISH NEWS.   1921— .
P.O. Box 529, Canton, Ohio 44701
    Editor: Leonard J. Leopold   Language: English
    Circulation: 1,200   Frequency: Monthly   Subscription: $4.00

This community-oriented monthly covers Jewish events within the
Canton area. Includes announcements on births, deaths, social news,
and individuals. Also features a cooking column.

524. ST. LOUIS JEWISH LIGHT.   1947— .
1347 Railway Exchange Bldg., 611 Olive Street, St. Louis, Missouri 63101
    Editor: Robert A. Cohn   Language: English
    Sponsor: Jewish Federation of St. Louis
    Circulation: 16,000   Frequency: Semi-monthly   Subscription: $3.50

Provides comprehensive coverage of news relating to local, national, and
world events of interest to the Jewish community. Also publishes editorials,
book reviews, and youth features.

525. SYNAGOGUE LIGHT.   1933— .
47 Beekman Street, New York, New York 10002
    Editor: Rabbi Meyer Hager   Language: English
    Sponsor: Union of Chassidic Rabbis
    Circulation: 17,000   Frequency: Monthly   Subscription: $5.00

Contains articles and commentaries on Judaism and the Jewish faith.
Outstanding individuals of the Jewish religion are profiled in each issue.

526. SYNAGOGUE SCHOOL.   1942— .
218 East 70th Street, New York, New York 10021
    Editor: Morton Siegel   Language: English
    Sponsor: United Synagogue Commission on Jewish Education
    Circulation: 1,170   Frequency: Quarterly   Subscription: $2.50

The main objective of this publication is "to provide a readership in the
Jewish educational constituency with both theoretical and practical
discussion of the needs of Jewish education as viewed from the vantage
point of the Conservative Movement in Judaism" [editor's statement].

527. TEXAS JEWISH POST.   1947— .
P.O. Box 742, Fort Worth, Texas 76101
    Editor: Jimmy Wisch   Language: English
    Circulation: 7,000   Frequency: Weekly   Subscription: $7.00

General news on international, national, and local affairs of interest to
the Jewish population.

528. TOLEDO JEWISH NEWS.   1951— .
2506 Evergreen Road, Toledo, Ohio 43606
    Editor: Burt Silverman   Language: English
    Sponsor: Jewish Welfare Federation
    Circulation: 2,500   Frequency: Monthly   Subscription: $3,00

Coverage of local, national, and international news of special interest to
the Jewish community. Activities of the United Jewish Fund are also
covered.

529. THE TORCH.   1941— .
3080 Broadway, New York, New York 10027
    Editor: Mannye London   Language: English
    Sponsor: National Federation of Jewish Men's Clubs
    Circulation: 46,000   Frequency: Quarterly   Subscription: $8.00

Contains by-lined articles on a variety of topics related to Judaism and
Jewish issues, as well as reports on the NFJMC, editorials, and letters to
the editor.

530. TRADITION.   1959— .
220 Park Avenue South, New York, New York 10003
    Editor: Walter S. Wurzburger   Language: English
    Sponsor: Rabbinical Council of America
    Circulation: 4,000   Frequency: Quarterly   Subscription: Unknown

This quarterly presents an analysis of traditional Judaism on current
theological, philosophical, political, and social issues.

531. TULSA JEWISH REVIEW.   1930— .
P.O. Box 2647, Tulsa, Oklahoma 74101
    Editor: Greg Broad   Language: English
    Sponsor: National Council of Jewish Women, Tulsa Section
    Circulation: 885   Frequency: Monthly   Subscription: $4.00

Review of general news and features relating to the Jewish community.
Critical editorial column on a specific issue. Special holiday issues.

UNDZER WEG.   See Jewish Publications in Yiddish and Yiddish-English.

532. UNITED SYNAGOGUE REVIEW.   1957—.
    3080 Broadway, New York, New York 10027
        Editor: Rabbi Alvin Kass   Language: English
        Sponsor: United Synagogue of America
        Circulation: 250,000   Frequency: Quarterly   Subscription: $1.00

    Contains articles on various issues of interest to the Jewish people, with
    the emphasis on Conservative Judasim. Stresses important events of the
    United Synagogue of America.

533. VOICE.   1941—.
    2395 West Marlton Pike, Cherry Hill, New Jersey 08034
        Editor: Bernard Dubin   Language: English
        Sponsor: Jewish Federation of Camden County
        Circulation: 5,800   Frequency: Semi-monthly   Subscription: $2.00

    Presents news of the activities of the Jewish Federation of Camden County,
    plus national and international news with the emphasis on Israel. Also
    included are articles and editorials on issues that are significant to the
    Jewish community.

534. WESTCHESTER JEWISH TRIBUNE.   1945—.
    95-20 63rd Road, Rego Park, New York 11374
        Editor: Rabbi Abraham Shoulson   Language: English
        Sponsor: Zionist Region in Westchester
        Circulation: 7,800   Frequency: Monthly   Subscription: $2.00

    This monthly publishes national and international news of special
    interest to the Jewish people, with the emphasis on local Jewish community
    activities and events. Coverage includes by-lined articles on various issues,
    youth features, and book reviews.

535. WISCONSIN JEWISH CHRONICLE.   1921—.
    340 North Milwaukee Street, Milwaukee, Wisconsin 53202
        Editor: Edwarde F. Perlson   Language: English
        Sponsor: Wisconsin Jewish Chronicle
        Circulation: Unknown   Frequency: Weekly   Subscription: $7.50

    Provides coverage of Jewish news of a local, national, and international
    nature. Publishes editorials and by-lined articles on a variety of Jewish
    issues. Also includes coverage of organizations and personalities, and
    book reviews.

536. WOMEN'S AMERICAN ORT REPORTER.   1949— .
     1250 Broadway, New York, New York 10001
          Editor: Elie Faust   Language: English
          Sponsor: Women's American Organization for Rehabilitation through
               Training
          Circulation: 140,000   Frequency: Bi-monthly
          Subscription: Unknown

     This publication reports on the activities of ORT sponsored shcools.
     Provides coverage of Jewish communities as well as national and inter-
     national news of special interest to the Jewish population.

537. WOMEN'S LEAGUE OUTLOOK.   1930— .
     48 East 74th Street, New York, New York 10021
          Editor: Mrs. Harold Kamsler   Language: English
          Sponsor: National Women's League of the United Synagogue of America
          Circulation: 169,000   Frequency: Quarterly   Subscription: $1.00

     Oriented toward the preservation of Conservative Judaism, this quarterly
     presents articles dealing with the Jewish past and conservatism. Included
     are reports on the activities of the Sisterhoods (800) of the Conservative
     Movement of Judaism; articles on education, homemaking, art, and
     travel; and book reviews.

538. WOMEN'S WORLD.   1951— .
     1640 Rhode Island Avenue, N.W., Washington, D.C. 20036
          Editor: Elizabeth Bilanow   Language: English
          Sponsor: B'nai B'rith Women
          Circulation: 140,000 Frequency: Monthly   Subscription: Free to members

     This monthly provides comprehensive reports on the activities of chapter,
     district, national, and international levels of the organization. Articles on
     current subjects of interest in the areas of public affairs and Jewish educa-
     tion are included.

539. WORLD OVER.   1940— .
     426 West 58th Street, New York, New York 10019
          Editors: Ezekiel Schloss and Morris Epstein   Language: English
          Sponsor: Board of Jewish Education, Inc.
          Circulation: 100,000   Frequency: Unknown   Subscription: $3.50

     Aimed at the 9 to 13 year old Jewish school child, this publication "attempts
     to present a portrait of Jewish life, past and present, in text, art, and photos"
     [editor's statement]. Principal objective is to foster an appreciation of the
     Jewish cultural and religious heritage and contribution.

540. YAVNEH REVIEW.   1965– .
    84 Fifth Avenue, New York, New York 10011
        Editor: Levi Meier   Language: English
        Sponsor: Yavneh-Religious Jewish Students Association
        Circulation: 1,500   Frequency: Annually   Subscription: $1.50

    A student journal of Jewish studies, this annual publishes scholarly
    articles on Jewish topics, especially on theological issues. The articles
    are written exclusively by students. Reviews are also published.

YEDIES FUN YIVO.   See Jewish Publications in Yiddish and Yiddish-English.

YIDDISH LINGO.   See Jewish Publications in Yiddish and Yiddish-English.

DI YIDDISHE HEIM.   See Jewish Publications in Yiddish and Yiddish-English.

541. YONKERS JEWISH CHRONICLE.   1969– .
    122 South Broadway, Yonkers, New York 10701
        Editor: Louis Schrier   Language: English
        Sponsor: Jewish Federation of Yonkers
        Circulation: 7,500   Frequency: Weekly   Subscription: $2.00

    This newspaper is the "official voice of the Jewish community and is
    published by the Jewish Federation, which consists of 44 organizations
    and synagogues in the city" [editor's statement]. It includes news of
    local, national, and international events of interest to the Jewish people.

YOUNG JUDEAN.   See Jewish Publications in Hebrew and Hebrew-English.

542. YOUNG ISRAEL VIEWPOINT.   1952– .
    3 West 16th Street, New York, New York 10011
        Editor: Joel Saibel   Language: English
        Sponsor: National Council of Young Israel
        Circulation: 31,500   Frequency: Monthly   Subscription: $2.50

    This is the house organ of the NCYI, covering activities of the organiza-
    tion and students, and Jewish activities worldwide.

543. YOUNGSTOWN JEWISH TIMES.   1935— .
P.O. Box 777, Youngstown, Ohio 44501
    Editor: Harry Alter   Language: English
    Circulation: 8,975   Frequency: Bi-weekly   Subscription: $3.00

This publication provides coverage of Jewish activities on a local, national, and international level.

544. YOUR CHILD.   1968— .
218 East 70th Street, New York, New York 10021
    Editor: Rabbi Chaim Rozwaski   Language: English
    Sponsor: United Synagogue Commission on Jewish Education
    Circulation: 2,100   Frequency: Quarterly   Subscription: $1.75

Aimed at the Jewish parent of students of all ages and levels, this quarterly provides information on the developments in Jewish education.

545. YOUTH AND NATION.   1968— .
150 Fifth Avenue, Room 709, New York, New York 10071
    Editor: Edward Anzel   Language: English
    Sponsor: Hashomer Hatzair Socialist Zionist Youth Movement
    Circulation: 2,500   Frequency: Bi-monthly   Subscription: $1.50

This is a journal of opinion on various Jewish issues, with a socialist orientation.

Jewish Publications in German

546. AUFBAU.   Reconstruction.   1934— .
2121 Broadway, New York, New York 10023
    Editor: Dr. Hans Steinitz   Language: German
    Sponsor: New World Club, Inc.
    Circulation: 31,000   Frequency: Weekly   Subscription: $10.50

See also GERMAN PRESS.

547. JEWISH WAY.   1941— .
870 Riverside Drive, New York, New York 10032
    Editor: Mrs. Alice Oppenheimer   Language: English and German
    Sponsor: The Way in America Publishing Company
    Circulation: 8,000   Frequency: Monthly   Subscription: $2.00

A religious monthly.

KOREAN PRESS

Korean Publications in Korean and Korean-English

548. GONG GAE PYUN JI.   Korean Open Letter.   1942— .
    351 Newman Drive, South San Francisco, California 94080
       Editor: Hon. Young Han Choo   Language: Korean
       Sponsor: Private and Public Service
       Circulation: 2,800   Frequency: Bi-monthly   Subscription: Free

This publication is the successor to the *Min On* weekly, and its purpose
is "to promote the reunification sentiment and spirit among the Koreans"
[editor's statement]. It contains international, national, and local news of
interest to Koreans.

549. THE HANKOOK ILBO.   The Korea Times.   1965— .
    11638 Ventura Boulevard, Studio City, California
       Editor: Jae Ku Chang   Language: Korean
       Circulation: 2,500   Frequency: Daily   Subscription: $44.00

This publication, the only Korean daily in the United States, carries
international, national, and local news of interest to the Korean community. Illustrated.

550. THE KOREAN PACIFIC WEEKLY.   1913— .
    931 North King Street, Honolulu, Hawaii 96817
       Editor: Donald Chung Won Kim   Language: Korean and English
       Sponsor: Korean Dongji Hoi
       Circulation: 120   Frequency: Weekly   Subscription: $10.00

551. THE NEW KOREA.   1905— .
    1368 West Jefferson Boulevard, Los Angeles, California 90007
       Editor: Lee K. Park   Language: Korean and English
       Sponsor: Korean National Association
       Circulation: 494   Frequency: Bi-weekly   Subscription: $15.00

Korean Publications in English

552. KOREA WEEK.   1968– .
757 National Press Bldg., 14th and F Streets, N.W., Washington, D.C. 20004
  Editor: Po Sung Philip Kim   Language: English
  Circulation: 1,154   Frequency: Semi-monthly   Subscription: $5.50

"Covers developments in Korea, news in the U.S. related to Korea and the
Korean community in the U.S." [editor's statement]. Also includes news
from Japan related to Korea. Special features include historical articles
dealing with political, diplomatic, and commercial topics. Special emphasis
is placed on United States–Korea relations.

553. KOREAN REPORT.   1952– .
1145 19th Street, N.W., Washington, D.C. 20036
  Editor: Po Sung Kim   Language: English
  Sponsor: Korean Research and Information Office, Embassy of Korea
  Circulation: 33,000   Frequency: Quarterly   Subscription: Free

This is a general newsletter on Korea.

LATVIAN PRESS

See also LITHUANIAN PRESS, Number 594 and Number 595.

554. AMERIKAS LATVIETIS.   American Latvian.   1905– .
Box 23, Roxbury, Massachusetts 02119
  Editor: Edward Maurin   Language: Latvian
  Sponsor: Baltica Publishing Company
  Circulation: 500   Frequency: Semi-monthly   Subscription: $3.00

This publication is devoted to political, cultural, and other activities of
Latvians in the United States. It also includes poetry and fiction by Latvian
authors. Illustrated.

555. LAIKS.   Time.   1949– .
267 Ovington Avenue, Brooklyn, New York 11209
  Editor: Arturs Strautmanis   Language: Latvian
  Sponsor: Helmars Rudzitis, publisher
  Circulation: 12,650   Frequency: Semi-weekly   Subscription: $19.00

Presents general, national, and local news coverage, as well as news and
articles concerning Latvians in the United States.

LEBANESE PRESS

see ARAB PRESS

LITHUANIAN PRESS

Lithuanian and Lithuanian-English Publications

556. AIDAI.   Echoes.   1950– .
680 Bushwick Avenue, Brooklyn, New York 11221
    Editor: Dr. Juozas Girnius   Language: Lithuanian
    Sponsor: Franciscan Fathers
    Circulation: 1,900   Frequency: Monthly   Subscription: $7.00

This cultural magazine deals with all aspects of Lithuanian arts and science.
It includes book reviews and information on Lithuanian activities in
various countries.

557. AKECIOS.   The Harrow.   1965– .
680 Bushwick Avenue, Brooklyn, New York 11221
    Editor: Dr. Benvenutas Ramanauskas   Language: Lithuanian
    Circulation: Unknown   Frequency: Quarterly   Subscription: $7.00

Humorous, satirical magazine.

558. AKIRAČIAI.   Horizons.   1968– .
6821 South Maplewood, Chicago, Illinois 60629
    Editor: Dr. T. Remeikis   Language: Lithuanian
    Sponsor: Viewpoint Press, Inc.
    Circulation: 1,350   Frequency: Monthly   Subscription: $6.00

Provides non-partisan coverage of social, cultural, economic, and political
life under Soviet rule, as well as reports on the activities of Lithuanians
abroad.

559. ATEITIS.   The Future.   1911– .
7235 South Sacramento Avenue, Chicago, Illinois 60629
    Editor: Jonas Soliunas   Language: Lithuanian
    Sponsor: Lithuanian Catholic Youth Association
    Circulation: 1,500   Frequency: Monthly   Subscription: $5.00

This is a publication for Lithuanian Catholic youth.

560. DARBININKAS.   Worker.   1915— .
   910 Willoughby Avenue, Brooklyn, New York 11221
      Editor: Rev. Dr. Cornelius Bučmys, O.F.M.   Language: Lithuanian
      Sponsor: Franciscan Fathers
      Circulation: 17,000   Frequency: Semi-weekly   Subscription: $8.00

This Catholic-oriented publication covers general, international, national, and local news. Information on Lithuanian activities in the United States and other countries is also provided.

561. DIRVA.   The Field.   1915— .
   6907 Superior Avenue, Cleveland, Ohio 44103
      Editor: Vytautas Gedgaudas   Language: Lithuanian
      Sponsor: Viltis Printing, Inc.
      Circulation: 4,200   Frequency: Semi-weekly   Subscription: $13.00

This illustrated national Lithuanian magazine covers contemporary news.

562. DRAUGAS.   Lithuanian Daily "Friend."   1909— .
   4545 West 63rd Street, Chicago, Illinois 60629
      Editor: F. Garsva, Mic.   Language: Lithuanian
      Sponsor: Lithuanian Catholic Press
      Circulation: 13,000   Frequency: Daily   Subscription: $15.00

This daily provides general news coverage and features articles on the Lithuanian community in the United States and in the world. A book review section is also included. "Combatting communism everywhere" [editor's statement] is its aim. The Saturday issue contains a separate section dealing with art and literature.

563. EGLUTE.   The Little Fir.   1950— .
   Putnam, Connecticut 06260
      Editor: Sister Ann Mikaila   Language: Lithuanian
      Sponsor: Sisters of the Immaculate Conception
      Circulation: 1,500   Frequency: Monthly   Subscription: $5.00

A children's magazine.

564. ELTA INFORMATION SERVICE.   1949— .
   29 West 57th Street, Fl. 1p, New York, New York 10019
      Editor: Editorial Board   Language: English
      Sponsor: Supreme Committee for Liberation of Literature
      Circulation: 1,000   Frequency: Monthly   Subscription: $12.00

Contains material regarding the present political status of Lithuania. Published also in Lithuanian, Spanish, Italian, and French.

565. GARSAS.   The Echo.   1917— .
P.O. Box 32, Wilkes-Barre, Pennsylvania 18703
    Editor: Matas Zujus   Language: Lithuanian and English
    Sponsor: Lithuanian R. C. Alliance of America
    Circulation: 7,950   Frequency: Bi-monthly   Subscription: $2.00

Contains "articles and news about Lithuanian religious, national, cultural,
social, and fraternal activities in the United States and other countries;
news from Soviet occupied Lithuania; and general news" [editor's statement] .

566. GIRIOS AIDAS.   Echo of the Forest.   1950— .
2740 West 43rd Street, Chicago, Illinois 60632
    Editor: J. Kuprionis   Language: Lithuanian
    Sponsor: Association of Lithuanian Foresters in Chicago
    Circulation: 200   Frequency: Bi-annually   Subscription: $6.00

Lithuanian forestry journal.

567. I LAISUE.   Toward Freedom.   1943— .
P.O. Box 77048, Los Angeles, California
    Editor: Leonardas Valiukas   Language: Lithuanian
    Circulation: Unknown Frequency: Quarterly   Subscription: $5.00

Covers cultural and historical topics and contemporary activities of
Lithuanians.

568. KARYS.   Warrior.   1950— .
916 Willoughby Avenue, Brooklyn, New York 11221
    Editor: Z. Raulinaitis   Language: Lithuanian
    Sponsor: Association of Lithuanian Veterans
    Circulation: 1,350   Frequency: Monthly   Subscription: $7.00

Features articles on Lithuanian history, military history, and veterans' news.

569. KELEIVIS.   Traveler.   1905— .
636 Broadway, South Boston, Massachusetts 02127
    Editor: Jackus Sonda   Language: Lithuanian
    Sponsor: Keleivis Publishing Company
    Circulation: 3,600   Frequency: Weekly   Subscription: $6.00

This weekly, sponsored by the Lithuanian Socialist Union, covers international, national, and local news.

570. LAIŠKAI LIETUVIAMS.   Letters to Lithuanians.   1950— .
2345 West 56th Street, Chicago, Illinois 60636
Editor: Joseph Vaišnys, S.J.
Sponsor: Lithuanian Jesuit Fathers
Circulation: 4,000   Frequency: Monthly   Subscription: $5.00

Includes articles on religious, educational, political, and youth topics.
The main objective is "to help Lithuanian immigrants to solve their
problems in foreign countries" [editor's statement].

571. LAISVE.   Liberty.   1911— .
102-02 Liberty Avenue, Ozone Park, New York 11417
Editor: Anthony Bimba   Language: Lithuanian
Sponsor: The Lithuanian Cooperative Publishing Society, Inc.
Circulation: Unknown   Frequency: Semi-weekly   Subscription: $9.00

Provides general news with a communist orientation.

572. LAISVOJI LIETUVA.   Free Lithuania.   1946— .
2618 West 71st Street, Chicago, Illinois 60629
Editor: V. Simkus   Language: Lithuanian
Sponsor: Lithuanian Regeneration Association
Circulation: 1,806   Frequency: Bi-weekly   Subscription: $6.00

An anti-communist paper which provides general news.

573. LAIVAS.   The Ship.   1921— .
4545 West 63rd Street, Chicago, Illinois 60629
Editor: Rev. C. Baras   Language: Lithuanian
Sponsor: Marian Fathers
Circulation: 5,000   Frequency: Semi-monthly   Subscription: $5.00

Catholic magazine for the Lithuanians in the United States.

574. LIETUVIU DIENOS.   Lithuanian Days.   1946— .
4364 Sunset Boulevard, Hollywood, California 90029
Editor: Bernaras Brazdzionis   Language: Lithuanina and English
Circulation: 5,000   Frequency: Monthly   Subscription: $6.00

Contains contemporary materials on Lithuanians in the world. Illustrated.

575. METMENYS.   Plan of Literature.   1958— .
2606 Princeton Avenue, Evanston, Illinois 60202
    Editor: Dr. Vytautas Kavolis   Language: Lithuanian
    Sponsor: Metmenys, Inc.
    Circulation: 900   Frequency: Semi-annually   Subscription: $10.00

Contains articles on Lithuanian culture, politics, history, and literature, plus book reviews and contemporary Lithuanian poetry.

576. MOTERU DIRVA.   Women's Field.   1914— .
3005 North 124th Street, Brookfield, Wisconsin 53005
    Editor: Mrs. Dale Murray   Language: Lithuanian and English
    Sponsor: American-Lithuanian Roman Catholic Women's Alliance
    Circulation: 2,150   Frequency: Monthly   Subscription: $2.50

In addition to organizational information and chapter news, this monthly publishes stories, poetry, and any items of interest to women.

577. MUSU SPARTAI.   Our Wings.   1950— .
5718 South Richmond Street, Chicago, Illinois 60629
    Editor: Povilas Dilys   Language: Lithuanian
    Circulation: Unknown   Frequency: Quarterly   Subscription: Unknown

A Lithuanian evangelical religious quarterly.

578. MUSU VYTIS.   Our Knight.   1951— .
6744 South Oakley Avenue, Chicago, Illinois 60636
    Editor: Ramune Kviklyte   Language: Lithuanian
    Sponsor: Lithuanian Student Scout Association
    Circulation: 490   Frequency: Bi-monthly   Subscription: $4.00

A Lithuanian Scout magazine.

579. MUZIKOS ZINIOS.   Musical News.   1935— .
209 Clark Place, Elizabeth, New Jersey 07206
    Editor: Juozas Kreivenas   Language: Lithuanian
    Sponsor: Lithuanian Organist Alliance of America
    Circulation: 550   Frequency: Quarterly   Subscription: $2.00

This is a musical quarterly dealing with Lithuanian musical culture.

580. NAUJIENOS.   The Lithuanian Daily.   1914— .
1739 South Halsted Street, Chicago, Illinois 60608
    Editor: Dr. Pius Grigaitis   Language: Lithuanian
    Sponsor: Lithuanian News Publishing Company
    Circulation: 30,540   Frequency: Daily   Subscription: $18.00
Contains national, international, and Lithuanian news.

581. SANDARA.   The League.   1914— .
840 West 33rd Street, Chicago, Illinois 60608
    Editor: Michael Vaidyla   Language: Lithuanian
    Sponsor: Lithuanian National League of America
    Circulation: Unknown   Frequency: Weekly   Subscription: $5.00
General news coverage, with an emphasis on the local Lithuanian
community.

582. SEJA.   The Sowing.   1953— .
1649 North Broadway, Melrose Park, Illinois 60160
    Editor: Antanas Rukas   Language: Lithuanian
    Sponsor: Varpininku Leidiniu Fondas
    Circulation: Unknown   Frequency: Bi-monthly   Subscription: $5.00
National democratic paper.

583. SV. FRANCISKAUS VARPELIS.   The Bell of St. Francis.   1942— .
Franciscan Monastery, Kennebunkport, Maine 04046
    Editor: Rev. Victor Gidziunas, O.F.M.   Language: Lithuanian
    Sponsor: Franciscan Fathers
    Circulation: 3,050   Frequency: Monthly   Subscription: $3.00
This religious monthly is read primarily by members of the Lithuanian
St. Francis order in the United States and other countries.

584. SVIESA.   The Light.   1934— .
102-02 Liberty Avenue, Ozone Park, New York 11417
    Editor: Anthony Bimba   Language: Lithuanian
    Sponsor: American Lithuanian Literary Association, Inc.
    Circulation: Unknown   Frequency: Quarterly   Subscription: Members only
American-Lithuanian cultural communist magazine.

585. TAUTOS PRAEITIS.   The Past of a Nation.
4439 South Talmon Avenue, Chicago, Illinois 60632
    Editor: Jonas Dainauscas   Language: Lithuanian
    Sponsor: Lithuanian Historical Society
    Circulation: Unknown   Frequency: Irregular   Subscription: $16.00

This scholarly historical publication includes various historical materials on Lithuania.

586. TECHNIKOS ZODIS.   Engineering Word.   1951— .
208 West Natoma Avenue, Addison, Illinois 60101
    Editor: G. Lazauskas   Language: Lithuanian
    Sponsor: American Lithuanian Engineers and Architects Association
    Circulation: Unknown   Frequency: Bi-monthly   Subscription: $5.00

587. TEVYNE.   Motherland.   1889— .
307 West 30th Street, New York, New York 10001
    Editor: Joseph Petrenas   Language: Lithuanian
    Sponsor: Lithuanian Alliance of America
    Circulation: 5,728   Frequency: Weekly   Subscription: $4.00

This weekly publishes general news and news of Lithuanian affairs.

588. TEVYNES SARGAS.   Guardian of the Fatherland.   1896— .
894 East 223rd Street, Euclid, Ohio 44123
    Editor: D. Jasaitis, M.D.   Language: Lithuanian
    Sponsor: Lithuanian Christian Democratic Union
    Circulation: 685   Frequency: Annually   Subscription: $3.00

This political magazine, from the Lithuanian Christian Democratic Union, covers all aspects of Lithuanian life.

589. TIESA.   Truth.   1930— .
104-07 102nd Street, Ozone Park, New York 11417
    Editors: John Liurba (Lithuanian) and Anne Yakstis (English)
    Language: Lithuanian and English
    Sponsor: Association of Lithuanian Workers
    Circulation: 3,000   Frequency: Monthly
    Subscription: Free to members

This monthly, which has a Socialist orientation, provides general news.

590. VARPAS. Bell. 1889— .
1214 North 16th Avenue, Melrose Park, Illinois 60160
Editor: Antanas Kucys   Language: Lithuanian
Sponsor: Lithuanian Alumni Association, Varpas
Circulation: 1,000   Frequency: Annually   Subscription: $2.50

"Journal for propagation of freedom and independence of Lithuania, individual and national freedom, Lithuanian culture and liberal ideology" [editor's statement].

591. VIENYBE. Unity. 1886— .
192 Highland Boulevard, Brooklyn, New York 11207
Editor: Jonas Valaitis   Language: Lithuanian
Circulation: 2,530   Frequency: Bi-weekly   Subscription: $7.00

The oldest Lithuanian newspaper. This publication provides general news and Lithuanian news.

592. VILNIS. Surge. 1920— .
3116 South Halsted Street, Chicago, Illinois 60608
Editor: Stanislovas Jokubka   Language: Lithuanian
Sponsor: The Workers Publishing Association, Inc.
Circulation: 3,550   Frequency: Daily   Subscription: $12.00

This communist-oriented daily publishes general, national, and international news.

593. VYTIS. The Knight. 1915— .
c/o I. K. Sankus, 2520 West 68th Street, Chicago, Illinois
Editor: Irene K. Sankus   Language: English and Lithuanian
Sponsor: Knights of Lithuania
Circulation: 1,600
Frequency: Monthly, October-May; Bi-monthly, June-September
Subscription: $4.00

This is the house organ of the Knights of Lithuania organization.

Lithuanian Publications in English

594. THE BALTIC REVIEW. 1945— .
29 West 57th Street, New York, New York 10019
Editor: Bronius Nemickas   Language: English
Sponsor: Committee for a Free Estonia, Latvia and Lithuania
Circulation: 1,000   Frequency: 3 times/year   Subscription: Unknown

This publication features historical, political, sociological articles on the Baltic States. A section of book reviews is also included.

595. LITUANUS.   1954— .
P.O. Box 9318, Chicago, Illinois 60690
    Editor: Dr. A. Klimas   Language: English
    Sponsor: Lituanus Foundation, Inc.
    Circulation: 5,000   Frequency: Quarterly   Subscription: $5.00

"Baltic States journal of arts and sciences, the only English language quarterly about Lithuania, Latvia, and Estonia, presenting a forum for free-world scholars to express their views on the history and people of the Baltic area" [editor's statement].

596. THE MARIAN.   1948— .
4545 West 63rd Street, Chicago, Illinois 60629
    Editor: Rev. Joseph Prunskis   Language: English
    Sponsor: St. Casimir American Province of the Congregation of
            Marian Fathers
    Circulation: 11,000   Frequency: Monthly   Subscription: $4.00

597. VILTIS.   Hope.   1942— .
P.O. Box 1226, Denver, Colorado 80201
    Editor: V. F. Beliajus   Language: English
    Sponsor: Mart Printers
    Circulation: 2,110   Frequency: Bi-monthly   Subscription: $5.00

This publication is devoted to folk customs and arts. Each issue covers a certain nationality and its customs, especially descriptions of folk dancing.

LUXEMBOURG PRESS

598. LUXEMBOURG NEWS OF AMERICA.   1966— .
496 North Northwest Highway, Park Ridge, Illinois 60068
    Editor: Victor Jacoby   Language: English
    Sponsor: Luxembourgers of America
    Circulation: 650   Frequency: Monthly   Subscription: $5.00

"Communication medium for Luxembourgers living in the United States; also their descendents and friends. News items of Luxembourg Societies. Also anything of general interest in the Grand Duchy of Luxembourg" [editor's statement].

MEXICAN PRESS

see SPANISH PRESS

NORWEGIAN PRESS

Norwegian and Norwegian-English Publications

599. DECORAH-POSTEN OG VED ARNEN. The Decorah-Post and By the
Fireside.   1874– .
108 Washington Street, Decorah, Iowa 52101
Editor: Rasmus Dahle-Melsaether   Language: Norwegian and English
Sponsor: The Anundsen Publishing Company
Circulation: 6,276   Frequency: Weekly   Subscription: $10.00

This paper was founded as a literary magazine (*Ved Arnen*). It contains a
news section on national and international affairs, local news from northwestern states, and a page with news from Norway and Denmark; it also
publishes various articles dealing with politics, culture, and social issues.
Each weekly issue contains a literary section, "Ved Arnen." Special
features include weekly letters from correspondents in Norway, a weekly
sermonette, and illustrations. On some occasions a few articles appear
in English.

600. MINNESOTA POSTEN.   Minnesota Post.   1956– .
1455 West Lake Street, Minneapolis, Minnesota 55408
Editor: Jenny A. Johnsen   Language: Norwegian
Sponsor: Friend Publishing Company
Circulation: 4,840   Frequency: Weekly   Subscription: $5.00

This publication contains cultural news from Norway and news concerning
Norwegian activities in the United States. Articles inform readers about the
industry, government, and social thinking of Norway. Pertinent articles
from American publications are occasionally reprinted, and Norwegian
organizational activities of the Twin Cities area are publicized and promoted.

601. NORDISK TIDENDE.   The Norwegian News.   1891– .
8104 Fifth Avenue, Brooklyn, New York 11209
Editor: Ragnar Busch   Language: Norwegian and English
Sponsor: Norse News, Inc.
Circulation: 10,500   Frequency: Weekly   Subscription: $10.00

This weekly provides local news about Norwegians, mainly in the Greater New York area. Also, it includes information concerning American relations with Norway. A special feature is church news. Sometimes a few articles are published in English. Illustrated.

602. NORSK UNGDOM.   Norwegian Young People.   1913– .
1134 South Eighth Street, Minneapolis, Minnesota 55404
Editor: Ingolf Marthinussen   Language: Norwegian
Sponsor: Lutheran Mission Societies, Inc.
Circulation: 2,465   Frequency: Monthly   Subscription: $2.00

A religious monthly dedicated to the interpretation of the Gospel of Jesus Christ, this paper also includes news from Norway and news about various Christian groups and religious life around the world.

603. WESTERN VIKING.   1889– .
2040 N.W. Market Street, Seattle, Washington 98107
Editor: Henning C. Boe   Language: Norwegian and English
Circulation: 3,080   Frequency: Weekly   Subscription: $9.00

Provides news from Norway and from many Norwegian societies and lodges in the cities along the Pacific Coast, including Canada and Mexico. Contains a special section in English, "News of Norway," issued by the Norwegian Information Service. The main objective of this weekly is "to maintain the interest for Norwegian culture . . . , as well as maintaining contact with the native country . . ." [editor's statement]. Illustrated.

Norwegian Publications in English

604. THE AUGSBURG NOW.   1929– .
701-707 21st Avenue South, Minneapolis, Minnesota 55404
Editor: Unknown   Language: English
Sponsor: Augsburg College and Theological Seminary
Circulation: Unknown   Frequency: Monthly   Subscription: $3.00

605. EBENEZER.   1934– .
5214 Tenth Avenue South, Minneapolis, Minnesota 55417
Editor: Fernanda U. Malmin   Language: English
Sponsor: Ebenezer Home Society
Circulation: 25,000   Frequency: Quarterly   Subscription: $1.00

This illustrated house organ contains news of interest to members of the Ebenezer Home Society.

606. FAITH AND FELLOWSHIP.   1920– .
Box 655, Fergus Falls, Minnesota 56537
     Editor: Rev. Robert Overgaard   Language: English
     Sponsor: Lutheran Brethern Publishing Company
     Circulation: 2,800   Frequency: Bi-weekly   Subscription: $3.50

Publishes articles on religious and literary subjects.

607. NEWS OF NORWAY.   1941– .
3401 Massachusetts Avenue, Washington, D.C.   20007
     Editor: Einar Bergh   Language: English
     Sponsor: Norwegian Embassy Information Service
     Circulation: 7,000   Frequency: Semi-monthly   Subscription: Free

Contains news on various developments in Norway. Special features
include a column on "Books and Articles."

608. NORTHWOOD EMISSAEREN.   The Northwood Emissary   1914– .
Northwood, North Dakota 58267
     Editor: Rev. John O. Johanson   Language: English and Norwegian
     Sponsor: Northwood Deaconess Hospital and Home
     Circulation: 1,510   Frequency: Monthly   Subscription: $1.00

The purpose of this house organ is "to tell the story and to reflect the
activities of the Northwood Deaconess Hospital and Home" [editor's
statement].

609. NORWEGIAN AMERICAN STUDIES.   1925– .
St. Olaf College, Northfield, Minnesota
     Editor: Kenneth O. Bjork   Language: English
     Sponsor: Norwegian-American Historical Association
     Circulation: 1,155   Frequency: Irregular   Subscription: Varies

This is a series of publications by the Norwegian-American Historical
Association (organized in 1925). The Association publishes the following
series: 1. *Studies and Records* (vol. 1, 1926–). 2. *Travel and Description
Series* (vol. 1, 1926–). 3. *Authors' Series.* The *Studies and Records*
contains scholarly articles and source material on Norwegian immigration.

610. SANGER HILSEN.   Singers' Greeting.   1894– .
3133 Humbold Avenue South, Minneapolis, Minnesota 55408
     Editor: Erling Stone   Language: English
     Sponsor: Norwegian Singers Association of America
     Circulation: 1,005   Frequency: Bi-monthly   Subscription: Unknown

611. THE SONS OF NORWAY VIKING.   1903— .
     1455 West Lake Street, Minneapolis, Minnesota 55408
       Editor: Bent Vanberg   Language: English
       Sponsor: Sons of Norway
       Circulation: 44,300   Frequency: Monthly   Subscription: $4.00

"Primarily a membership magazine for Sons of Norway members, *The Viking* is also the main publication for all Norwegian-American-Canadian cultural and educational interests" [editor's statement]. Includes articles on Norway and Norwegians in America.

POLISH PRESS

Polish and Polish-English Publications

612. AMERYKA-ECHO.   America-Echo.   1886— .
     1521 West Haddon, Chicago, Illinois 60622
       Editor: Joseph Bialasiewicz   Language: Polish
       Sponsor: Ameryka-Echo, Inc.
       Circulation: 9,200   Frequency: Weekly   Subscription: $12.00

This weekly contains international, national, and local news of interest to Polish-Americans. Special emphasis is placed on Polish activities in the United States and in Poland. Articles cover political, historical, religious, cultural, and other topics. Aimed at the "old generation of Polish American" [editor's statement]. Illustrated.

613. APOSTOL.   The Apostle.   1890— .
     P.O. Box 87, Detroit, Michigan 48232
       Editor: John J. Koschella   Language: Polish
       Sponsor: Marianhill Mission Society
       Circulation: 8,000   Frequency: Bi-monthly   Subscription: Unknown

614. AVE MARIA.   Hail Mary.   1924— .
     600 Doat Street, Buffalo, New York 14211
       Editor: Sister Mary Donata, C.S.S.F.
       Sponsor: Felician Sisters
       Circulation: 7,225   Frequency: Bi-monthly   Subscription: $1.50

This publication presents articles dealing with religious, moral, and social issues. Aimed at the elderly. Popular presentation.

615. BIULETYN—INSTYTUT JOZEFA PILSUDSKIEGO V AMERYCE.
Jozef Pilsudski Institute of America Bulletin.   1944— .
381 Park Avenue South, New York, New York 10016
Editor: Dr. Jan Fryling   Language: Polish and English
Sponsor: Pilsudski Institute of America
Circulation: 1,000   Frequency: Annually
Subscription: Free to members

Published by the Jozef Pilsudski Institute of America (established 1943),
which is a major Polish scholarly organization in the United States. The
Bulletin is sent free of charge to all members of the Institute. It contains
annual reports, statements, obituaries, and historical or educational
articles.

616. CZAS.   The Times.   1905— .
142 Grand Street, Brooklyn, New York 11211
Editor: Jozef A. Glowacki   Language: Polish and English
Sponsor: Polish National Assiance of Brooklyn
Circulation: 9,100   Frequency: Weekly   Subscription: $5.00

This is the official organ of one of the largest Polish fraternal organizations in the United States. Mainly includes news items concerning Polish
National Alliance of Brooklyn, financial statements, reports, etc. A small
portion of this weekly is published in English. Contains some articles on
Poland and Polish-Americans.

617. DZIENNIK CHICAGOSKI.   Polish Daily News.   1890— .
1521 West Haddon Avenue, Chicago, Illinois 60622
Editor: Joseph Bialasiewicz, Executive Editor; Peter Fiolek, Editor
Language: Polish
Sponsor: Polish Publishing Company
Circulation: 15,387   Frequency: Daily   Subscription: $16.00

Covers international, national, and regional news, with special emphasis
on the activities of American Poles and Poland. Features articles on
political, cultural, social, and religious developments. Includes valuable
information on Poles in Chicago. The weekend edition contains an
additional section dedicated to special topics (e.g., literature, religious
life, and others). Illustrated.

618. DZIENNIK POLSKI.   Polish Daily News.   1904— .
2310 Cass, Detroit, Michigan 48201
Editor: Stanley Krajewski   Language: Polish
Sponsor: Polish Daily News, Inc.
Circulation: 16,100   Frequency: Daily   Subscription: $24.00

This daily includes international and national news, while also covering the activities of Polish organizations and Poles in the United States. It also "helps candidates of Polish descent in their bids for elective or appointive office" [editor's statement]. Illustrated.

619. DZIENNIK ZWIAZKOWY.   Polish Daily Zgoda.   1908— .
1201 North Milwaukee Avenue, Chicago, Illinois 60622
    Editor: John F. Krawiec   Language: Polish
    Sponsor: Alliance Printers and Publishers, Polish National Alliance
    Circulation: 20,000   Frequency: Daily   Subscription: $18.75

One of the major Polish dailies in the United States, this paper provides international, national, and local news coverage. It contains feature articles on politics, culture, literature, economy, sports, and other topics, as well as valuable material on the activities of Polish organizations and people in the United States. The Sunday edition includes a special supplement. Illustrated.

620. GAZETA POLONII.   Polish American Gazette.   1913— .
610 Dorchester Avenue, Boston, Massachusetts 02127
    Editor: Karol T. Jaskolski   Language: Polish and English
    Sponsor: Polish American News, Inc.
    Circulation: 5,000   Frequency: Weekly   Subscription: $7.00

The emphasis is placed on Polish-American life in New England, while a special section carries news from Poland and from the world. A small portion of the material is presented in English. Illustrated.

621. GLOS NARODU.   The Voice of the People.   1900— .
410 Matchaponix Avenue, Jamesburg, New Jersey 08831
    Editor: Kaz. Kolodziejczyk   Language: Polish
    Circulation: 4,900   Frequency: Weekly   Subscription: $5.00

General and local news of interest to the Polish community in the United States. Includes material on the activities of Polish religious and other organizations, as well as news on Poland. Illustrated.

622. GLOS LUDOWY.   The People's Voice.   1909— .
5854 Chene Street, Detroit, Michigan 48211
    Editors: Conrad Komorowski and Stanley Nowak
    Language: Polish and English
    Circulation: 3,150   Frequency: Weekly   Subscription: Unknown

This weekly contains general news, as well as articles on political, cultural, social, and other activities.

623. GLOS POLEK.   Polish Women's Voice.   1910— .
1309 North Ashland Avenue, Chicago, Illinois 60622
    Editors: Maria Lorys (Polish) and A. Lagodzinska (English)
    Language: Polish and English
    Sponsor: Polish Women's Alliance of America
    Circulation: 65,000   Frequency: Semi-monthly
    Subscription: Membership

This is the official semi-monthly publication of the Polish Women's
Alliance of America. While the major portion of the publication is
devoted to P.W.A.A. activities, it also aims at preserving Polish customs,
tradition, and language. Illustrated.

624. GWIAZDA.   Polish Star.   1902— .
3022 Richmond Street, Philadelphia, Pennsylvania 19134
    Editor: Gertrude Nowaczyk   Language: Polish
    Sponsor: Union of Polish Women in America
    Circulation: 9,005   Frequency: Weekly   Subscription: Unknown

A fraternal magazine.

625. GWIAZDA POLARNA.   Northern Star.   1908— .
1516 Frontenac Avenue, Stevens Point, Wisconsin 54481
    Editor: Adam Bartosz   Language: Polish and English
    Sponsor: Worzalla Publishing Company
    Circulation: 19,300   Frequency: Weekly   Subscription: $10.00

This weekly contains national, international, and local news. Articles
cover historical, political, social, cultural, and other topics, and a special
section contains information on Polish activities in America. A small
portion of material is published in English. Illustrated.

626. JASNA GORA.   Bright Hill.   1959— .
P.O. Box 151, Doylestown, Pennsylvania 18901
    Editor: Fr. Sales T. Strzelec   Language: Polish and English
    Sponsor: National Shrine of Our Lady of Czestochowa (Pauline Fathers)
    Circulation: 5,000   Frequency: Monthly   Subscription: $2.50

Published ten times yearly by the Pauline Fathers, this publication
features articles about the Blessed Virgin and other religious topics.
Includes news on "activities at the National Shrine of Our Lady of
Czestochowa in Doylestown, Pennsylvania" [editor's statement].
Illustrated.

627. JEDNOSC POLEK.   Unity of Polish Women.   1924— .
7526 Broadway Avenue, Cleveland, Ohio 44105
    Editor: Frances Tesny   Language: Polish
    Sponsor: Association of Polish Women of the United States
    Circulation: 1,329   Frequency: Semi-monthly   Subscription: $3.00

A fraternal magazine.

628. KURYER ZJEDNOCZENIA.   Courier of the Union.   1923— .
6805 Lansing Avenue, Cleveland, Ohio 44105
    Editor: Roman Trepczyk   Language: Polish
    Sponsor: Union of Poles in America
    Circulation: 20,945   Frequency: Semi-monthly   Subscription: Unknow

A fraternal magazine.

629. LEGIONNAIRE.   1943— .
6009 Fleet Avenue, Cleveland, Ohio 44105
    Editor: Julian S. Kubit   Language: Polish and English
    Sponsor: Polish Legion of American Veterans of U.S.A.
    Circulation: 2,500   Frequency: Bi-monthly   Subscription: Unknown

630. MIESIECZNIK FRANCISZKANSKI.   Franciscan Monthly.   1907— .
Pulaski, Wisconsin 54162
    Editor: Rev. Sebastian M. Kus, O.F.M.   Language: Polish
    Sponsor: Province of the Franciscan Fathers at Pulaski
    Circulation: 16,200   Frequency: Monthly   Subscription: $3.00

This religious monthly features articles on current religious, moral, and
social problems. Since it is aimed at readers of Polish descent, it includes,
from time to time, articles on Polish culture and history. Popular presentation. Illustrated.

631. MORZE.   The Sea.   1940— .
1082 Milwaukee Avenue, Chicago, Illinois 60622
    Editor: Albin B. Syc   Language: Polish
    Sponsor: Sea League of America
    Circulation: Unknown Frequency: Monthly   Subscription: $3.00

632. NAROD POLSKI.   The Polish Nation.   1886—.
984 Milwaukee Avenue, Chicago, Illinois 60622
Editor: Zygmunt J. Stefanowicz   Language: Polish and English
Sponsor: Polish Roman Catholic Union of America
Circulation: 57,268   Frequency: Semi-monthly
Subscription: $.60 for members

This official organ of the Polish Catholic Union features informative material on the Catholic Church and on the activities of the Union and its membership. The English section also includes "Sports Briefs." Illustrated.

633. NASZE SPRAWY.   Our Affairs.   1962—.
6550 San Vicente Boulevard, Los Angeles, California 90048
Editor: Tadeusz Zielinski   Language: Polish
Circulation: Unknown   Frequency: Monthly   Subscription: Unknown

634. NOWINY MINNESOCKIE.   Minnesota News.   1915—.
440 Thomas Avenue, St. Paul, Minnesota 55103
Editor: J. M. Koleski   Language: Polish
Sponsor: Polish Fraternal, Social, and Civic Organizations
Circulation: 1,595   Frequency: Weekly   Subscription: Unknown

635. NOWY DZIENNIK.   Polish Daily News.   1971—.
253 Washington Street, Jersey City, New Jersey 07302
Editor: Editorial Board   Language: Polish
Sponsor: Bicentennial Publishing Corporation
Circulation: Unknown   Frequency: Daily   Subscription: $26.00

This daily continues the tradition of *Nowy Swiat* and is similar to it in scope. See next entry.

636. NOWY SWIAT.   The Polish Morning World.   1896—1970.
40 West 21st Street, New York, New York 10010
Editor: Wladyslaw Borzecki   Language: Polish
Circulation: 6,533   Frequency: Daily   Subscription: $27.00

One of the oldest Polish dailies, this publication included national, international, and local news. Articles covered historical, political, cultural, social, and other topics. Emphasis on the activities of Polish organizations and Poles in the United States, especially in the eastern states. Was founded in 1896 as *Typodnik Nowojorski*; in 1914 it became the *Telegram Codzienny*; in 1920, *Nowy Swiat* (merged with *Telegram Codzienny*). Ceased publication December 1970; *Nowy Dziennik* began on February 27, 1971.

637. OBYWATEL AMERYKANSKI.   American Citizen.
410 Matchaponix Avenue, Jamesburg, New Jersey 08831

Circulation: 4,900   Frequency: Weekly   Subscription: $5.00

This weekly contains international, national, and local news, emphasizing the activities of Polish organizations and Poles in general in the United States. Illustrated.

638. PATRON.   1943—.
607 Humboldt Street, Brooklyn, New York 11222
Editor: Rev. Carol J. Wawak, C.M.   Language: Polish and English
Sponsor: St. Stanislaus Kostka Parish
Circulation: 1,200   Frequency: Weekly   Subscription: $3.00

This house organ features parish announcements, parish activities, and other material relevant to the members of the Stanislaus Kostka parish.

639. PITTSBURCZNIN.   The Pittsburgher.   1920—.
3515 Butler Street, Pittsburgh, Pennsylvania 15201
Editor: Dora M. Alski   Language: Polish
Sponsor: Pittsburgh Polish Daily Publishing Company, Inc.
Circulation: 10,456   Frequency: Weekly Subscription: $5.00

Containing general and local news, this weekly serves Polish-Americans in western Pennsylvania by promoting Polish culture and language.

640. POLAK AMERYKANSKI.   Polish American.   1919—.
410 Matchaponix Avenue, Jamesburg, New Jersey 08831
Editor: Kaz. Kolodziejczyk   Language: Polish
Circulation: 4,900   Frequency: Weekly Subscription: Unknown

641. POLKA.   Polish Woman.   1935—.
529 East Locust Street, Scranton, Pennsylvania 18505
Editor: J. Mastalski   Language: Polish and English
Sponsor: United Women's Societies of the Most Blessed Sacrament
Circulation: Unknown   Frequency: Quarterly Subscription: $1.00

This journal, devoted to the Polish-American woman, contains articles on the family, and on the role of women in society, as well as items on the activities and events of the Society.

642. POLONIA GAZETTE.   Polish and Slavonic Community Gazette. 1968– .
     1103 Wolf Street, Syracuse, New York 13208
        Editor: Clarence Kadys   Language: Polish and English
        Sponsor: Polonia Gazette
        Circulation: 5,000   Frequency: Monthly   Subscription: $3.00
     Informative items on a variety of topics.

643. POLONIAN.   1969– .
     767 Market Street, San Francisco, California 94103
        Editor: Dalegor Wladyslaw Suchecki   Language: English and Polish
        Sponsor: Polish Community Service Center
        Circulation: 5,500   Frequency: Bi-monthly   Subscription: $5.00
     Items on topics that have general ethnic group interest, especially to the
     Polish communities in northern California.

644. POSLANIEC MATKI BOSKIEJ SALETYNSKIEJ.   Messenger of
        Virgin Mary.
     Twin Lakes, Wisconsin 53131
        Editor: Rev. Saletyni Missionaries   Language: Polish
        Sponsor: La Salette Missionary Fathers
        Circulation: Unknown Frequency: Monthly   Subscription: Unknown

645. PRZEWODNIK POLSKI.   The Polish Guide.   1899– .
     1308 Cass Avenue, St. Louis, Missouri 63106
        Editor: H. Moczydlowski   Language: Polish
        Sponsor: Polish Publishing Company
        Circulation: Unknown Frequency: Weekly Subscription: Unknown

646. ROLA BOZA.   God's Field.   1923– .
     529 East Locust Street, Scranton, Pennsylvania 18505
        Editor: Rt. Rev. Anthony M. Rysz Language: Polish and English
        Sponsor: Polish National Catholic Church
        Circulation: 6,200   Frequency: Bi-weekly   Subscription: $5.00
     This Polish-English bi-weekly is primarily devoted to religious issues,
     including the activities and events of various Polish parishes. It is the
     official organ of the Polish National Catholic Church.

647. ROZE MARYI.   Roses of Mary.   1944— .
The Marian Fathers, Eden Hill, Stockbridge, Massachusetts 01262
    Editor: Brother Albin Larwa, M.I.C.   Language: Polish
    Sponsor: Association of Marian Helpers
    Circulation: 8,000   Frequency: Monthly   Subscription: $2.00

This religious Catholic weekly published by the Marian Fathers contains popular articles.

648. SODALIS.   1920— .
Orchard Lake, Michigan 48033
    Editor: Rt. Rev. Valerius J. Jasinski, S.T.D. Language: Polish
    Sponsor: SS. Cyril and Methodius Seminary
    Circulation: 1,658   Frequency: Monthly   Subscription: $3.00

This faculty publication deals with religious, social, pedagogic, and historical topics of interest to American Catholics of Polish descent.

649. SOKOL POLSKI.   Polish Falcon.   1896— .
97 South 18th Street, Pittsburgh, Pennsylvania 15203
    Editor: Mieczyslaw J. Wasilewski   Language: Polish and English
    Sponsor: Polish Falcons of America
    Circulation: 16,500   Frequency: Semi-monthly
    Subscription: Membership

The official publication of the Polish Falcons of America, this paper features news and articles on the Falcon (Sokol) organization and its members. Sometimes includes valuable historical material. Illustrated.

650. STRAZ.   The Guard.   1897— .
R.D. 1, Gouldsboro, Pennsylvania 18424
    Editor: Joseph Mastalski   Language: Polish and English
    Sponsor: Polish National Union of America
    Circulation: 12,100   Frequency: Weekly   Subscription: $4.00

Official weekly of the Polish National Union, featuring general and local news. Includes various polemic material aimed against the Roman Catholic Church and supporting the Polish National Catholic Church. Illustrated.

651. UNIA POLSKA.   Polish Union.   1920— .
761 Fillmore Avenue, Buffalo, New York 14212
    Editor: Thaddeus L. Sielski   Language: Polish and English
    Sponsor: Polish Union of America
    Circulation: 6,600 Frequency: Semi-monthly Subscription: Membership

This is the official organ of the Polish Union of America. Its contents are primarily devoted to presenting the various fraternal activities of the Union and of individual members.

652. WETERAN.   Veteran.   1921– .
17 Irving Place, New York, New York 10003
   Editor: Zbigniew A. Konikowski   Language: Polish
   Sponsor: Polish Army Veterans Association of America, Inc.
   Circulation: 4,950   Frequency: Monthly   Subscription: $4.00

The official organ of the Polish Army Veterans Association of America, this monthly covers historical, military, and current events, as well as news of various Polish veterans' organizations around the world.

653. ZGODA.   Unity.   1881– .
1201 North Milwaukee Avenue, Chicago, Illinois 60622
   Editor: Joseph Wiewiora   Language: English and Polish
   Sponsor: Polish National Alliance
   Circulation: 160,000   Frequency: Semi-monthly
   Subscription: Membership

This, the official publication of the Polish National Alliance, provides coverage of fraternal, cultural, sports, and general news. It includes features on prominent Americans of Polish descent and places emphasis on "Polish-American participation in the mainstream of American life" [editor's statement].

654. ZWIAZKOWIEC.   The Alliancer.   1913– .
6966 Broadway Avenue, Cleveland, Ohio 44105
   Editor: K. J. Zielecki   Language: Polish
   Sponsor: Alliance of Poles in America
   Circulation: 5,774   Frequency: Semi-monthly   Subscription: $7.00

Polish Publications in English

655. AMERICAN POLONIA REPORTER.   1957– .
21 East 17th Street, New York, New York 10003
   Editor: Leopold Dende   Language: English
   Sponsor: Amerpol Publishing Corporation
   Circulation: 3,250   Frequency: Quarterly   Subscription: Unknown

656. AM-POL EAGLE.   1960– .
1335 East Delavan Avenue, Buffalo, New York 14215
    Editor: Matthew W. Pelczynski   Language: English
    Circulation: 7,200   Frequency: Weekly   Subscription: $6.50

This newspaper is published primarily for Polish-Americans who reside in western New York. It includes general news items of special interest to Polish-Americans and provides coverage of the activities of Polish clubs, parishes, societies, and organizations.

657. FRANCISCAN MESSAGE.   1947– .
Franciscan Printery, Pulaski, Wisconsin 54162
    Editor: Rev. Felician Tulko, O.F.M.   Language: English
    Sponsor: Franciscan Fathers
    Circulation: 5,600   Frequency: Monthly   Subscription: $3.50

658. GAZETA READINGSTA.   Reading Newspaper.   1909– .
810 Franklin, Reading, Pennsylvania 19603
    Editor: S. B. Fruchter   Language: English
    Sponsor: Metropolitan Publishing Company
    Circulation: 5,400   Frequency: Monthly   Subscription: $1.00

Provides news of local interest to the Polish community.

659. KOSCIUSZKO FOUNDATION MONTHLY NEWSLETTER.   1946– .
15 East 65th Street, New York, New York 10021
    Editor: Dr. Eugene F. Kusielewicz   Language: English
    Sponsor: The Kosciuszko Foundation (American Center for Polish
           Culture)
    Circulation: 2,000   Frequency: Monthly   Subscription: Membership

This is a monthly bulletin of the Kosciuszko Foundation, which describes the activities of the Foundation and its members.

660. THE NATIONAL P.L.A.V.   1958– .
6073 Edgebrook Boulevard, Cleveland, Ohio 44130
    Editor: Julian S. Kubit   Language: English
    Sponsor: Polish Legion of American Veterans of U.S.A.
    Circulation: Unknown Frequency: Quarterly Subscription: Unknown

661. PERSPECTIVES.   A Polish-American Educational and Cultural Quarterly.   1971–
Apt. 732, 700 Seventh Street S.W., Washington, D.C. 20024
    Editor: Mrs. Marta Korwin-Rhodes, A.C.S.W.   Language: English
    Sponsor: Board of Editors
    Circulation: 5,000   Frequency: Quarterly   Subscription: $2.00

"Perspectives is an independent apolitical non-profit quarterly devoted
mainly to the current social and cultural scene. It aims at the cultivation
of the Polish-American heritage" [editor's statement]. Contains valuable
historical and other material on Polish life in America. Special features
include a book review section.

662. POLISH AMERICAN.   1963– .
1521 West Haddon Avenue, Chicago, Illinois 60622
    Editor: Rev. Peter A. Fiolek   Language: English
    Sponsor: Polish Publishing Company
    Circulation: Unknown   Frequency: Weekly   Subscription: Unknown

The principal objectives of this newspaper are "to appreciate the Polish
heritage, to initiate and support programs and representation of Poles in
American life, and to support causes for the betterment of the Polish
community" [editor's statement]. Contains articles on national, international, and local events of special interest to Polish-Americans. Sections are also devoted to editorials, book reviews, sports, and letters to
the editor, plus announcements on the activities of individuals.

663. POLISH AMERICAN CONGRESS NEWSLETTER.   1959– .
1200 North Ashland Avenue, Chicago, Illinois 60622
    Editor: Valentine Janicki   Language: English
    Sponsor: Polish American Congress
    Circulation: Unknown   Frequency: Quarterly
    Subscription: Free to members

This is the official organ of the Polish American Congress, a secular central
organization of Americans of Polish descent. It is primarily devoted to
presenting items of interest to Poles on the organization's various
activities.

664. POLISH AMERICAN HISTORICAL ASSOCIATION BULLETIN.   1945– .
St. Mary's College, Orchard Lake, Michigan 48034
    Editor: Dr. Anthony Milnar   Language: English
    Sponsor: Polish Institute of Arts & Sciences
    Circulation: 1,000   Frequency: Quarterly
    Subscription: Free to members

665. POLISH-AMERICAN JOURNAL.   1911– .
     409-415 Cedar Avenue, Scranton, Pennsylvania 18505
         Editor: Henry J. Dende   Language: English
         Sponsor: Dende Press, Inc.
         Circulation: 26,639   Frequency: Bi-weekly   Subscription: $3.00

This is the official organ of the Polish Union of the United States and
the Polish Beneficial Organization (fraternal-insurance organizations).
It carries international, national, and local news of special interest to
Americans of Polish descent. Included are sections devoted to letters to
the editor, achievements of individuals of Polish descent, news of various
organizations, church news, sports, women's corner, and educational notes.

666. POLISH AMERICAN STUDIES.   1943– .
     St. Mary's College, Orchard Lake, Michigan 48034
         Editor: Rev. Joseph Swastek   Language: English
         Sponsor: Polish American Historical Association of the Polish Institute
                 of Arts and Sciences
         Circulation: Unknown   Frequency: Semi-annually   Subscription: Unkno

A literary and historical magazine.

667. POLISH AMERICAN WORLD.   1959– .
     3100 Grand Boulevard, Baldwin, New York 11510
         Editor: Thomas Poster   Language: English
         Sponsor: Polish American World
         Circulation: 5,000   Frequency: Weekly   Subscription: $4.00

This weekly provides coverage of events and activities occurring in Polish-
American communities in the United States, plus commentaries on political matters which affect Americans of Polish descent. It also contains
reports on events occurring in Poland.

668. THE POLISH REVIEW.   1956– .
     59 East 66th Street, New York, New York 10021
         Editor: Dr. Ludwik Krzyzanowski   Language: English
         Sponsor: The Polish Institute of Arts & Sciences in America, Inc.
         Circulation: 1,450   Frequency: Quarterly   Subscription: $8.00

This scholarly quarterly centers on East European affairs, primarily Polish,
covering the humanities and social sciences. It deals with relations of other
countries to Poland, and provides up-to-date chronicles of events based on
Polish sources; extensive bibliographies pertaining to English language
publications concerning Polish affairs constitute regular and important
features. Includes book reviews and notices of East European studies.

669. POST EAGLE.   1963— .
    800 Van Houten Avenue, Clifton, New Jersey 07013
        Editor: Chester Grabowski   Language: English
        Sponsor: Post Publishing Company, Inc.
        Circulation: 6,000   Frequency: Weekly   Subscription: $4.00

    Provides news coverage of social, organizational, political, cultural, fraternal, and business activities of Polish communities and individuals.

670. THE QUARTERLY REVIEW.   1948— .
    Apt. 732, 700 Seventh Street S.W., Washington, D.C. 20024
        Editor: Marta Korwin-Rhodes   Language: English
        Sponsor: American Council of Polish Cultural Clubs
        Circulation: Unknown   Frequency: Quarterly   Subscription: $2.00

    This is the official organ of the American Council of Polish Cultural Clubs, a confederation of 25 affiliates in 21 cities. The purpose of this publication is to propagate "the knowledge and appreciation of the culture and civilization of Poland" [editor's statement]. It contains articles on Polish culture in the United States and on the activities of Polish cultural clubs, plus editorials, letters to the editor, and book reviews.

PORTUGUESE PRESS

Portuguese Publications in Portuguese and Portuguese-English

671. BOLETIM DA S.P.R.S.I.   Bulletin.   1899— .
    3031 Telegraph Avenue, Oakland, California 94609
        Editor: Marie L. Wilson   Language: English and Portuguese
        Sponsor: Conselho Supremo Da S.P.R.S.I.
        Circulation: Unknown   Frequency: Monthly
        Subscription: Free to members

    This is the official organ of the Sociedade Portuguesa Rainha Santa Isabel—a fraternal organization—containing society and membership news. The major portion of the publication is in English.

672. CORREIO OPERARIO NORTEAMERICANO.   North American
Labor News.   1963— .
815 16th Street N.W., Washington, D.C. 20006
Editor: George Meany   Language: Portuguese
Sponsor: AFL-CIO
Circulation: 14,000   Frequency: Semi-monthly   Subscription: Free

This publication provides pertinent labor news from North America
to organized labor in Brazil.

673. DIARIO DE NOTICIAS.   The Daily News.   1919— .
93 Rivet Street, New Bedford, Massachusetts 02742
Editor: Joao R. Rocha   Language: Portuguese
Sponsor: Daily News Publishing Company
Circulation: 7,263   Frequency: Daily   Subscription: $23.00

General, local, and group news of interest to Portuguese communities.

674. JORNAL PORTUGUÊS.   Portuguese Journal.   1888— .
3240 East 14th Street, Oakland, California 94601
Editor: Alberto Dos Santos Lemos   Language: Portuguese and English
Sponsor: Portuguese Journal
Circulation: 3,700   Frequency: Weekly   Subscription: $6.00

This weekly presents news items on events and activities within Portuguese
communities in the United States and Canada and also includes news from
Portugal, Portuguese Africa, and Brazil. Its objective is to "keep alive
Portuguese and Brazilian traditions and culture" [editor's statement].

675. LUSO-AMERICANO.   1928— .
88 Ferry Street, Newark, New Jersey 07105
Editor: Vasco Jardim, Jr.   Language: Portuguese
Sponsor: Luso-Americano Company, Inc.
Circulation: 5,250   Frequency: Weekly   Subscription: $6.00

Provides general and local news, plus special features of interest to the
Portuguese-speaking communities in America.

676. A LUTA.   The Struggle.   1937— .
443 East 135th Street, Bronx, New York 10454
Editor: Rt. Rev. Msgr. Joseph Cacella   Language: Portuguese
Sponsor: St. Anthony Center
Circulation: 4,600   Frequency: Semi-monthly   Subscription: $4.00

Publishes primarily religious material.

677. VOZ DE PORTUGAL.   Voice of Portugal.   1960– .
     370 A Street, Hayward, California 94541
          Editor: Gilberto Lopes Aguiar   Language: Portuguese
          Circulation: 3,970   Frequency: 3 times/month   Subscription: $6.00

     General, local, and group news of interest to Protuguese-speaking people.

Portuguese Publications in English

678. OUR LADY OF FATIMA MAGAZINE.   1932– .
     443 East 135th Street, Bronx, New York 10454
          Editor: Rt. Rev. Msgr. Joseph Cacella   Language: English
          Sponsor: St. Anthony Center
          Circulation: 10,550   Frequency: Monthly   Subscription: $3.00

     This monthly, religious in nature, is the "official organ for the propaga-
     tion of the devotion of Our Lady of Fatima" [editor's statement] .

ROMANIAN PRESS

Romanian Publications in Romanian and Romanian-English

679. AMERICA.   1906– .
     15 Lawrence Avenue, Detroit, Michigan 48202
          Editor: Eugene J. Popescu   Language: Romanian
          Sponsor: Union and League of Romanian Societies of America
          Circulation: 3,000   Frequency: Bi-weekly   Subscription: $6.00

     The main objective of this publication is "to promote the interest of the
     Union and League to keep active the national consciousness among the
     Romanians in America" [editor's statement] . It provides news items on
     Romanian organizations and group activities in the United States.

680. AMERICAN-ROMANIAN NEWS.   1906– .
     5701-03 Detroit Avenue, Cleveland, Ohio 44102
          Editor: Peter Lucaci   Language: Romanian
          Sponsor: Union and League of Romanian Societies of America
          Circulation: 2,970   Frequency: Weekly   Subscription: $7.00

     A fraternal newspaper.

681. LUMINATORUL.   Illuminator.   1926— .
      7009 Detroit Avenue, Cleveland, Ohio 44102
          Editor: Dr. Luca Sezonov   Language: Romanian and English
          Sponsor: Romanian Baptist Association of the United States
          Circulation: Unknown   Frequency: Monthly   Subscription: $7.50

      This religious weekly is primarily concerned with religious issues and the
      Romanian Baptist Church in the United States. A small section is
      published in English.

682. ROMANIA.   1956— .
      157 West 57th Street, New York, New York 11019
          Editor: Editorial Committee   Language: Romanian
          Sponsor: Rumanian National Committee
          Circulation: 2,000   Frequency: Bi-monthly   Subscription: Unknown

683. SOLIA.   The Herald.   1936— .
      11341 Woodward Avenue, Detroit, Michigan 48202
          Editor: Rt. Rev. Valerian D. Trifa   Language: Romanian and English
          Sponsor: Romanian Orthodox Episcopate of America
          Circulation: 4,350   Frequency: Semi-monthly   Subscription: $5.00

      This is the official organ of the Romanian Orthodox Episcopate of
      America. It features articles on the Orthodox faith, on church activities,
      and on religious education.

684. UNIREA.   The Union.   1950— .
      823 South Military Avenue, Dearborn, Michigan 48124
          Editor: Rev. Mircea Todericiu   Language: Romanian
          Sponsor: Association of Romanian Catholics of America, Inc.
          Circulation: Unknown   Frequency: Monthly   Subscription: Unknown

Romanian Publications in English

685. ROMANIAN BULLETIN.   1968— .
      1607 23rd Street N.W., Washington, D.C. 20008
          Editor: Unknown   Language: English
          Sponsor: Embassy of the Socialist Republic of Romania
          Circulation: Unknown   Frequency: Monthly   Subscription: Free

      This communist publication provides information on current events in
      Romania.

RUSSIAN PRESS

Russian Publications in Russian and Russian-English

686. BULLETIN.   1934— .
   97 Fort Washington Avenue, New York, New York 10032
   Editor: George C. Dvorjitsky   Language: Russian
   Sponsor: Association of Russian Imperial Naval Officers, Inc.
   Circulation: 500   Frequency: 3 times/year   Subscription: Free

   This bulletin is intended "to maintain contact among former Russian Imperial Naval Officers" [editor's statement] and to aid needy officers. It includes photographs, biographies, and addresses of many officers and also contains articles on historical topics, reminiscences, and events of current naval and political interest, including some translations from other publications.

687. EVANGELSKOYE SLOVO.   Gospel Word.   1942— .
   P.O. Box 35220, Chicago, Illinois 60635
   Editor: Rev. Stephen I. Lipen   Language: Russian
   Sponsor: World Fellowship of Slavic Evangelical Christians
   Circulation: Unknown   Frequency: 3 times/year   Subscription: Unknown

   A religious magazine.

688. KORPUSNIK.
   349 West 86th Street, New York, New York 10024
   Editor: Dimitry Vertepov   Language: Russian
   Sponsor: St. Alexander Nevsky Foundation, Inc.
   Circulation: 650   Frequency: Monthly   Subscription: Free

689. NASHI DNI.   Our Days.   1967— .
   4540 Marion Court, Sacramento, California 95822
   Editor: Nikolai Wodnevsky-Waden   Language: Russian
   Sponsor: Pacific Coast Slavic Baptist Association
   Circulation: 1,670   Frequency: Weekly   Subscription: $10.00

   This is a religious magazine which presents interpretations of the teachings of the Bible.

690. NASHI VESTI.   Our News.   1945— .
349 West 86th Street, New York, New York 10024
Editor: Dimitry Vertepov   Language: Russian
Sponsor: Russian Corps Combatants, Inc.
Circulation: 670   Frequency: Monthly   Subscription: Unknown

This is a magazine for Russian veterans.

691. NOVAYA ZARYA.   New Dawn.   1928— .
2078 Sutter Street, San Francisco, California 94115
Editor: G. T. Soohoff   Language: Russian
Circulation: 2,818   Frequency: Daily   Subscription: $8.50

This independent Russian daily provides general news coverage.

692. NOVOYE RUSSKOYE SLOVO.   New Russian Word.   1910— .
243 West 56th Street, New York, New York 10019
Editor: Mark Weinbaum   Language: Russian
Sponsor: Novoye Russkoye Slovo Publishing Corporation
Circulation: 28,505   Frequency: Daily   Subscription: $28.00

This daily provides readers with national and international news as well
as news of Russian-oriented activities in the United States. Features
articles on politics, culture, history, and other topics of interest to the
Russian community. Special features include "articles on Russian literature and publication of underground material which we receive from the
Soviet Union via our own sources of communication" [editor's statement].

693. NOVYJ ZHURNAL.   The New Review.   1942— .
2700 Broadway, New York, New York 10019
Editor: Roman B. Goul   Language: Russian
Sponsor: The New Review, Inc.
Circulation: 1,580   Frequency: Quarterly   Subscription: $10.00

694. PO STOPAM KHRISTA.   Following the Steps of Christ.   1950— .
1908 Essex Street, Berkeley, California 94703
Editor: V. Rev. N. Vieglais   Language: Russian
Sponsor: Orthodox Press
Circulation: 900   Frequency: Quarterly   Subscription: $2.00

This quarterly features religious news and guidance to followers of the
Orthodox faith. It includes international news of Orthodox churches, hymns
and publications of interest, and commentaries by members of the clergy.
Since 1957 each issue contains a supplement with church music.

695. PODSNEZHNIK.   Snowdrop.   1954—59, 1970— .
361 Van Siclen Avenue, Brooklyn, New York 11207
    Editor: Unknown   Language: Russian
    Sponsor: St. Joseph's School
    Circulation: Unknown   Frequency: Monthly Subscription: Unknown

Features stories, poetry, puzzles, sketches, humor, and drawings by
students of the school. Brief news of events and schedules at the school
is also given.

696. PRAVOSLAVNAYA RUS.   Orthodox Russia.   1928— .
Holy Trinity Monastery, Jordanville, New York 13361
    Editor: Fr. Constantine   Language: Russian
    Sponsor: Holy Trinity Monastery
    Circulation: 1,600   Frequency: Semi-monthly   Subscription: $8.00

Features articles and news on Eastern Orthodoxy "from the view of the
Russian Orthodox Church outside Russia" [editor's statement].

697. PRAVOSLAVNAYA ZHIZN'.   Orthodox Life.   1950— .
Holy Trinity Monastery, Jordanville, New York 13361
    Editor: Fr. Constantine   Language: Russian
    Sponsor: Holy Trinity Monastery
    Circulation: 1,650   Frequency: Monthly   Subscription: $3.00

"Lives of Saints and features of the Eastern Orthodox Christianity of
the Russian Orthodox Church outside Russia" [editor's statement].

698. RODINA.   Fatherland.   1950— .
Chadwick Street 20, Glen Cove, New York 11542
    Editor: Dr. Boris Solonevitch   Language: Russian
    Circulation: 200   Frequency: Bi-monthly   Subscription: Free

This "Russian independent anticommunist magazine" is non-commercial
and is intended for Russian emigrees and all "serious readers of anti-
communist thought" [editor's statement]. It stresses political theory and
opinion, often on a particular theme. Articles discuss both historical and
current topics.

699. RODNIYE DALI.   Native Vistas.   1954— .
1117 North Berendo Street, Los Angeles, California 90029
    Editor: Editorial Committee   Language: Russian
    Sponsor: Rodniye Dali Company
    Circulation: Unknown   Frequency: Monthly   Subscription: Unknown

700. ROSSIYA.   Russia.   1933— .
216 West 18th Street, New York, New York 10011
   Editor: George Alexandrovsky   Language: Russian
   Sponsor: Newspaper Rossiay Company
   Circulation: 1,650   Frequency: Semi-weekly   Subscription: $18.00

General news coverage.

701. ROSSIYSKAYA NEZAVISIMOST.   Russian Independence.   1955— .
495 Glenmore Avenue, Brooklyn, New York 11207
   Editor: Editorial Board   Language: Russian
   Circulation: Unknown   Frequency: 3 times/year
   Subscription: Unknown

This is a literary and political magazine.

702. RUSSKAYA ZHIZN'.   Russian Life.   1920— .
2458 Sutter Street, San Francisco, California 94115
   Editor: Mrs. Ariadna Delianich   Language: Russian
   Sponsor: Russian Life, Inc.
   Circulation: 2,500   Frequency: 5 times/week   Subscription: $25.00

This publication is dedicated to "serving the American-Russian community
and Russian nationals abroad to preserve the Russian language, culture,
and literature" [editor's statement] from a "conservative, American"
point of view. It gives worldwide news of politics, literature, history,
science, and social events. Includes news of emigree organizations,
Orthodox churches, and accomplishments of members of the Russian
emigree community.

703. RUSSKY GOLOS.   Russian Voice.   1917— .
69 Tiemann Place, New York, New York
   Editor: Victor A. Yakhontoff   Language: Russian
   Circulation: 2,584   Frequency: Weekly   Subscription: $9.00

General, international, national, and local news coverage. Provides
coverage also of Russian life in the United States.

704. RUSSKO-AMERIKANSKY PRAVOSLAVNY VESTNIK.   The
   Russian-American Orthodox Messenger.   1904— .
59 East Second Street, New York, New York 10003
   Editor: V. Rev. Cyril Fotiev   Language: Russian
   Sponsor: Orthodox Church in America
   Circulation: 1,200   Frequency: Monthly   Subscription: $6.00

Features religious news and guidance for the Russian Orthodox clergy and laity. It reports events, activities, appointments, and transfers of clergy from Orthodox churches all over the world. It also includes doctrinal instruction, biographies of religious figures, and messages from members of the clergy.

705. RUSSKOYE DELO.   The Russian Cause.   1958— .
349 West 86th Street, New York, New York 10024
    Editor: Alexander V. Rummel   Language: Russian
    Sponsor: Russian Immigrants Representative Association in America, Inc.
    Circulation: 656   Frequency: Monthly   Subscription: $4.00

"Critical analysis of the theory, practice and propaganda of communism. Survey of the current political events from the anti-communist point of view and immigrants' life chronicle" [editor's statement].

706. SOGLASIYE.   Harmony.   1950— .
1414 Maltman Avenue, Los Angeles, California 90026
    Editor: George P. Apanasenko   Language: Russian
    Circulation: 675   Frequency: Monthly   Subscription: $5.00

Anti-communist political magazine. Serves "special needs of the new-coming emigrants and special needs of Russian cultural activities in the U.S.A." [editor's statement].

707. STRANNIK.   Pilgrim.   1945— .
P.O. Box 206, Garfield, New Jersey 07026
    Editor: A. V. Chubkowsky   Language: Russian
    Sponsor: Christian Evangelical Pentecostal Faith
    Circulation: 2,000   Frequency: Quarterly Subscription: Unknown

708. TSERKOVNAYA ZHIZN'.   Church Life.   1934— .
75 East 93rd Street, New York, New York 10028
    Editor: Synod of Bishops of the Russian Orthodox Church
    Language: Russian
    Sponsor: Synod of Bishops of the Russian Orthodox Church
    Circulation: 350   Frequency: Irregular   Subscription: $3.00

Contains "information of Church events and commentary of ecclesiastical issues; publication of documents" [editor's statement].

709. VESTNIK OBSHCHESTVA RUSSKIKH VETERANOV VELIKOI
VOINY.   Messenger of the Russian Veterans of World War I.
1926— .
2041 Lyon Street, San Francisco, California 94115
Editor: Collegia   Language: Russian
Sponsor: Society of Russian Veterans of World War I
Circulation: 200   Frequency: Irregular   Subscription: $.35/copy

The main objective of this publication is "to save memoirs of military character by members of the Society and other men of different Russian armies" [editor's statement].

710. ZNAMYA ROSSII.   The Banner of Russia.   1946— .
3544 Broadway, New York, New York 10031
Editor: Nicholas N. Chuhnov   Language: Russian
Circulation: 1,200   Frequency: Monthly   Subscription: $4.00

This publication is "an organ of Russian independent monarchical thought dedicated to anticommunist political views" [editor's statement]. It has articles on socio-political topics, both historical and current, relating to Russia and Russian emigrees. Includes international news, a chronicle of Russian life, information on funds for emigrees, and occasional political poems.

Russian Publications in English

711. ONE CHURCH.   1930— .
P.O. Box 363, East Lansing, Michigan 48823
Editor: Rt. Rev. Archpriest Photius Donahue   Language: English
Sponsor: Patriarchal Russian Orthodox Vicariate in America
Circulation: 2,500   Frequency: Bi-monthly   Subscription: $4.00

Contains religious news and guidance for followers of the Orthodox faith. News articles include information on church life and political developments around the world. Editorials, sermons, commentaries on current events, and answers to doctrinal questions provide spiritual guidance. Book and record reviews are also included. Occasionally a Russian section is featured.

712. THE ORTHODOX HERALD.   1952— .
116 Eastridge Drive, San Antonio, Texas 78227
Editor: V. Rev. W. Basil Stroyen   Language: English
Sponsor: The Orthodox Herald, Inc.
Circulation: 5,020   Frequency: Monthly   Subscripton: $1.25

Features news of the Orthodox world and spiritual guidance for followers of the Orthodox faith. It includes international news of recent events, religious discussions and quizzes, answers to doctrinal questions, and Bible reading schedules. Religious poetry, recipes for Russian dishes, and light articles are also included.

713. ORTHODOX LIFE.   1950— .
Holy Trinity Monastery, Jordanville, New York 13361
    Editor: V. Rev. Archimandrite Constantine   Language: English
    Sponsor: Holy Trinity Monastery
    Circulation: 700   Frequency: Bi-monthly   Subscription: $3.00

"Dedicated to the preservation of traditional Orthodox Christianity of the Russian Church" [editor's statement].

714. THE RUSSIAN REVIEW.   1941— .
The Hoover Institution, Stanford, California 94305
    Editor: Dimitri von Mohrenschildt   Language: English
    Sponsor: The Russian Review, Inc.; The Hoover Institution
    Circulation: 1,850   Frequency: Quarterly   Subscription: $9.00

An interdisciplinary quarterly which aims at providing a broad survey of the Russian scene: political, historical, economic, and cultural. Contains an extensive book review section and occasionally publishes important historical and literary documents.

715. ST. VLADIMIR'S THEOLOGICAL QUARTERLY.   1952— .
575 Scarsdale Road, Crestwood, New York 10707
    Editor: John Meyendorf   Language: English
    Sponsor: St. Vladimir's Orthodox Theological Seminary
    Circulation: 1,300   Frequency: Unknown   Subscription: $4.00

716. TOLSTOY FOUNDATION NEWS LETTER.   1939— .
250 West 57th Street, New York, New York 10019
    Editor: Mrs. Tatiana Schaufuss   Language: English and Russian
    Sponsor: Tolstoy Foundation, Inc.
    Circulation: Unknown   Frequency: Semi-annually   Subscription: Free

This well-illustrated newsletter reports on the activities, accomplishments, and present needs of the Tolstoy Foundation.

SCANDINAVIAN PRESS

see DANISH, NORWEGIAN, and SWEDISH PRESS

SERBIAN PRESS

Serbian Publications in Serbian, Serbian-English, and South Slavonian

717. AMERIKANSKI SRBOBRAN.   The American Serb Defender.   1929-
3414 Fifth Avenue, Pittsburgh, Pennsylvania 15213
      Editor: Robert Rade Stone   Language: Serbian and English
      Sponsor: Serb National Federation
      Circulation: 9,100   Frequency: 3 times/week   Subscription: $8.00

This publication is "the oldest and largest Serbian newspaper in America," and its purpose is "to keep alive traditions and ideals of Serbian people and to promote 100 per cent Americanism" [editor's statement]. It has many articles on people and events in the Serbian community in the United States. As an organ of the Serb National Federation, it also publicizes its national sports program. Monday and Friday issues are published in Serbian, Wednesday issues in English.

718. RADNICKA BORBA.   Workers' Struggle.   1907—.
14302 Schoolcraft, Detroit, Michigan 48227
      Editor: Peter Slepcevich   Language: South Slavonian
      Sponsor: South Slavonian Federation of the Socialist Labor Party
      Circulation: Unknown   Frequency: Semi-monthly   Subscription: $2.0C

Political party newspaper of the Yugoslav Federation of the Socialist Labor Party (Socialist Labor Party of America). Its articles are largely devoted to political theory, political news, and news of meetings and events. A column is regularly devoted to letters from readers.

719. SERBIA.   Voice of Serbian Freedom Fighters.   1960—.
9663 Maple Avenue, Gary, Indiana 46403
      Editor: Momchilo Djujich   Language: Serbian
      Sponsor: Serbian Chetniks
      Circulation: 3,500   Frequency: Bi-monthly   Subscription: Unknown

Political magazine of anti-communist orientation.

720. SLOBODA.   Liberty.   1952— .
3090 West North Avenue, Chicago, Illinois 60647
    Editor: Miomir Radovanovic   Language: Serbian
    Sponsor: Serbian National Defense Council
    Circulation: 2,000   Frequency: Weekly   Subscription: Unknown

721. SRPSKA BORBA.   The Serbian Struggle.   1946— .
448 Barry Avenue, Chicago, Illinois 60657
    Editor: Dr. Slobodan M. Draskovich   Language: Serbian and English
    Sponsor: Serbian Literary Association
    Circulation: 16,160   Frequency: Unknown   Subscription: $12.00

The purpose of this publication is "to preserve, strengthen, and develop
the spirit of freedom, individual and national, among all Serbs scattered
in thirty-six countries of the free world, as well as in communist-occupied
Yugoslavia" [editor's statement]. Every issue has a review of world
events. Articles cover historical, political, social, literary, theatrical, and
other topics. Social and political aspects of the United States are also
explained.

722. YUGOSLOVENSKI AMERICKI GLASNIK.   Yugoslav-American
    Herald.   1909— .
235 Starbird Drive, Monterey Park, California 91754
    Editor: Mike Perko   Language: English and Serbo-Croatian
    Sponsor: Yugoslav-American Publishers, Inc.
    Circulation: 1,700   Frequency: Monthly   Subscription: $5.00

Provides political, social, religious, and cultural news to all peoples of
Yugoslav origin, attempting to give equal coverage to each. It includes
information on activities and meetings, laws and rights in the United
States, and churches and sports. It also advertises books and records
available in Yugoslav languages.

SLOVAK PRESS

see also CZECH PRESS

Slovak Publications in Slovak and Slovak-English

723. AVE MARIA.   1916— .
2900 East Boulevard, Cleveland, Ohio 44104
    Editor: Rev. Andrew Pier   Language: Slovak
    Sponsor: Slovak Benedictine Fathers
    Circulation: Unknown   Frequency: Monthly   Subscription: Unknown

724. BRATSTVO.   Brotherhood.   1898— .
205 Madison Street, Passaic, New Jersey 07055
    Editor: Stefan J. Tkac   Language: Slovak and English
    Sponsor: Pennsylvania Slovak Catholic Union
    Circulation: 3,754   Frequency: Monthly   Subscription: $2.00

This fraternal publication provides general news coverage of interest to the Slovak community. Includes reports of the activities of the Union.

725. CALVIN.   1907— .
342 Boulevard of Allies, Pittsburgh, Pennsylvania 15222
    Editor: George Virchick, Jr.   Language: Slovak and English
    Sponsor: Presbyterian Beneficial Union
    Circulation: 1,034   Frequency: Monthly   Subscription: $1.25

Prior to June 1960 this publication went under the title *Slovak Presbyterian.* It is fraternal in nature and publishes articles and reports on the activities of the Union.

726. DOBRY PASTIER.   Good Shepherd.   1927— .
205 Madison Street, Passaic, New Jersey 07055
    Editor: Rev. Joseph Altany   Language: Slovak and English
    Sponsor: Slovak Catholic Federation of America
    Circulation: 4,000   Frequency: Monthly   Subscription: $2.00

727. FLORIDSKY SLOVAK.   Floridian Slovak.   1952— .
Rt. 1, Box 39, Maitland, Florida 32751
    Editor: Charles Belohlavek   Language: Slovak and English
    Circulation: Unknown   Frequency: Quarterly   Subscription: Unknown

This house organ includes news of special interest to retired Slovaks, especially articles on Slovak culture.

728. JEDNOTA.   Union.   1893— .
1001 Rosedale Avenue, Middletown, Pennsylvania 17057
    Editor: Joseph C. Krajsa   Language: Slovak
    Sponsor: First Catholic Slovak Union
    Circulation: 40,000   Frequency: Weekly   Subscription: $4.00

This is the official organ of the first Catholic Slovak Union, a fraternal life insurance company. Objectives are "to promote and preserve the Catholic faith of the Slovac people, their language, and identity" [editor's statement]. Also provides news of the fraternity.

729. KATOLICKY SOKOL.   Catholic Falcon.   1915— .
205 Madison Street, Passaic, New Jersey 07055
Editor: John C. Sciranka   Language: Slovak and English
Sponsor: Slovak Catholic Sokol
Circulation: 19,200   Frequency: Weekly   Subscription: $3.50

A fraternal publication.

730. LISTY SVATEHO FRANTISKA.   Leaflets of St. Francis.   1924— .
232 South Home Avenue, Pittsburgh, Pennsylvania 15202
Editor: Rev. Rudolf Dilong, O.F.M.   Language: Slovak
Sponsor: Slovak Franciscan Fathers
Circulation: 3,000   Frequency: Monthly   Subscription: $3.00

Contents are primarily of a religious and spiritual nature, although some educational materials are also published.

731. LUDOVE NOVINY.   People's News.   1905— .
1510 West 18th Street, Chicago, Illinois 60608
Editor: Paul Hodos   Language: Slovak
Circulation: 1,200   Frequency: Weekly   Subscription: $6.00

Provides general news coverage of special interest to Slovaks.

732. MOST.   Bridge.   1954— .
2900 East Boulevard, Cleveland, Ohio
Editor: Nicholas Sprinc   Language: Slovak
Sponsor: The Slovak Institute
Circulation: 1,000   Frequency: Quarterly   Subscription: $5.00

This cultural and literary quarterly features articles on Slovak literature, fine arts, history, social sciences, and philosophy by Slovak authors outside Slovakia.

733. NARODNE NOVINY.   National News.   1910— .
516 Court Place, Pittsburgh, Pennsylvania 15219
Editor: John Mihal   Language: Slovak and English
Sponsor: National Slovak Society
Circulation: 10,000   Frequency: Semi-monthly
Subscription: Membership dues

This publication emphasizes the events and activities of the fraternal organization.

734. NEW YORSKY DENIK.   New York Daily.   1912— .
283-5 Oak Street, Perth Amboy, New Jersey 08861
    Editor: Karol Bednar   Language: Slovak
    Sponsor: Universum Press Company
    Circulation: 2,400   Frequency: Weekly   Subscription: Unknown

735. PRIATEL DIETOK.   The Children's Friend.   1911— .
205 Madison Street, Passaic, New Jersey 07055
    Editor: John C. Sciranka   Language: Slovak
    Sponsor: Junior Slovak Catholic Sokol
    Circulation: 8,336   Frequency: Monthly   Subscription: $1.00

A children's magazine.

736. SION.   Zion.   1929— .
342 Boulevard of the Allies, Pittsburgh, Pennsylvania 15222
    Editor: Rev. John Kovacik and Rev. Jan Adam   Language: Slovak
    Sponsor: Slovak Zion Synod
    Circulation: 1,771   Frequency: Monthly   Subscription: $2.00

A religious magazine.

737. SLOVAK V AMERIKE.   Slovak in America.   1889— .
313 Ridge Avenue, Middletown, Pennsylvania 17057
    Editor: Draga Pauco   Language: Slovak
    Sponsor: Joseph Pauco, Publisher
    Circulation: 1,980   Frequency: Weekly   Subscription: $6.00

This is the oldest Slovak newspaper in America, providing coverage of
national, international, and local news of special concern to its Slovak
readers. It "champions the right of Slovak people to the re-establishment
of their own national state" [editor's statement].

738. SLOVENSKA OBRANA.   Slovak Defense.   1913— .
4 Fairlawn Drive, Pittston, Pennsylvania 18640
    Editor: Edward Kovac, Jr.   Language: Slovak
    Sponsor: Bosak Publications, Inc.
    Circulation: 4,950   Frequency: Weekly   Subscription: $12.00

This weekly publishes general, national, and local news, and features
articles on Slovak activities and organizations in the United States.

739. SLOVENSKY SOKOL.   Sokol Times   1905– .
276 Prospect Street, East Orange, New Jersey 07019
Editor: Karol Bednar   Language: English and Slovak
Sponsor: Slovak Gymnastic Union Sokol of U.S.A.
Circulation: 11,000   Frequency: Weekly   Subscription: $6.00

Official publication of a fraternal and physical education organization.
Articles on history and program of the Sokol movement, gymnastics,
and sports.

740. SVEDOK.   The Witness.   1906– .
342 Boulevard of the Allies, Pittsburgh, Pennsylvania 15222
Editor: Rev. John J. Pelikan, Sr.   Language: Slovak
Sponsor: Synod of Evangelical Lutheran Churches
Circulation: 1,925   Frequency: Monthly   Subscription: $1.50

A magazine for Lutheran Slovaks.

741. SVORNOST.   Harmony.   1912– .
342 Boulevard of the Allies, Pittsburgh, Pennsylvania 15222
Editor: Rev. Thomas Harnyak   Language: Slovak
Sponsor: Catholic Slovak Brotherhood
Circulation: 981   Frequency: Bi-monthly   Subscription: $1.00

A fraternal religious magazine.

742. UNITED LUTHERAN.   1893– .
1701 Banksville Road, Pittsburgh, Pennsylvania
Editor: Daniel M. Zornan   Language: Slovak and English
Sponsor: United Lutheran Society
Circulation: 8,200   Frequency: Monthly   Subscription: Free

This is the official organ of the United Lutheran Society.

743. ZENSKA JEDNOTA.   1913– .
5340 Mary Ann Lane, Gary, Indiana 45409
Editor: Mrs. Anne Fusillo   Language: Slovak and English
Sponsor: First Catholic Slovak Ladies Association
Circulation: 35,100   Frequency: Monthly   Subscription: $1.50

The name of this official organ of a fraternal insurance society has been
changed from *Zenska Jednota* to *Fraternally Yours.* Articles cover the
activities of the Association, Slovak culture, and Slovak leaders.

744. ZIVENA.   1908— .
342 Boulevard of the Allies, Pittsburgh, Pennsylvania 15222
Editor: John Cieker   Language: Slovak and English
Sponsor: Zivena Beneficial Society
Circulation: 1,975   Frequency: Monthly   Subscription: Unknown
A fraternal publication.

745. ZORNICKA.   Morning Star.   1941— .
Box 168, Middletown, Pennsylvania 17057
Editor: Edward Kovac, Jr.   Language: Slovak
Sponsor: Ladies Pennsylvania Slovak Catholic Union
Circulation: 5,000   Frequency: Monthly   Subscription: $.50
This fraternal monthly publishes general news and news of the Union.

Slovak Publications in English

746. SLOVAKIA.   1951— .
313 Ridge Avenue, Middletown, Pennsylvania 17057
Editor: Joseph Pauco   Language: English
Sponsor: Slovak League of America
Circulation: 2,240   Frequency: Irregular   Subscription: $3.00

The editorial objective of this publication is to "support freedom and
political independence for Slovakia and promote a better understanding
of the Slovak nation" [editor's statement]. Covers Slovak history, culture,
politics, and other relevant topics. Book review section. Scholarly publication.

SLOVENIAN PRESS

Slovenian Publications in Slovenian and Slovenian-English

747. AMERIKANSKI SLOVENEC-GLASILO K.S.K. JEDNOTE.   American
Slovenian-Herald.   1891— .
6117 St. Clair Avenue, Cleveland, Ohio 44103
Editor: Ivan Racic   Language: Slovenian and English
Sponsor: American Slovenian Catholic Union
Circulation: 16,770   Frequency: Weekly   Subscription: $5.00

Provides general and local news of special interest to Slovenian readers,
as well as fraternal news.

748. AMERISKA DOMOVINA.   American Home.   1898— .
6117 St. Clair Avenue, Cleveland, Ohio 44103
   Editors: Vinko Lipovee (Slovenian) and Mary Debevec (English)
   Language: Slovenian and English
   Sponsor: American Home Publishing Company
   Circulation: 5,000   Frequency: Daily   Subscription: $16.00

This publication, the oldest Slovenian daily, provides general, national, and local news of interest to readers, including coverage of national Slovenian organizations.

749. AVE MARIA.   M ·   1909— .
1400 Main Street, Lemont, Illinois 60439
   Editor: Fortunat Zorman   Language: Slovenian
   Sponsor: Slovene Franciscan Fathers
   Circulation: 3,529   Frequency: Monthly   Subscription: $2.50

This Catholic monthly publishes materials about the Catholic faith and life. A special news section is entitled "The Church in the World."

750. FRATERNAL VOICE.   1908— .
5809 West 38th Avenue, Denver Colorado 80212
   Editors: Ed Krasovich (English) and Anthony Jersin (Slovenian)
   Language: English and Slovenian
   Sponsor: The Western Slavonic Association
   Circulation: 3,783   Frequency: Monthly   Subscription: $1.20

The purpose of this fraternal publication is to "unite our whole membership and develop fraternity, brotherhood, and cooperation to the highest degree" [editor's statement] .

751. NAS GLAS.   Our Voice.   1939— .
6401 St. Clair Avenue, Cleveland, Ohio 44103
   Editor: S. J. Modic   Language: Slovenian and English
   Sponsor: American Mutual Life Association
   Circulation: 7,500   Frequency: Semi-monthly
   Subscription: Free to members

This fraternal publication promotes fraternalism and Slovenian culture.

752. NOVA DOBA.   New Era.   1925— .
6233 St. Clair Avenue, Cleveland, Ohio 44103
    Editor: Julia Pirc   Language: Slovene
    Sponsor: American Fraternal Union
    Circulation: 8,578   Frequency: Semi-monthly Subscription: $1.50

A fraternal publication which provides general news coverage.

753. NOVI SVET.   New World Herald.   1938— .
2032 West Cermak Road, Chicago, Illinois 60608
    Editor: Dr. Ludwig A. Leskovar   Language: Slovene and English
    Sponsor: Novi Svet Publishing Company
    Circulation: 1,700   Frequency: Quarterly   Subscription: $1.00

This quarterly features articles on educational topics and family life.

754. PROSVETA.   Enlightenment.   1906— .
2657 South Lawndale Avenue, Chicago, Illinois 60623
    Editor: Louis Beniger   Language: Slovene and English
    Sponsor: Slovene National Benefit Society
    Circulation: 8,832   Frequency: Daily   Subscription: $15.00

This daily covers general, national, and international news of interest to
the Slovenian community, as well as fraternal news.

755. VOICE OF YOUTH.   1922— .
2657 South Lawndale Avenue, Chicago, Illinois 60623
    Editor: Louis Beniger   Language: English and Slovenian
    Sponsor: Slovene National Benefit Society
    Circulation: 11,350   Frequency: Monthly   Subscription: $3.00

A youth magazine.

756. ZARJA.   The Dawn.   1927— .
1937 West Cermak Road, Chicago, Illinois 60608
    Editor: Corinne Leskovar   Language: English and Slovenian
    Sponsor: Slovenian Women's Union of America
    Circulation: 11,150   Frequency: Monthly   Subscription: $3.00

The objective of this official publication of the Slovenian Women's Union
of America is to uphold "the ideals of sisterhood and perpetuate the
traditions of the Slovenian nationality" [editor's statement] .

SPANISH PRESS

Editor's note: This section includes ethnic Spanish publications of Mexican-American, Puerto Rican-American, and Cuban-American orientations published in the United States

Spanish Publications in Spanish and Spanish-English

757. ALIANZA.   Alliance.   1909— .
      P.O. Box 1671, Tucson, Arizona 85702
          Editor: Beatriz Yslas   Language: Spanish
          Sponsor: Alianza
          Circulation: Unknown   Frequency: Quarterly
          Subscription: Membership dues

758. AMERICA SPANISH NEWS.   1953— .
      2448 Mission Street, San Francisco, California 94110
          Editor: Dr. Felipe Marquez   Language: Spanish and English
          Circulation: 25,000   Frequency: Bi-weekly Subscription: Unknown

      Provides general, national, international, and local news coverage.

759. BERNALILLO TIMES.   1931— .
      P.O. Box B, Bernalillo, New Mexico 87004
          Editor: Cruz Segura   Language: Spanish and English
          Sponsor: Independent Publishing Company
          Circulation: 720   Frequency: Weekly   Subscription: $2.50

760. BUEN HOGAR.   Good Home.   1966— .
      5535 N.W. 7th Avenue, Miami, Florida 33127
          Editor: Frank Calderon   Language: Spanish
          Sponsor: Continental Publishing Company, Inc.
          Circulation: 375,000   Frequency: Monthly   Subscription: $6.00

      This family magazine provides articles on food, fashion, beauty, home furnishings, health and medicine, children and babies, horoscopes, family problems, along with novels and feature stories. Edited for the 18 to 35 year old married women in the rising middle-income category. Covers all Spanish-speaking countries of Latin America, plus the United States.

761. EL CENTINELA Y HERALDO DE LA SALUD.   Sentinel and Herald
     of Health.   1895– .
     1350 Villa Street, Mountain View, California 94040
         Editor: Fernando Chaij   Language: Spanish
         Sponsor: Pacific Press Publishing Company
         Circulation: 110,000   Frequency: Monthly   Subscription: $4.00

     Along with international and national news coverage, this monthly
     publishes articles on religious liberty, temperance, health, and other
     topics.

762. EL CONTINENTAL.   Continental.   1925– .
     909 East San Antonio Street, El Paso, Texas 79901
         Editor: Raul Cuellar   Language: Spanish
         Sponsor: El Continental Publishing Company
         Circulation: 8,000   Frequency: Daily   Subscription: $16.00

     The objectives of this daily are to provide "general information to the
     public with news from all over the world. This is a modern newspaper
     that works like any other regular daily in the U.S.A." [editor's state-
     ment].

763. CORPUS CHRISTI AMERICANO.
     1012 Leopard Street, Corpus Christi, Texas 78401
         Editor: P. R. Ochoa   Language: Spanish
         Sponsor: Ochoa Newspapers
         Circulation: Unknown   Frequency: Weekly   Subscription: Unknown

764. EL DIARIO–LA PRENSA.   Daily Press.   1913– .
     181 Hudson Street, New York, New York 10025
         Editor: Sergio Santelices   Language: Spanish
         Circulation: 82,613   Frequency: Daily   Subscription: $28.00

     This daily newspaper is published for the Spanish-speaking population
     of New York and surrounding areas. International, national, and local
     news coverage.

765. DIARIO DE LAS AMERICAS.   Daily of the Americas.   1953– .
     4349 N.W. 36th Street, Miami, Florida 33166
         Editor: Horacio Aguirre   Language: Spanish
         Sponsor: Americas Publishing Company
         Circulation: 36,665   Frequency: Daily   Subscription: $24.00

     International, national, and local news; emphasis is on inter-American news.

766. LA ESPAÑA LIBRE.   Free Spain.   1936— .
231 West 18th Street, New York, New York 10011
   Editor: Marcos C. Marí   Language: Spanish and English
   Sponsor: Confederated Spanish Societies of U.S.A.
   Circulation: 2,500   Frequency: Bi-monthly   Subscription: $5.00

767. LA GACETA.   The Gazette.   1922— .
2015 15th Street, Tampa, Flroida 33605
   Editor: Roland Manteiga   Language: Spanish, English, Italian
   Sponsor: La Gaceta Publishing Company
   Circulation: 9,825   Frequency: Weekly   Subscription: $5.00

768. EL HERALDO DE BROWNSVILLE.   Brownsville Herald.   1892— .
13th and Adams Streets, Brownsville, Texas 78520
   Editor: D. R. Segal   Language: Spanish and English
   Sponsor: Freedom Newspapers, Inc.
   Circulation: 12,800   Frequency: Daily   Subscription: $26.00

769. EL HISPANO.   The Spanish-American.   1966— .
416 Luna N.W., Albuquerque, New Mexico 87102
   Editor: A. B. Collado   Language: Spanish
   Sponsor: El Hispano, Inc.
   Circulation: 7,000   Frequency: Weekly   Subscription: $3.00

This weekly newspaper carries many ads and legal notices, as well as local news of special interest to the Spanish-speaking population. Includes local sports news and syndicated columns on women's and entertainment news.

770. EL INDEPENDIENTE.   The Independent.   1885— .
114 Grand Avenue N.W., Albuquerque, New Mexico 87101
   Editor: Mary Beth Acuff   Language: English and Spanish
   Sponsor: Independent Publishing Company
   Circulation: 1,000   Frequency: Weekly   Subscription: $3.00

"Legal newspaper containing political commentary and problems of the legal profession. . . . Our papers serve lawyers and political activists of all ethnic groups" [editor's statement].

771. LA JUSTICIA.   Justice.   1933— .
1710 Broadway, New York, New York 10019
    Editor: Anthony Lespier   Language: Spanish
    Sponsor: International Ladies' Garment Workers' Union
    Circulation: 83,000   Frequency: Monthly   Subscription: $2.00

This monthly is "primarily an organ of union information. All aspects
of union news. Also editorial comment on national and local issues.
Political education, rights and responsibilities and involvement in
community affairs" [editor's statement].

772. LA LUZ.   The Light.   1931— .
8259 Niles Center Road, Skokie, Illinois 60076
    Editor: Jorge J. Rodriguez-Florido   Language: Spanish
    Sponsor: National Textbook Company
    Circulation: 16,000   Frequency: Monthly   Subscription: $4.00

A magazine for high school students of Spanish. Includes news articles
of interest to teenagers, historical articles, short stories, cartoons, movie
and book reviews, and sports stories. Also includes articles on the customs
and culture of Spanish-speaking countries.

773. LA LUZ APOSTÓLICA.   The Apostolic Light.   1916— .
230 Meadowood Lane, San Antonio, Texas 78216
    Editor: H. C. Ball   Language: Spanish
    Sponsor: The Latin American District Council of the Assemblies of God
    Circulation: 3,320   Frequency: Monthly   Subscription: $1.50

This religious monthly is "the official organ of the Spanish Assemblies of
God in all states west of the Mississippi River and also in Wisconsin and
Michigan in the U.S.A." [editor's statement].

774. EL MUNDO DE NUEVA YORK.   New York World.   1970— .
115 East 69th Street, New York, New York 10021
    Editor: Stanley Ross   Language: Spanish
    Sponsor: El Mundo Enterprises
    Circulation: Unknown   Frequency: Monthly   Subscription: Unknown

This general magazine, aimed primarily at the Spanish-speaking population of New York City, contains local news of the more sensational type,
state and national news, feature articles, and news from Spanish-speaking
countries. Feature articles include some true-confession type material
with quite sensational illustrations.

775. MUNDO HISPANO.   Spanish World.   1970— .
2448 Mission Street, San Francisco, California 94110
   Editors: Dr. Felipe Marquez and Thomas Berkley
   Language: Spanish
   Sponsor: Alameda Publishing Company
   Circulation: 10,000   Frequency: Weekly   Subscription: $7.50

This weekly newspaper contains local, state, national, and international news, both general and of special appeal to Spanish-speaking population. Contains all regular newspaper features such as editorials, women's news, etc.

776. LA OPINION.   The Opinion.   1926— .
1436 South Main Street, Los Angeles, California 90015
   Editor: Ignacio E. Lozano, Jr.   Language: Spanish
   Sponsor: Lozano Enterprises
   Circulation: 15,927   Frequency: Daily   Subscription: $24.00

"*La Opinion* is a daily newspaper of general interest and content, published in the Spanish language. It covers local, national and international news, with emphasis on news of particular interest to the Spanish-speaking community of Southern California" [editor's statement].

777. LA PALABRA DIARA.   Daily Word.   1955— .
Unity Village, Missouri 64063
   Editor: Martha Smock   Language: Spanish
   Sponsor: Unity School of Christianity
   Circulation: 20,500   Frequency: Monthly   Subscription: $2.00

Religious non-denominational monthly.

778. PALADIN & DON QUIXOTE.   1963— .
21 East Santa Clara Street, San Jose, California 95113
   Editor: P. C. Ramirez   Language: Spanish
   Sponsor: MIM Diaz-Infante, Publisher
   Circulation: 5,000   Frequency: Semi-monthly   Subscription: Unknown

This publication includes general and local news of interest to the Spanish-speaking community in California.

779. EL PORVENIR.   The Outlook.   1934— .
200 East Third Street, Mission, Texas 78572
    Editor: Rogelio Cantu   Language: Spanish
    Sponsor: Border Printing Service
    Circulation: 4,500   Frequency: Bi-weekly   Subscription: Unknown

780. THE POST—EL INFORMADOR.   1967— .
2973 Sacramento Street, Berkeley, California 94701
    Editor: Thomas L. Berkley   Language: Spanish and English
    Circulation: 40,000   Frequency: Monthly   Subscription: $7.80

This monthly provides general news and items of group interest.

781. TAMPA INDEPENDENT.   El Tampa Independiente.
P.O. Box 1838, Tampa, Florida 33601
    Editor: Robert L. Jerome, Jr.   Language: Spanish
    Sponsor: Tampa Independent Publishers
    Circulation: 1,496   Frequency: Weekly   Subscription: Unknown

782. THE TAOS NEWS.   Las Noticias de Taos.   1959— .
P.O. Box 1005, Taos, New Mexico 87571
    Editor: J. E. Peeler   Language: English and Spanish
    Sponsor: Taos Publishing Corporation
    Circulation: 1,800   Frequency: Weekly   Subscription: $7.00

This regular weekly newspaper contains local and national news, without
any special emphasis on news of interest to the Spanish-speaking
community.

783. TEMAS.   Topics.   1950— .
1560 Broadway, New York, New York 10036
    Editor: José de la Vega   Language: Spanish
    Sponsor: Club Familiar, Inc.
    Circulation: 78,200   Frequency: Monthly   Subscription: $4.00

This publication is "a family magazine containing general information,
special features, interviews, beauty and health topics" [editor's state-
ment]. Also contains entertainment news, women's features, etc.

784. EL TIEMPO.   The Times.   1963— .
116 West 14th Street, New York, New York 10011
    Editor: Stanley Ross   Language: Spanish
    Circulation: 45,000   Frequency: Daily   Subscription: $30.00

785. EL TIEMPO DE LAREDO.   Laredo Times.   1886— .
P.O. Box 29, Laredo, Texas 78040
    Editor: James H. Hale   Language: English and Spanish
    Sponsor: Laredo Newspapers, Inc.
    Circulation: 18,000   Frequency: Daily   Subscription: $25.80

"Standard daily newspaper. Spanish pages utilize local news copy, the
A.P., and Copley News Service. No special interests or axes to grind"
[editor's statement].

786. LA TRIBUNA DE NORTH JERSEY.   North Jersey Tribune.   1950— .
70 Kossuth Street, Newark, New Jersey
    Editor: Carlos Bidot   Language: Spanish
    Circulation: 50,000   Frequency: Monthly   Subscription: $2.00

Contains information of interest to the Spanish-speaking population.
Editorials are published on a variety of subjects.

787. LA TROMPETA.   The Trumpet.   1912— .
905 Bluntzer Street, Corpus Christi, Texas 78405
    Editor: Rev. Maurice M. Caldwell   Language: Spanish
    Sponsor: Christian Triumph Company
    Ciruclation: 200   Frequency: Monthly   Subscription: Free

788. LA VERDAD.   The Truth.   1940— .
910 Francisca Street, Corpus Christi, Texas 78405
    Editor: Santos de la Paz   Language: Spanish and English
    Sponsor: Santos de la Paz, Owner
    Circulation: 7,000   Frequency: Weekly   Subscription: $3.50

This right-wing publication contains heavily editorialized articles on
labor, welfare, etc. Some local news.

789. THE VOICE.   La Voz.   1959— .
6201 Biscayne Boulevard, Miami, Florida 33138
    Editor: George H. Monahan   Language: English and Spanish
    Circulation: 63,212   Frequency: Weekly   Subscription: $5.00

"*The Voice* is the official publication of the Catholic Archdiocese of
Miami. Its news function is that of bringing developments within the
Church to the people of South Florida. Also . . . emphasis on social
action problems . . . articles concerning the plight of the poor, of migrants,
of the Cuban refugees, the Spanish-speaking members of the younger
generation who are estranged from society, etc." [editor's statement].

Spanish Publications in English

790. COSTILLA COUNTY FREE PRESS.   1948— .
P.O. Box 116, San Luis, California 81152
  Editor: Alfonso J. LaCombe   Language: English and Spanish
  Circulation: Unknown   Frequency: Weekly   Subscription: $2.00

An independent weekly which publishes general and local news.

791. DEFENSOR-CHIEFTAIN.   Socorro County News.   1904— .
P.O. Box Q, 204 Manzanares N.E., Socorro, New Mexico 87801
  Editor: Robert Klipsch   Language: English
  Circulation: 1,843   Frequency: Semi-weekly   Subscription: $6.50

792. RIO GRANDE HERALD.   1923— .
102 North Corpus, P.O. Box 452, Rio GRande City, Texas 78582
  Editor: Cris Quintxnilla   Language: English
  Sponsor: Starr County Publishing Company
  Circulation: 910   Frequency: Weekly   Subscription: $6.50

793. RIO GRANDE SUN.   1956— .
Box 790, Española, New Mexico 87532
  Editor: Robert Trapp   Language: English and Spanish
  Sponsor: Sun Company, Inc.
  Circulation: 2,979   Frequency: Weekly   Subscription: $4.00

This independent newspaper provides general and local coverage.

794. SANTA ROSA NEWS.   1924— .
P.O. Drawer P, Santa Rosa, New Mexico 88435
  Editor: Darrel Freeman   Language: English
  Circulation: 1,800   Frequency: Weekly   Subscription: $4.00

This weekly features general and local news of interest to the Santa
Rosa community.

795. THE TIMES.   1935— .
P.O. Box 856, 683 West Main Street, Raymondville, Texas 78580
  Editor: A. R. Rodriguez   Language: English
  Circulation: 820   Frequency: Weekly   Subscription: $3.00

SWEDISH PRESS

Swedish Publications in Swedish and Swedish-English

796. THE LEADING STAR.   Ledstjarnan.   1920— .
    1410 Fifth Avenue, Seattle, Washington 98101
        Editor: Carl L. Helgren   Language: English and Swedish
        Sponsor: Order of Runeberg
        Circulation: 3,600   Frequency: Monthly   Subscription: $1.50

    This is the official organ of the international order of Runeberg, a
    fraternal order of Swedish-Finnish origin.

797. MUSIKTIDNING.   Music Tidings.   1905— .
    6132 North Winchester Avenue, Chicago, Illinois 60626
        Editor: Gunnar A. Bloom   Language: English and Swedish
        Sponsor: American Union of Swedish Singers
        Circulation: 1,100   Frequency: Monthly   Subscription: $3.00

    Promotes teaching and cultivation of chorus singing, principally in
    Swedish.

798. NORDEN.   The North.   1896— .
    4816 Eighth Avenue, Brooklyn, New York 11220
        Editor: Erik R. Hermans   Language: Swedish
        Sponsor: Norden News, Inc.
        Circulation: 1,720   Frequency: Weekly   Subscription: $10.00

    Contains news from Finland and from different immigrant colonies in
    the United States and Canada, and general news. "The main objective
    is to give the fewer and fewer immigrants a newspaper that is written
    in their mother tongue. This paper is the only news medium for Swedish
    speaking people from Finland" [editor's statement].

799. NORDSTJERNAN-SVEA.   The North Star-Svea.   1872— .
    4 West 22nd Street, New York, New York 10010
        Editor: Gerhard T. Rooth   Language: English and Swedish
        Circulation: 11,000   Frequency: Weekly   Subscription: $8.00

    This weekly, the oldest Swedish newspaper in the United States, provides
    general, national, and local news coverage.

800. SVENSKA AMERIKANAREN TRIBUNEN.   Swedish American
Tribune.   1876— .
916 West Belmont Avenue, Chicago, Illinois 60657
Editor: Einar O. Enard   Language: Swedish
Sponsor: Swedish American Newspaper Company
Circulation: 19,435   Frequency: Weekly   Subscription: $7.00

Provides extensive coverage of Swedish life in the United States, as well
as general news coverage. Independent in religion and politics.

801. SVENSKA POSTEN.   Swedish Post.   1886— .
2228 First Avenue, Seattle, Washington 98121
Editor: Harry Fabbe   Language: Swedish
Sponsor: Consolidated Press Printing Company
Circulation: 2,668   Frequency: Weekly   Subscription: $6.00

This weekly publishes international, national, and local news, with
particular attention to events in Sweden and Swedish life in the United
States.

802. VESTKUSTEN.   West Coast.   1885— .
435 Duboce Avenue, San Francisco, California 94117
Editor: Karin Person   Language: Swedish
Circulation: 1,994   Frequency: Weekly   Subscription: $6.00

803. THE WESTERN NEWS.   1888— .
1210 California, Denver, Colorado 80204
Editor: Glenn D. Peterson   Language: English and Swedish
Sponsor: Enoch Peterson
Circulation: 1,050   Frequency: Semi-monthly   Subscription: $3.00

Provides information on Swedish, Norwegian, Danish, and Finnish
people and their clubs, lodges, and churches.

Swedish Publications in English

804. THE AMERICAN-SCANDINAVIAN REVIEW.   1911— .
127 East 73rd Street, New York, New York 10021
Editor: Erik J. Friis   Language: English
Sponsor: The American-Scandinavian Foundation
Circulation: 6,100   Frequency: Quarterly   Subscription: $7.50

Features articles on Scandinavia, its people, culture, and history.

805. BETHPAGE MESSENGER.   1913— .
Bethpage Mission, Axtell, Nebraska 68924
    Editor: Robert Turnquist   Language: English
    Sponsor: Bethpage Mission
    Circulation: 14,000 Frequency: Monthly   Subscription: $.25

806. CALIFORNIA COVENANTER.   1916— .
P.O. Box 1007, Turlock, California 95380
    Editor: Virgil Hanson   Language: English
    Sponsor: California Conference of the Evangelical Covenant Church
    Circulation: 5,689   Frequency: Bi-weekly Subscription: $3.00

A religious magazine.

807. CALIFORNIA VECKOBLAD.   California Weekly.   1910— .
P.O. Box 3156 Terminal Annex, Los Angeles, California 90054
    Editor: Mary Hendricks   Language: English
    Circulation: 2,200   Frequency: Weekly   Subscription: $5.00

This independent weekly provides general and local news.

808. EVANGELICAL BEACON.   1931— .
1515 East 66th Street, Minneapolis, Minnesota 55423
    Editor: Mel Larson   Language: English
    Sponsor: Evangelical Free Church of America
    Circulation: 23,000 Frequency: Bi-weekly Subscription: Unknown

809. HERALD OF FAITH.   1934— .
P.O. Box 118, Prairie View, Illinois 60069
    Editor: Joseph Mattsson-Boze   Language: English
    Sponsor: Full Gospel Faith and Fellowship—Herald of Faith, Inc.
    Circulation: 6,950   Frequency: Monthly   Subscription: Unknown

810. SCAN.   1940?— .
127 East 73rd Street, New York, New York 10021
    Editor: Gene G. Gage   Language: English
    Sponsor: American-Scandinavian Foundation
    Circulation: 6,300   Frequency: Monthly   Subscription: Free

Contains information on the activities of the American-Scandinavian Foundation.

811. SCANDINAVIAN-AMERICAN BULLETIN.   1965– .
     5817 Eighth Avenue, Brooklyn, New York 11220
     Editor: Erik J. Friis   Language: English
     Circulation: Unknown   Frequency: Monthly   Subscription: Unknown

812. SCANDINAVIAN STUDIES.   1910– .
     127 East 73rd Street, New York, New York 10021
     Editor: George Schoolfield   Language: English
     Sponsor: Society for the Advancement of Scandinavian Study
     Circulation: 700   Frequency: Quarterly   Subscription: $10.00

This scholarly journal, devoted to Scandinavian studies, features articles
on history, literature, philology, and other relevant topics. Book reviews
are included.

813. THE SVITHIOD JOURNAL.   1898– .
     5520 West Lawrence Avenue, Chicago, Illinois 60630
     Editor: Harold Wennersten   Language: English
     Sponsor: Independent Order of Svithiod
     Circulation: 7,200   Frequency: Monthly   Subscription: $.50

A fraternal publication originally published in Swedish, now entirely in
English. Information is provided on the activities of the lodges, including
financial reports, etc.

814. THE STANDARD.   1910– .
     1233 Central, Evanston, Illinois
     Editor: Donald E. Anderson   Language: English
     Sponsor: Harvest Publications, Baptist General Conference
     Circulation: 27,000   Frequency: Bi-weekly   Subscription: $4.00

This religious publication was originally Swedish and printed in Swedish.

815. SWEDISH INSTITUTE YEARBOOK.
     639 38th Street, Rock Island, Illinois 61201
     Editor: Unknown   Language: English
     Sponsor: Augustana College
     Circulation: 500   Frequency: Irregular   Subscription: Unknown

Consists of essays by Swedish authors on Swedish-Americans and
Sweden. Objective is "to preserve elements of the Swedish heritage
in America" [editor's statement].

816. THE SWEDISH PIONEER HISTORICAL QUARTERLY.   1950– .
5125 North Spaulding Avenue, Chicago, Illinois 60625
    Editor: Dr. Franklin D. Scott   Language: English
    Sponsor: Swedish Pioneer Historical Society, Inc.
    Circulation: 1,825   Frequency: Quarterly   Subscription: $7.00

This quarterly features scholarly historical articles on the Swedish
community in the United States. Its objective is "to promote Swedish-
American historical research and literary work in literature, art, culture,
education and religion" [editor's statement].

817. VASASTJÄRNAN.   Vasa Star.   1908– .
10219 South Union Avenue, Chicago, Illinois 60628
    Editor: Ruth Peterson   Language: English
    Sponsor: Vasa Order of America
    Circulation: 30,000   Frequency: Monthly   Subscription: Unknown

A fraternal publication.

818. VIKINGEN.   Vikings.   1901– .
157 East Ohio Street, Chicago, Illinois 60611
    Editor: William A. Johnson   Language: English
    Sponsor: Grand Lodge of Independent Order of Vikings
    Circulation: 9,100   Frequency: Monthly   Subscription: Unknown

A fraternal monthly.

SWISS PRESS

Swiss Publications in German and German-English-Italian

819. AMERIKANISCHE SCHWEIZER ZEITUNG.   American-Swiss
    Gazette.   1868– .
One Union Square West, New York, New York 10003
    Editor: Max E. Ammann   Language: English and German
    Sponsor: Swiss Publishing Company
    Circulation: 2,000   Frequency: Weekly   Subscription: $12.00

This weekly provides coverage of Switzerland (politics, culture, finance,
local news, sports) and news of the Swiss in the United States (Swiss
clubs, Swiss companies, and other). Also includes general and United
States news. About half the paper is published in German.

820. SWISS JOURNAL.   1918— .
548 Columbus Avenue, San Francisco, California 94133
Editor: Mario Muschi   Language: English, German, Italian
Sponsor: Swiss Journal Company
Circulation: 3,000   Frequency: Weekly   Subscription: $8.00

General news on Switzerland, Swiss people, and Swiss organizations in
the United States.

Swiss Publications in English

821. THE SWISS AMERICAN.   1869— .
33 Public Square, Room 1008, Cleveland, Ohio 44113
Editor: Anton Haemmerle   Language: English
Sponsor: The North American Swiss Alliance
Circulation: 3,600   Frequency: Monthly   Subscription
Subscription: Membership

This fraternal monthly promotes fraternalism and good-fellowship among
the Swiss, Swiss-Americans and their descendants. Includes information
on social activities of various Swiss societies, financial reports, etc.

SYRIAN PRESS

see ARABIC PRESS

TURKISH PRESS

Turkish Publications in Turkish and English

822. TURKIYE.   Turkey.   1970— .
7676 New Hampshire Avenue, Suite 120, Langley Park, Maryland 20783
Editor: Akif Leblebicioglu   Language: Turkish and English
Sponsor: Turkiye Magazine and Publishing Corporation
Circulation: 4,697   Frequency: Quarterly   Subscription: $15.00

This quarterly includes a broad range of general news articles on
Turkey and Turkish activities in the United States.

UKRAINIAN PRESS

Ukrainian Publications in Ukrainian and Ukrainian-English

823. AMERYKA.   America.   1912— .
817 North Franklin Street, Philadelphia, Pennsylvania 19123
   Editor: Lew Shankowsky   Language: Ukrainian and English
   Sponsor: The Providence Association of Ukrainian Catholics in America
   Circulation: 6,500   Frequency: Daily   Subscription: $15.00

This is the only Ukrainian Catholic daily. It publishes news on international, national, and local events of special interest to Ukrainians. Emphasis is placed on developments within the Ukrainian Catholic Church. Cultural, educational, political, and other activities and events by Ukrainian organizations and individuals within Ukrainian communities in the United States, Canada, and Europe are also covered. Includes editorials, commentaries, letters to the editor, and by-lined articles on a variety of topics. There is a special English language edition.

824. BIBLOS.   1954— .
238 East Sixth Street, New York, New York 10003
   Editor: Nicholas Sydor-Czartorysky   Language: Ukrainian
   Circulation: 1,000   Frequency: Quarterly.   Subscription: $4.00

This bibliographical trade magazine includes news items on Ukrainian publications outside the Ukraine, bibliographical listings, and brief book reviews.

825. BIULETEN'.   Bulletin.   1962— .
P.O. Box 3295 Country Fair Station, Champaign, Illinois 61820
   Editor: Dmytro Shtohryn   Language: Ukrainian
   Sponsor: Ukrainian Librarians' Association of America
   Circulation: 300   Frequency: Irregular
   Subscription: Free to members

This is the official organ of the Ukrainian Librarians' Association of America. Includes news on activities of the Association, bibliographical notes, and brief articles.

BIULETEN' TOVARYSTVA ABSOL'VENTIV UHA-UTHI.   Bulletin
for the Alumni of the Technological Academy—Ukrainian Technical
University.

See TOVARYSTVO ABSOL'VENTIV UHA-UTHI. BIULETEN'.

BIULETEN' TOVARYSTVA UKRAINSKYCH INZHINERIV AMERYKY.
Bulletin of Ukrainian Engineers Society of America.

See TOVARYSTVO UKRAINSKYCH INZHINERIV AMERYKY.
BIULETEN'.

BIULETEN'. UKRAINSKE HENEALOHICHNE I HERALDYCHNE
TOVARYSTVO. Bulletin of the Ukrainian Genealogical and Heraldic Society

See UKRAINSKE HENEALOHICHNE I HERALDYCHNE
TOVARYSTVO. BIULETEN'.

BIULETEN'. UKRAINSKE ISTORYCHNE TOVARYSTVO.   Bulletin of
the Ukrainian Historical Association.

See UKRAINSKE ISTORYCHNE TOVARYSTVO. BIULETEN'.

826. CERKOVNYJ VISNYK.   Church Herald.   1968— .
2247 West Chicago Avenue, Chicago, Illinois 60622
    Editor: Vasyl Markus   Language: Ukrainian
    Sponsor: Sts. Volodymyr and Olha Ukrainian Catholic Parish
    Circulation: 2,500   Frequency: Bi-monthly   Subscription: $5.00

Religious periodical with the stress on the problems of the Ukrainian
Catholic Church and its autonomous status. Contains current general
local and religious news relevant to the Ukrainian Catholic community.
Emphasizes topics of national and ethnic education and cultural preservation.

827. EKRAN. ILLUSTROVANYI, DVO-MISIACHNYK UKRAINSKOHO
    ZYTTIA. Screen, Illustrated Bimonthly of Ukrainian life. 1960— .
2102 West Chicago Avenue, Chicago, Illinois 60622
    Editor: A. Antonovych   Language: Ukrainian
    Sponsor: Ukrainian School Societies of Chicago
    Circulation: 3,000   Frequency: Irregular   Subscription: $4.00

This is an illustrated Ukrainian magazine for youth and adults. Illustrations represent historical, religious, cultural, and political events in
the Ukrainian community in the United States and other countries.

828. FENIKS—ZHURNAL MOLODYKH.   Phoenix—Journal of Social and
Political Thought.   1951— .
P.O. Box 141, Riverton, New Jersey 08077
Editor: Nicholas G. Bohatiuk   Language: Ukrainian and English
Sponsor: The Michnowsky Ukrainian Students Association
Circulation: 1,000   Frequency: Irregular   Subscription: $2.00

Includes articles on several aspects of Ukrainian culture, history,
politics, humanities, and social thought. Also contains occasional book
reviews and news about the activities of the Michnowsky Ukrainian
Students Association.

829. HOLOS LEMKIVSHCHYNY.   The Lemko Voice.   1963— .
417 Nepperhan Avenue, Yonkers, New York 10703
Editor: Stephan Zenecky   Language: Ukrainian
Sponsor: The Karpaty Publishers
Circulation: 4,000   Frequency: Monthly   Subscription: $3.00

This independent Ukrainian monthly is dedicated to Lemko's affairs
in the Ukraine, Poland, America, and other parts of the world. General
and local news coverage is also provided.

830. HOTUJS'.   Be Ready.   1958— .
1,58 East Seventy Street, Apt. 3A, New York, New York 10009
Editor: Lesja Chraplyva   Language: Ukrainian
Sponsor: Plast, Inc.
Circulation: 1,000   Frequency: Monthly   Subscription: $3.00

Magazine for Ukrainian children who are members of the Plast youth
organization.

831. HROMADSKYJ HOLOS.   Voice of the Commonwealth.   1941— .
Box 218, Cooper Station, New York, New York 10003
Editor: Vladimir Levitsky   Language: Ukrainian
Sponsor: Ukrainian Publishing Association
Circulation: 1,600   Frequency: Bi-monthly   Subscription: $2.50

This communist-oriented publication features articles on Ukrainian
political and social events.

832. HUTSULIYA.   1967— .
2453 West Chicago Avenue, Chicago, Illinois 60622
    Editor: N. Domashevsky   Language: Ukrainian
    Sponsor: Hutsul Association, Inc.
    Circulation: 1,150   Frequency: Quarterly   Subscription: $5.00

Dedicated to the study of the Ukrainian ethnic Hutsul group, their land,
history, art, and culture. Includes news on the activities of the Hutsul
Association in the United States and Hutsul life in the Ukraine.

833. KRYLATI.   The Winged Ones.   1963— .
315 East Tenth Street, New York, New York 10009
    Editor: Editorial Committee   Language: Ukrainian
    Sponsor: Central Committee of Ukrainian American Youth Association
    Circulation: 6,000   Frequency: Monthly   Subscription: $5.00

This youth magazine features articles on Ukrainian history and culture,
and on current events in the Ukrainian community and the Ukrainian
American Youth Association.

834. KRYZA.   Crisis.   1971— .
140-142 Second Avenue, New York, New York 10003
    Editors: Roman Kupchynsky, Iu. Karpynsky, Roman Petyk
    Language: Ukrainian and English
    Circulation: Unknown   Frequency: Monthly   Subscription: $3.00

Features articles concerning the crisis in the Ukrainian Catholic Church,
including critical articles on the Ukrainian Catholic hierarchy in the
United States. Supports the creation of a Ukrainian Catholic Patriarchate.

835. LEMKIVS'KI VISTI.   Lemko News.   1950— .
P.O. Box 202, Camillus, New York 13031
    Editor: John Hvosda   Language: Ukrainian
    Sponsor: Organization for the Defense of Lemkivshchyna
    Circulation: 2,200   Frequency: Monthly   Subscription: $4.00

This Ukrainian newspaper is "devoted to the affairs of the Ukrainian
ethnographic territory Lemkivshchyna, as well as to the inhabitants
thereof" [editor's statement]. Serves Ukrainian Lemkos in the United
States, Canada, and Europe.

836. LIKARSKYI VISNYK ZHURNAL UKRAINSKOHO LIKARSKOHO
TOVARYSTVA PIVNICHNOI AMERYKY.   Journal of the
Ukrainian Medical Association of North America, Inc.   1954—.
Two East 79th Street, New York, New York 10021
Editor: Paul J. Dzul, M.D.   Language: Ukrainian
Sponsor: Ukrainian Medical Association of North America, Inc.
Circulation: 1,200   Frequency: Quarterly   Subscription: $12.00

Publishes scientific medical papers in Ukrainian. Includes Ukrainian
medical terminology.

837. LITOPYS BOYKIVSHCHYNY.   Journal Boykivshchyna.   1969—.
2222 Brandywine Street, Philadelphia, Pennsylvania 19130
Editor: Alexander Bereznyckyj   Language: Ukrainian
Sponsor: Association "Boykivshchyna"
Circulation: 575   Frequency: Quarterly   Subscription: $4.00

Dedicated to the study of the Ukrainian Boikian ethnic group and the
Boikian land (Boykivshchyna). Features historical, ethnological articles,
and other relevant materials.

838. LYS MYKYTA.   The Fox.   1951—.
4933 Larkins, Detroit, Michigan 48210
Editor: Edward Kozak   Language: Ukrainian
Sponsor: "The Fox," Ukrainian Publishing Company
Circulation: 2,800   Frequency: Monthly   Subscription: $4.50

Satirical periodical with numerous illustrations and short stories.

839. MISIIA UKRAINY.   Mission of Ukraine.   1957—.
P.O. Box 38, Greenpoint Station, Brooklyn, New York 11222
Editor: Valentyn Koval   Language: Ukrainian
Sponsor: Association for the Liberation of Ukraine
Circulation: 2,500   Frequency: Irregular   Subscription: $2.00

Features articles on political, cultural, and social topics related to
Ukraine and to the activities of the Association.

840. MISIONAR.   The Missionary.   1917—.
1825 West Lindley Avenue, Philadelphia, Pennsylvania 19141
Editor: Sister M. Modesta, O.S.B.M.   Language: Ukrainian
Sponsor: Sisters of St. Basil the Great
Circulation: 1,600   Frequency: Monthly   Subscription: $2.00

841. MYRIANYN.   The Layman.   1968— .
1219 North Avers Avenue, Chicago, Illinois 60651
    Editor: Jurij Teodorovych   Language: Ukrainian
    Circulation: 1,000   Frequency: Monthly   Subscription: $6.00

842. NARODNA VOLYA.   The People's Will.   1911— .
524 Olive Street, Scranton, Pennsylvania 18509
    Editor: Wasyl M. Werhan   Language: Ukrainian and English
    Sponsor: Ukrainian Workingmen's Organization
    Circulation: 5,000   Frequency: Weekly   Subscription: $4.00

This fraternal weekly features articles on Ukrainian affairs in the past
and present (history, politics, literature, social issues). Includes information on Ukrainian life in the United States and other parts of the world,
as well as on the activities of the Ukrainian Workingmen's Association.
Each issue has an English supplement.

843. NASH SVIT.   Our World.   1958— .
98 Second Avenue, New York, New York 10003
    Editor: Michael Ostrowercha   Language: Ukrainian
    Sponsor: "Selfreliance," Association of American Ukrainians
    Circulation: 3,425   Frequency: Bi-monthly   Subscription: $7.00

Journal of "Selfreliance," a cooperative fraternity. Features articles on
Ukrainian economic life in the United States.

844. NASHA BATKIVSHCHYNA.   Our Fatherland.   1962— .
133 East Fourth Street, New York, New York 10003
    Editor: Sydir Krawec   Language: Ukrainian
    Sponsor: Batkivshchyna (Fatherland), Inc.
    Circulation: 1,700   Frequency: Semi-monthly   Subscription: $7.00

General, national, and local news of interest to the Ukrainian community
of the Orthodox faith. Features articles on Ukrainian history, political
life, culture, and religious life.

845. NASHE ZHYTTIA.   Our Life.   1944— .
4936 North 13th Street, Philadelphia, Pennsylvania 19141
    Editor: Mrs. Lydia Burachynska   Language: Ukrainian and English
    Sponsor: Ukrainian National Women's League of America, Inc.
    Circulation: 4,600   Frequency: Monthly   Subscription: $6.00

Features organizational articles, as well as articles on Ukrainian literature, folk art, and other topics. Each issue includes a separate children's
section and a "practical section" (articles on hygiene, recipes, etc.).
One section in the magazine is in English.

846. NAZARETH.   1971— .
2208 West Chicago Avenue, Chicago, Illinois 60622
    Editor: Editorial Board   Language: Ukrainian
    Sponsor: Ecumenical Center of St. Atanazii Velykyi
    Circulation: Unknown   Frequency: Monthly   Subscription: $1.00/copy

Ukrainian Catholic missionary magazine.

847. NOTATKY Z MYSTECTVA.   Ukrainian Art Digest.   1963— .
1022 North Lawrence Street, Philadelphia, Pennsylvania 19123
    Editor: Petro Mehyk   Language: Ukrainian
    Sponsor: Ukrainian Artists' Association in USA—Philadelphia Branch
    Circulation: 1,000   Frequency: Irregular   Subscription: $3.00/copy

The purpose of this publication is to acquaint the reader with many
aspects of art. "The emphasis is on Ukrainian art and its artists. Activities and works of students of the Ukrainian Art Studio are also included"
[editor's statement]. Color and black and white plates of paintings.

848. NOTATNYK.   Diary.   1961— .
Box 2325, Grand Central Station, New York, New York 10017
    Editor: L. Lyman   Language: Ukrainian
    Sponsor: Notatnyk
    Circulation: Unknown   Frequency: Monthly   Subscription: $2.00

Features brief articles on Ukrainian affairs in the Ukraine and in other
countries.

849. NOVA ZORYA.   New Star.   1965— .
2203 West Chicago Avenue, Chicago, Illinois 60622
    Editor: Rev. Jaroslav Swyschuk   Language: Ukrainian and English
    Sponsor: St. Nicholas Diocese Press
    Circulation: 6,000   Frequency: Weekly   Subscription: $6.00

This Ukrainian Catholic weekly includes articles on Catholic and other
churches, education, religion, and Ukrainian culture.

850. NOVI NAPRIAMY.   New Directions.   1969— .
140-142 Second Avenue, New York, New York 10003
    Editor: Christine Lukomsky   Language: Ukrainian and English
    Sponsor: New York City Ukrainian Student Hromada, Inc.
    Circulation: 2,000   Frequency: Bi-monthly   Subscription: $2.00

A student magazine which "attempts to provide a free forum for the
discussion of contemporary problems facing the Ukrainian community"
[editor's statement].

851. OVYD.   Horizon.   1949— .
2226 West Chicago Avenue, Chicago, Illinois
    Editor: Mykola Denysiuk   Language: Ukrainian
    Sponsor: Mykola Denysiuk Publishing Company
    Circulation: 1,200   Frequency: Quarterly   Subscription: $4.00

Contains literary works (poetry and short stories), articles on Ukrainian
literature and culture, art, politics, and social issues. It is moderately
illustrated.

852. OZNAKY NASHOHO CHASU.   Sings of Our Time.   1930— .
1350 Villa Street, Mountain View, California 94040
    Editor: Nicholas Ilchuk   Language: Ukrainian
    Sponsor: Pacific Press Publishing Association
    Circulation: 3,500   Frequency: Monthly   Subscription: $4.00

This religious magazine is dedicated to the interpretation of the Bible.

853. PISLANETS' PRAVDY.   Messenger of Truth.   1927— .
247 East Roland Road, Parkside, Chester, Pennsylvania 19015
    Editor: Dr. Leon Zabko-Potapovich   Language: Ukrainian
    Sponsor: Ukrainian Baptist Convention in the U.S.A.
    Circulation: 1,000   Frequency: Bi-monthly   Subscription: $3.00

This is the official organ of the Ukrainian Baptist Churches outside the
Ukraine. It includes articles on religion, education, and other topics
relevant to Ukrainian Baptists.

854. PRAVNYCHYI VISNYK.   Law Journal.   1955— .
536 East 14th Street, New York, New York 10003
    Editor: Editorial Board   Language: Ukrainian
    Sponsor: The Ukrainian Lawyers' Organization in the U.S.
    Circulation: 500   Frequency: Irregular   Subscription: Unknown

Contains scholarly articles on Ukrainian law and history, book reviews, and bibliographies. Resumes in English.

855. PRAVOSLAVNYI UKRAINETS'.   Orthodox Ukrainian.   1952– .
2710 West Iowa Street, Chicago, Illinois 60622
    Editor: Alexander Bykowetz   Language: Ukrainian
    Sponsor: Ukrainian Autocephalous Church in the U.S.A.
    Circulation: 700   Frequency: Quarterly   Subscription: Unknown

Official organ of the Ukrainian Autocephalous Church in the U.S.A.

856. SAMOSTIJNA UKRAINA.   Independent Ukraine.   1948– .
2315 West Chicago Avenue, Chicago, Illinois 60622
    Editor: Michael Panasiuk   Language: Ukrainian
    Sponsor: Organization for the Rebirth of the Ukraine
    Circulation: 1,500   Frequency: Monthly   Subscription: $6.00

This monthly is devoted to Ukrainian affairs in the Ukraine and abroad. It includes articles on Ukrainian history, political life, culture, and social issues, as well as information on the activities of the Organization for the Rebirth of the Ukraine and its members. Supports the ideology and activities of the Ukrainian Nationalist Organization (OUN).

857. SHLAKH.   The Way.   1940– .
805 North Franklin Street, Philadelphia, Pennsylvania 19123
    Editor: Dr. Lew Mydlowskyj   Language: Ukrainian and English
    Sponsor: Apostolate, Inc.
    Circulation: 12,356   Frequency: Weekly   Subscription: $5.00

The main objective of this Ukrainian Catholic weekly is to "support the religious and national education of Ukrainians in the U.S.A." [editor's statement].

858. SONIASHNYK.   Helianthus.   1970– .
Box 145 Student Center, Wayne State University, Detroit, Michigan
    Editor: Michael Berezowsky   Language: Ukrainian and English
    Sponsor: Ukrainian Student Organization of Nicholas Michnowsky–
                Detroit Branch
    Circulation: 450   Frequency: Quarterly   Subscription: $2.00

A student magazine which includes articles dealing with the Ukrainian community in the United States and its political and cultural aspects.

859. SVOBODA. UKRAINSKYI SHCHODENNYK.   Liberty. Ukrainian
Daily.   1893— .
81-83 Grand Street, Jersey City, New Jersey 07303
Editor: Anthony Dragan   Language: Ukrainian
Sponsor: Ukrainian National Association, Inc.
Circulation: 20,500   Frequency: Daily   Subscription: $18.00

This is the oldest Ukrainian daily in the United States. It provides international, national, and local news coverage, and features articles on
Ukrainian political, cultural, religious, and social life in America and in
the world. It "considers the Ukrainian people's current status as that of
a subjugated and oppressed nation, upholds Ukraine's rights and
aspirations for freedom and independence" [editor's statement]. The
paper maintains a non-partisan political view.

860. SUMIVETZ.   1953— .
315 East Tenth Street, New York, New York 10009
Editor: D. Motruk   Language: Ukrainian
Sponsor: Ukrainian American Youth Association
Circulation: Unknown   Frequency: Irregular   Subscription: Unknown

A Ukrainian youth magazine.

861. TEREM. PROBLEMY UKRAINSKOI KULTURY, NEPERIODYCHNYI
ILIUSTROVANYI ZHURNAL.   Terem. Problems of Ukrainian
Culture.   1962— .
13588 Sunset Street, Detroit, Michigan 48212
Editor: Yurij Tys-Krochmaluk   Language: Ukrainian
Sponsor: Institute of Ukrainian Culture
Circulation: 1,400   Frequency: Irregular   Subscription: $3.50/copy

This is the official publication of the Institute of Ukrainian Culture.
Its purpose is "to gather information on the status and growth of
Ukrainian culture in countries of the free world" [editor's statement].
Each issue is dedicated to an individual who has contributed to "the
constantly expanding sphere of Ukrainian culture in the Western Hemi-
sphere." Covers literature, art, and social sciences.

862. TOVARYSTVO ABSOL'VENTIV UHA-UTHI. BIULETEN'.   Bulletin
for the Alumni of the Ukrainian Technological Academy—Ukrainian
Technical University (Ukrainska Hospodarska Akademia and Ukrainskyi
Technichno Hospodarskyi Instytut).   1956— .
136-19 Cherry Avenue, Flushing, New York 11355

Editor: Alex Kozlowsky   Language: Ukrainian
Sponsor: Association of the Alumni of the Ukrainian Technological
Academy—Ukrainian Technical University
Circulation: 400   Frequency: Irregular   Subscription: $2.00

An alumni publication.

863. TOVARYSTVO UKRAINSKYCH INZHINERIV AMERYKY. BIULETEN'.
Bulletin of the Ukrainian Engineers Society of America.
Two East 79th Street, New York, New York 10021
Editor: Eugene Ivashkiv   Language: Ukrainian
Sponsor: Ukrainian Engineers Society of America
Circulation: 500   Frequency: Irregular   Subscription: $2.00

Features technological articles, news of the activities of UES members,
and organization news.

864. TRYZUB.   Trident.   1960— .
526 East 12th Street, New York, New York 10009
Editor: Editorial Board   Language: Ukrainian
Sponsor: Ukrainsko Nacionalno-Derzhavnyi Soiuz
Circulation: 750   Frequency: Bi-monthly   Subscription: $3.00

This political magazine of democratic orientation includes articles on
Ukrainian history and political life.

865. TSERKVA I ZHYTTIA.   Church and Life.   1957— .
1239 North Artesian Avenue, Chicago, Illinois 60622
Editor: A. I. Jaremenko   Language: Ukrainian
Sponsor: Ukrainian Orthodox Brotherhood of Metropolitan Vasil
Lypkivsky
Circulation: 1,000   Frequency: Bi-monthly   Subscription: $2.00

Orthodox religious magazine supporting the Ukrainian Orthodox Autocephalous Church. Includes articles on church history, biographies of
prominent orthodox leaders, and other relevant religious materials.

866. UKRAINSKA KNYHA.   The Ukrainian Book.   1971— .
4800 North 12th Street, Philadelphia, Pennsylvania 19141
Editor: Editorial Board   Language: Ukrainian
Sponsor: Shevchenko Scientific Society; Ukrainian Library Association
Circulation: 1,000   Frequency: Quarterly   Subscription: $3.00

This Ukrainian bibliographical quarterly features articles on historical bibliography, reviews, and retrospective bibliographies dealing with special topics (literature, history, and others).

867. UKRAINSKE HENEALOHICHNE I HERALDYCHNE TOVARYSTVO. BIULETEN'.   Ukrainian Genealogical and Heraldic Society. Bulletin.   1963— .
573 N.E. 102nd Street, Miami Shores, Florida 33138
    Editor: Dr. Roman O. Klimkevich   Language: Ukrainian
    Sponsor: Ukrainian Genealogical and Heraldic Society
    Circulation: 200   Frequency: Quarterly   Subscription: Membership

Official publication of the Society. Contains news items on the activities of the Society and its members.

868. UKRAINSKE ISTORYCHNE TOVARYSTVO. BIULETEN'.   Ukrainian Historical Association Bulletin.   1967— .
573 N.E. 102nd Street, Miami Shores, Florida 33138
    Editor: Dr. Roman O. Klimkevich   Language: Ukrainian
    Sponsor: Ukrainian Historical Association
    Circulation: 250   Frequency: Quarterly   Subscription: Membership

Official publication of the Ukrainian Historical Association. Includes materials on the activities of the Association and its members, as well as some articles on the present status of Ukrainian scholarship in the United States and in other countries.

869. UKRAINSKE KOZATSTVO.   Ukrainian Cossackdom.   1968— .
2100 West Chicago Avenue, Chicago, Illinois 60622
    Editor: Antin Kushchynskyj   Language: Ukrainian
    Sponsor: Veteran's Brotherhood, "Ukrainian Free Cossacks"
    Circulation: 800   Frequency: Quarterly   Subscription: $4.00

Magazine of Ukrainian veterans dedicated to the dissemination of the ideas of Ukrainian Cossacks. Contains articles on military Ukrainian history, Cossack traditions, and the activities of the "Ukrainian Free Cossacks Brotherhood."

870. UKRAINSKE NARODNE SLOVO.   Ukrainian National Word.   1915— .
P.O. Box 1948, Pittsburgh, Pennsylvania 15230
    Editor: Paul Marynec   Language: Ukrainian and English
    Sponsor: Ukrainian National Aid Association of America
    Circulation: 4,250   Frequency: Bi-weekly   Subscription: $2.50

A fraternal organ which includes information on activities of various Ukrainian organizations in the United States. One section is published in English.

871. UKRAINSKE PRAVOSLAVNE SLOVO. Ukrainian Orthodox Word. 1950– .
P.O. Box 595, South Bound Brook, New Jersey 08880
    Editor: Rev. M. Zemlachenko   Language: Ukrainian
    Sponsor: Ukrainian Orthodox Church of the U.S.A.
    Circulation: 2,000   Frequency: Monthly   Subscription: $5.00

This is the official organ of the Ukrainian Orthodox Church in the United States. It features articles on the Orthodox Church and religious education. There is a separate news section on the Ukrainian Orthodox Church and its activities.

872. UKRAINSKE ZHYTTIA.   Ukrainian Life.   1955– .
2532 West Chicago Avenue, Chicago, Illinois
    Editor: Dr. Toma Lapychak   Language: Ukrainian
    Sponsor: Ukrainian Life Cooperative Association
    Circulation: 1,600   Frequency: Weekly   Subscription: $5.00

This independent weekly publishes articles on political, cultural, and social events in the Ukraine and in other parts of the world. Promotes "democratic ideas and philosophy" [editor's statement].

873. UKRAINSKI VISTI.   Ukrainian News.   1920– .
85 East Fourth Street, New York, New York 10003
    Editor: Leon Tolopko   Language: Ukrainian
    Sponsor: Ukrainian Daily News, Inc.
    Circulation: 1,670   Frequency: Weekly   Subscription: $5.00

General and local news. Communist orientation.

874. UKRAINSKYI HOSPODARNYK.   The Ukrainian Economist.   1954– .
47 Ellery Avenue, Irvington, New Jersey 07111
    Editor: Mykola Yelychkivsky   Language: Ukrainian and English
    Circulation: 500   Frequency: Irregular   Subscription: $2.00

Journal of Ukrainian economists in the United States. Features articles on the economic development of the Ukrainian SSR, history of the Ukrainian economy, etc.

875. UKRAINSKYI FILATELIST.   The Ukrainian Philatelist.   1951— .
80-73 87th Avenue, Woodhaven, Jamaica, New York 11421
    Editor: Leo M. Popovich   Language: Ukrainian
    Sponsor: Society of Ukrainian Philatelists, Inc.
    Circulation: 500   Frequency: Irregular   Subscription: $1.00

Includes articles on Ukrainian stamps, descriptions of individual stamp
collections, medals, and other related topics. The objective is "to bring
together Ukrainian philatelists all over the world and to keep the level
of interest in this field growing" [editor's statement].

876. UKRAINSKYI ISTORYK.   Ukrainian Historian.   1963— .
P.O. Box 312, Kent, Ohio 44240
    Editor: Lubomyr R. Wynar   Language: Ukrainian and English
    Sponsor: Ukrainian Historical Association
    Circulation: 1,000   Frequency: Quarterly   Subscription: $10.00

Official journal of the Ukrainian Historical Association. It is devoted to
the study of East European and Ukrainian history, and emphasis is
placed on political, social, and cultural history. A special section includes
articles on auxiliary historical sciences, and archival materials. Reviews
and bibliographical notes are included in each issue. The major scholarly
journal of Ukrainian history outside the Soviet Ukraine.

877. UKRAINSKYI PRAVOSLAVNYI VISNYK.   Ukrainian Orthodox
    Herald.   1933— .
90-34 139th Street, Jamaica, New York 11435
    Editor: Very Rev. Ivan Tkaczuk   Language: Ukrainian and English
    Sponsor: Ukrainian Orthodox Church of U.S.A. and Canada
    Circulation: 1,000   Frequency: Quarterly   Subscription: $2.00

Official organ of the Ukrainian Orthodox Church in America in the
jurisdiction of the Ecumenical Patriarch. Includes articles on theological
and educational matters.

878. UKRAINSKYI ZHURNALIST. BIULETEN SPILKY UKRAINSKYCH
    ZHURNALISTIV AMERYKY.   The Ukrainian Journalist. 1967— .
14 Peck Avenue, Newark, New Jersey 07107
    Editors: Dr. Roman Kryshtalskyj, Dr. Jaroslaw Shawiak, M. Dolnyckyj
    Language: Ukrainian
    Sponsor: Ukrainian Journalist's Association of America
    Circulation: 135   Frequency: Irregular   Subscription: Unknown

Articles on journalism and events of interest to Association members.

879. VESELKA.   The Rainbow.   1954— .
81-83 Grand Street, Jersey City, New Jersey 07303
Editor: Wolodymyr Barahura   Language: Ukrainian
Sponsor: Ukrainian National Association
Circulation: 3,000   Frequency: Monthly   Subscription: $4.00

This illustrated children's monthly magazine includes materials for
pre-school and school age children (e.g., stories, fairy tales, puzzles,
etc.). "The content of the magazine is designed to cultivate and preserve the Ukrainian spiritual heritage" [editor's statement].

880. VILNA UKRAINA.   Free Ukraine.   1953— .
P.O. Box 4, Peter Stuyvesant Station, New York, New York 10009
Editor: Editorial Board   Language: Ukrainian
Sponsor: Ukrainian Free Society of America
Circulation: 700   Frequency: Quarterly   Subscription: $5.00

This quarterly political magazine features articles on Ukrainian history,
politics and social issues. Also has a book review section. Supports
Ukrainian socialist ideology.

881. VISNYK.   The Herald.   1947— .
P.O. Box 304 Cooper Station, New York, New York 10003
Editor: Unknown   Language: Ukrainian
Sponsor: Organization for Defense of Four Freedoms for Ukraine, Inc.
Circulation: 2,000   Frequency: Monthly   Subscription: $6.00

A political monthly which contains articles on Ukrainian political life,
history, culture, and social issues. Supports the ideology of the Ukrainian Nationalist Organization.

882. VISTI UKRAINSKYKH INZHINERIV.   Ukrainian Engineering
News.   1949— .
Two East 79th Street, New York, New York 10021
Editor: S. G. Prociuk   Language: Ukrainian
Sponsor: Ukrainian Engineers' Society of America
Circulation: 1,000   Frequency: Quarterly   Subscription: $5.00

Includes original research papers in the field of technical sciences and
articles on technological and economic developments in the Ukraine.
A book review section and current news on modern technology are
included.

883. VISTI UVAN.   News of Academy.   1970— .
206 West 100th Street, New York, New York 10025
Editor: Alexander Dombrovsky   Language: Ukrainian
Sponsor: The Ukrainian Academy of Arts and Sciences in the U.S.
Circulation: 1,000   Frequency: Irregular
Subscription: Free to members

Features articles on the activity of the Ukrainian Academy, biographical articles, bibliographies, and other news items.

884. YEVANHELSKY RANOK.   Evangelical Morning.   1905— .
22146 Kelly Road East, Detroit, Michigan 48021
Editor: Rev. Wladimir Borowsky   Language: Ukrainian
Sponsor: Ukrainian Evangelical Alliance of North America
Circulation: 800   Frequency: Bi-monthly   Subscription: $3.00

Official organ of the Ukrainian Evangelical Alliance. Articles on religious and educational topics.

885. ZA PATRIARCHAT.   For the Patriarchate.   1967— .
P.O. Box 11012, Philadelphia, Pennsylvania 19141
Editor: Stephan Procyh   Language: Ukrainian
Sponsor: Society for Promotion of the Patriarchal System in the
          Ukrainian Catholic Church
Circulation: 1,000   Frequency: Quarterly   Subscription: $2.00

Features historical and current materials on the status of the Ukrainian Catholic Church. Supports the establishment of Ukrainian Catholic Patriarchate.

886. ZA PRAVDU PRO UKRAINU. BIULETEN' UKRAINSKOHO
PUBLITSYSTYCHNO-NAUKOVOHO INSTYTUTU. For the
Truth About Ukraine. Bulletin of Ukrainian Research and Infor-
mation Institute.   1963— .
2534 West Chicago Avenue, Chicago, Illinois 60622
Editor: Dr. Toma Lapychak   Language: Ukrainian and English
Sponsor: Ukrainian Research and Information Institute
Circulation: 1,000   Frequency: Irregular   Subscription: Membership

The main objective of this publication is to correct major historical and political misconceptions regarding the Ukraine and Ukrainians as presented in English publications. Contains reprints of various authors and publishers concerning distortions of Ukrainian history.

887. ZAPYSKY. UKRAINSKE HENEALOHICHNE I HERALDYCHNE
TOVARYSTVO. Memoirs. Ukrainian Genealogical and Heraldic
Society. 1969— .
573 N.E. 102nd Street, Miami Shores, Florida 33138
Editor: Dr. Roman O. Klimkevich Language: Ukrainian
Sponsor: Ukrainian Genealogical and Heraldic Society
Circulation: 500 Frequency: Bi-monthly Subscription: $.50/copy

Covers Ukrainian genealogy, heraldry, sphragistics, and related subjects.
A special feature is the current bibliography of Ukrainian auxiliary
historical sciences.

888. ZHYTTIA I SHKOLA. Life and School. 1954— .
418 West Nittany Avenue, State College, Pennsylvania 16801
Editor: Dr. Wasyl Luciw Language: Ukrainian
Circulation: 1,000 Frequency: Bi-monthly Subscription: $4.00

This publication consists mainly of reprinted older articles from various
Ukrainian periodicals on Ukrainian culture, history, bibliography and
other subjects. It also carries original articles on the same subjects.

Ukrainian Publications in English

889. AMERYKA. America. 1912— .
817 North Franklin Street, Philadelphia, Pennsylvania 19123
Editor: Lew Shankovsky Language: English
Sponsor: Providence Association of Ukrainian Catholics
Circulation: 6,500 Frequency: Weekly Subscription: $4.00

Weekly English supplement of Ukrainian daily, *Ameryka.* See number 823.

890. ANNALS OF THE UKRAINIAN ACADEMY OF ARTS AND SCIENCES.
1951— .
206 West 100th Street, New York, New York 10025
Editor: Editorial Committee Language: English
Sponsor: Ukrainian Academy of Arts and Sciences in the U.S.
Circulation: 1,000 Frequency: Irregular
Subscription: Usually $8.00

A scholarly publication featuring articles on Ukrainian history, culture,
literature, and other subjects in the humanities, social sciences, and
sciences. Includes reviews, an obituary section, and a chronicle of
UVAN activities.

891. DIGEST OF THE SOVIET UKRAINIAN PRESS.   1956— .
875 West End Avenue, New York, New York 10025
    Editor: Myroslow Prokop   Language: English
    Sponsor: Prolog Research and Publishing Association, Inc.
    Circulation: Unknown   Frequency: Monthly   Subscription: $15.00

Features translated articles from the Ukrainian Soviet press. Annual index.

892. FORUM: A UKRAINIAN REVIEW.   1967— .
440 Wyoming Avenue, Scranton, Pennsylvania
    Editor: Andrew Gregorovich   Language: English
    Sponsor: Ukrainian Workingmen's Association
    Circulation: 1,450   Frequency: Quarterly   Subscription: $1.80

Publishes primarily articles on Ukraine and Ukrainians in Europe and
North America for young adult and university student readers. Covers
art, history, literature, biographies of outstanding people, sports, and
book reviews. Articles are written in a popular style.

893. RECENZIJA.   A Review of Soviet Ukrainian Scholarly Publications.
    1970— .
1737 Cambridge Street, Room 208, Cambridge, Massachusetts 02138
    Editors: Orest Subtelny and Lubomyr Hajda
    Language: English
    Circulation: 1,500   Frequency: Semi-annually   Subscription: $5.00

This publication, initiated by Ukrainian students at Harvard University,
features critical reviews of Ukrainian scholarly materials published in the
Soviet Ukraine.

894. THE UKRAINIAN QUARTERLY.   1944— .
302 West 13th Street, New York, New York 10014
    Editor: Dr. Walter Dushnyck   Language: English
    Sponsor: Ukrainian Congress Committee of America, Inc.
    Circulation: 5,000   Frequency: Quarterly   Subscription: $7.00

A journal of East European and Asian affairs. "Although in its editorial
treatment of Eastern Europe *The Ukrainian Quarterly* places special
emphasis on Ukraine, its overall editorial perspective embraces the other
captive nations in the USSR" [editor's statement]. Features articles on
history, politics, ethnography, sociology, literature, art, and culture.
A special feature is the chronicle of current events (Ukrainian life in
the United States and other countries).

895. THE UKRAINIAN WEEKLY. 1933– .
    81-83 Grand Street, Jersey City, New Jersey 07303
        Editor: Zenon Snylyk   Language: English
        Sponsor: Ukrainian National Association
        Circulation: 20,500 Frequency: Weekly   Subscription: $4.50

This is the English language supplement of the *Svoboda* daily. "The weekly is designed primarily as a vehicle of information and an opinion forum for the American-born generation of Ukrainians" [editor's statement]. Informative articles on Ukrainian affairs, creative literary pieces, social topics, sports news, and other relevant material.

WELSH PRESS

Welsh Publications in Welsh

896. DRYCH. 1850– .
    P.O. Box 313, Milwaukee, Wisconsin 53201
        Editor: Horace Breese Powell   Language: Welsh
        Sponsor: Drych Publishing Company
        Circulation: Unknown Frequency: Monthly   Subscription: $3.00

Items of general interest to the Welsh. Promotes the usage of the Welsh language.

YIDDISH PRESS

see JEWISH PRESS

YUGOSLAV PRESS

see CROATIAN, SERBIAN, and SLOVENIAN PRESS

ADDITIONS TO ITALIAN PRESS

Italian Publications in Italian and Italian-English

897. LA NOTIZIA. The News. 1916– .
    30-34 Battery St., G.P.O. Box 1870, Boston, Massachusetts
        Editor: G. N. Longarini   Language: Italian
        Circulation: 24,600 Frequency: Weekly   Subscription: $5.00

Provides coverage of national, international, and local news, plus information about public and private institutions. Serves as an aid for the Italian-speaking population in "adjusting to the new environment" (editor's statement).

898. LA NUOVA CAPITALE.   The New Capital.   1929— .
681 South Broad Street, Trenton, New Jersey 08611
Editor: Maurice Perilli   Language: Italian
Circulation: 2,595   Frequency: Monthly   Subscription: $2.00

899. LA PAROLA DEL POPOLO.   The Word of the People.   1908— .
627 West Lake Street, Chicago, Illinois 60606
Editor: E. Clemente   Language: Italian and English
Sponsor: La Parola Publishing Company
Circulation: 4,500   Frequency: Bi-monthly   Subscription: $4.00

A pro-labor, Democratic Socialist publication recognized by the
Socialist Labor International. News and commentaries on economic,
social, and political affairs of Italy and the United States.

Italian Publications in English

900. I.A.N.U. BULLETIN.   1926— .
30 West Washington Street, Suite 1007, Chicago, Illinois 60602
Editor: Anthony De Julio   Language: English
Sponsor: Italo-American National Union
Circulation: Unknown   Frequency: Quarterly   Subscription: $.50/yea

901. ITALIAN-AMERICAN REVIEW.   1958— .
111-113 Columbia Heights, Brooklyn, New York, 11201
Editor: John N. LaCorte   Language: English
Sponsor: Italian Historical Society
Circulation: Unknown Frequency: Bi-monthly   Subscription: Unknov

902. ITALIAN QUARTERLY.   1957— .
College of Letters and Sciences, University of California, Riverside, Cal. 925(
Editor: Carlo L. Golina   Language: English
Sponsor: University of California, Riverside
Circulation: 550   Frequency: Quarterly   Subscription: $6.00

Articles on Italy and Italian culture. Topics covered include literature,
economics, art, education, music, politics, and cinema.

903. THE ITALIAN TRIBUNE NEWS.   1931— .
427 Bloomfield, Newark, New Jersey, 07107
Editor: John J. Sileo   Language: English
Sponsor: Ace Alagna Publications
Circulation: 19,488   Frequency: Weekly   Subscription: Unknow

APPENDIX

ETHNIC PUBLICATIONS—STATISTICAL ANALYSIS

The following tables represent statistical analyses of individual ethnic presses arranged in alphabetical order. It should be noted that 97 titles out of 903 do not contain circulation figures. In most of these cases the editors or publishers did not supply this information. Entry for each individual ethnic press includes information on the frequency of publication in relation to language and circulation data. Also listed under each press are the titles for which circulation figures were not available.

ALBANIAN
(Albanian; Albanian and English)

	NATIVE LANGUAGE	
	Number of Publications	Circulation
Quarterly	3	2,600
	BI-LINGUAL	
Weekly	2	2,850
Monthly	1	1,200
(Subtotal)	(3)	(4,050)
TOTAL	6	6,650

Circulation not given for one publication:
    6. ZERI I BALLIT.

ARABIC
(Arabic; Arabic and English; English)

	NATIVE LANGUAGE	
	Number of Publications	Circulation
Semi-weekly	2	5,830
Weekly	4	3,510
(Subtotal)	(6)	(9,340)
	BI-LINGUAL	
Weekly	2	1,600

ARABIC (cont'd)

ENGLISH

	Number of Publications	Circulation
Weekly	5	24,700
Semi-monthly	2	21,900
Monthly	3	32,000
Quarterly	1	7,000
(Subtotal)	(11)	(85,600)
TOTAL	19	96,540

ARMENIAN
(Armenian; Armenian and English; English)

NATIVE LANGUAGE

	Number of Publications	Circulation
Daily	2	5,540
Semi-weekly	1	1,300
Weekly	1	
Monthly	1	
Quarterly	1	500
(Subtotal)	(6)	(7,340)

BI-LINGUAL

Semi-weekly	2	3,472
Weekly	2	2,050
Monthly	6	20,775
Bi-monthly	1	400
Quarterly	4	12,020
Semi-annual	1	2,500
(Subtotal)	(16)	(41,217)

ENGLISH

Weekly	3	8,600
Monthly	2	7,500
Quarterly	2	1,600
Unknown	1	500
(Subtotal)	(8)	(18,200)
TOTAL	30	66,757

Circulation not given for two publications:

45. SHOGHAKAT'

47. YERITASARD HAYASTAN

ASSYRIAN
(Assyrian and English)

BI-LINGUAL

	Number of Publications	Circulation
Bi-monthly	1	1,600
TOTAL	1	1,600

BELGIAN-FLEMISH
(Flemish)

NATIVE LANGUAGE

	Number of Publications	Circulation
Weekly	1	2,855
TOTAL	1	2,855

BULGARIAN
(Bulgarian; Bulgarian and English)

NATIVE LANGUAGE

	Number of Publications	Circulation
Monthly	1	465
Bi-monthly	1	5,000
(Subtotal)	(2)	(5,465)

BI-LINGUAL

Weekly	1	3,860
Semi-monthly	1	818
(Subtotal)	(2)	(4,678)
TOTAL	4	10,143

BYELORUSSIAN
(Byelorussian; Byelorussian and English)

NATIVE LANGUAGE

	Number of Publications	Circulation
Weekly	1	500
Monthly	1	2,100
Bi-monthly	1	400
Quarterly	2	500
Semi-annual	2	1,200
Annual	1	500
Irregular	2	300
(Subtotal)	(10)	(5,500)

BI-LINGUAL

Monthly	1	1,000
Quarterly	1	
Semi-annual	2	3,500
(Subtotal)	(4)	(4,500)

TOTAL	14	10,000

Circulation not given for three publications:

64. BARACBA
67. BYELORUSSIAN YOUTH
70. KAMUNIKATY

CARPATHO-RUTHENIAN
(Carpatho-Ruthenian; Carpatho-Ruthenian and English; Russian and English; English)

NATIVE LANGUAGE

	Number of Publications	Circulation
Weekly	1	18,000
Semi-monthly	1	2,488
Monthly	1	1,000
Bi-monthly	1	1,000
(Subtotal)	(4)	(22,488)

BI-LINGUAL

	Number of Publications	Circulation
Semi-monthly	2	1,915
Monthly	2	9,462
Bi-monthly	1	2,000
(Subtotal)	(5)	(13,377)

ENGLISH

	Number of Publications	Circulation
Weekly	2	33,875
Monthly	2	5,200
(Subtotal)	(4)	(39,075)

TOTAL	13	74,940

Circulation not given for two publications:
77. CERKOVNYJ VISTNIK
88. THE ORTHODOX CHURCH

CHINESE
(Chinese; Chinese and English; English)

NATIVE LANGUAGE

	Number of Publications	Circulation
Daily	6	43,137
Weekly	3	16,300
Semi-monthly	1	9,000
(Subtotal)	(10)	(68,437)

BI-LINGUAL

	Number of Publications	Circulation
Weekly	1	4,985
Monthly	1	
Irregular	1	1,500
(Subtotal)	(3)	(6,485)

ENGLISH

	Number of Publications	Circulation
Daily	5	42,465
Semi-weekly	1	3,100
Weekly	3	17,350
Monthly	2	221
Bi-monthly	1	195
(Subtotal)	(12)	(63,331)

TOTAL	25	138,253

Circulation not given for one publication: 95. GETTING TOGETHER

COSSACK
(Ukrainian, Russian, English)

BI-LINGUAL

	Number of Publications	Circulation
Quarterly	1	690
TOTAL	1	690

CROATIAN
(Croatian; Croatian and English; English)

NATIVE LANGUAGE

	Number of Publications	Circulation
Weekly	3	11,410
Monthly	1	2,000
Bi-monthly	1	2,000
(Subtotal)	(5)	(15,410)

BI-LINGUAL

Weekly	1	40,200
Bi-monthly	1	15,500
Quarterly	1	500
Irregular	1	500
(Subtotal)	(4)	(56,700)

ENGLISH

Annual	1	1,000
TOTAL	10	73,110

CZECH
(Czech; Czech and English; Czech and Slovak; English)

NATIVE LANGUAGE

	Number of Publications	Circulation
Daily	2	20,947
Semi-weekly	1	4,622
Weekly	7	12,699
Semi-monthly	1	12,050
Monthly	6	11,722
Bi-monthly	1	600
Quarterly	3	6,750
(Subtotal)	(21)	(69,390)

BI-LINGUAL

Weekly	3	27,347
Monthly	6	72,454
Bi-monthly	1	
Quarterly	1	
(Subtotal)	(11)	(99,801)

ENGLISH

Monthly	1	

TOTAL	33	169,191

Circulation not given for five publications:

134. HLAS JEDNOTY
148. SOKOL TYRS NEWSLETTER
152. TEXASKY ROLNIK
156. ZPRAVODAJ
158. AMERICAN BULLETIN

DANISH
(Danish; Danish and English; English)

NATIVE LANGUAGE

	Number of Publications	Circulation
Weekly	1	3,500

BI-LINGUAL

Semi-monthly	1	4,700

ENGLISH

Monthly	3	20,500
Bi-monthly	1	
(Subtotal)	(4)	(20,500)
TOTAL	6	28,700

Circulation not given for one publication: 164. PHOEBE

DUTCH
(Dutch; Dutch and English; English)

NATIVE LANGUAGE

	Number of Publications	Circulation
Semi-monthly	1	2,850

BI-LINGUAL

Monthly	1	4,000

ENGLISH

Weekly	2	52,640
Monthly	1	
Quarterly	1	1,500
(Subtotal)	(4)	(54,140)
TOTAL	6	60,990

Circulation not given for one publication:
167. ATLANTIC OBSERVER—KNICKERBOCKER
INTERNATIONAL

ESTONIAN
(Estonian)

NATIVE LANGUAGE

	Number of Publications	Circulation
Weekly	1	4,000
Monthly	1	800
Bi-monthly	1	1,026
(Subtotal)	(3)	(5,826)
TOTAL	3	5,826

FILIPINO
(English)

ENGLISH

	Number of Publications	Circulation
Semi-monthly	1	25,000
Monthly	5	23,750
(Subtotal)	(6)	(48,750)
TOTAL	6	48,750

FINNISH
(Finnish; Finnish and English; English)

NATIVE LANGUAGE

	Number of Publications	Circulation
Semi-weekly	3	10,650
Weekly	1	2,586
Monthly	1	750
Quarterly	1	6,000
3 times/week	1	2,080
(Subtotal)	(7)	(22,066)

BI-LINGUAL

Semi-weekly	1	2,548

FINNISH (cont'd)

ENGLISH

	Number of Publications	Circulation
Irregular	1	400
TOTAL	9	25,014

FRENCH
(French; French and English; English)

NATIVE LANGUAGE

	Number of Publications	Circulation
Weekly	5	47,627
Semi-monthly	1	3,500
Monthly	1	5,000
Quarterly	2	61,600
(Subtotal)	(9)	(117,727)

BI-LINGUAL

Bi-monthly	1	15,100

ENGLISH

Bi-monthly	1	1,500
3 times/year	1	
(Subtotal)	(2)	(1,500)
TOTAL	12	134,327

Circulation not given for one publication:
            199. AMERICAN SOCIETY LEGION OF HONOR
                 MAGAZINE

GEORGIAN
(Georgian)

NATIVE LANGUAGE

	Number of Publications	Circulation
Bi-monthly	1	1,000
TOTAL	1	1,000

GERMAN
(German; German and English; English)

NATIVE LANGUAGE

	Number of Publications	Circulation
Daily	3	55,000
Semi-weekly	1	8,800
Weekly	25	86,135
Semi-monthly	1	4,874
Monthly	10	57,950
Bi-monthly	1	28,880
Quarterly	1	1,200
Unknown	1	
(Subtotal)	(43)	(242,839)

BI-LINGUAL

Weekly	2	33,400
Monthly	4	20,225
(Subtotal)	(6)	(53,625)

ENGLISH

Weekly	2	49,300
Semi-monthly	1	
Monthly	11	77,094
Bi-monthly	1	15,298
Quarterly	2	11,510
(Subtotal)	(17)	(153,202)

TOTAL	66	449,666

Circulation not given for twelve publications:
- 206. BALTIMORE CORRESPONDENT
- 215. EVANGELISCH-LUTHERISCHES GEMEINDEBLATT
- 218. DAS FREIE WORT
- 223. KATHOLISCHER JUGENDFRUEND
- 228. MILWAUKEE DEUTSCHE ZEITUNG
- 243. THE SWISS AMERICAN
- 247. WASHINGTON JOURNAL
- 251. BAY AREA INTERNATIONAL MONTHLY
- 256. GERMAN AMERICAN TRADE NEWS
- 258. LUXEMBOURG NEWS
- 261. NINTH MANHATTAN MASONIC NEWS
- 264. STEUBEN NEWS

GREEK
(Greek; Greek and English; English)

NATIVE LANGUAGE

	Number of Publications	Circulation
Daily	1	14,337
Weekly	1	4,030
Semi-monthly	2	8,300
Monthly	4	5,299
(Subtotal)	(8)	(31,966)

BI-LINGUAL

Daily	1	14,583
Weekly	5	34,598
Semi-monthly	1	12,000
Monthly	3	23,750
Bi-monthly	1	3,000
5 times/year	1	
(Subtotal)	(12)	(87,931)

ENGLISH

Weekly	1	23,717
Semi-monthly	1	2,000
Monthly	1	2,000
Bi-monthly	3	35,570
Bi-annual	1	1,000
(Subtotal)	(7)	(64,287)

TOTAL	27	184,184

Circulation not given for five publications:

272. HELLAS
273. HELLENIC FREE PRESS
274. ILLUSTRATED ATLANTIS
285. THE TRIBUNE OF G.A.P.A.
292. THE LOGOS

HUNGARIAN
(Hungarian; Hungarian and English)

NATIVE LANGUAGE

	Number of Publications	Circulation
Daily	2	21,660
Weekly	8	28,307
Semi-monthly	4	29,948
Monthly	4	3,975
Unknown	1	1,000
(Subtotal)	(19)	(84,890)

BI-LINGUAL

Weekly	1	12,505
Monthly	4	23,786
Quarterly	1	1,000
(Subtotal)	(6)	(37,291)
TOTAL	25	122,181

Circulation not given for three publications:

307. MAGYAR UJSAG
308. NEMZETVEDELMI TAJEKOZTATO
317. WILLIAM PENN LIFE

ITALIAN
(Italian; Italian and English; English)

NATIVE LANGUAGE

	Number of Publications	Circulation
Daily	1	70,548
Weekly	9	58,449
Semi-monthly	2	4,531
Monthly	6	71,804
Bi-monthly	1	300
(Subtotal)	(19)	(205,632)

ITALIAN (cont'd)

BI-LINGUAL

	Number of Publications	Circulation
Weekly	7	65,455
Semi-monthly	3	15,355
Monthly	4	60,925
Bi-monthly	2	6,100
Quarterly	2	2,420
(Subtotal)	(18)	(150,255)

ENGLISH

Weekly	4	37,464
Semi-monthly	1	
Monthly	1	32,300
Bi-monthly	2	10,000
Quarterly	2	
Irregular	2	1,600
(Subtotal)	(12)	(81,914)
TOTAL	49	437,801

Circulation not given for three publications:

348. LA TRIBUAN ITALIANA
353. ACIM DESPATCH
356. COLUMBUS PRESS
900. I.A.N.U. BULLETIN
901. ITALIAN AMERICAN REVIEW

JAPANESE
(Japanese and English; English)

BI-LINGUAL

	Number of Publications	Circulation
Daily	7	65,919
Semi-weekly	1	4,050
Weekly	2	1,066
Monthly	1	1,100
3 times/week	1	910
(Subtotal)	(12)	(73,045)

JAPANESE (cont'd)

ENGLISH

	Number of Publications	Circulation
Weekly	2	21,419
Monthly	2	2,230
(Subtotal)	(4)	(23,649)
TOTAL	16	96,694

Circulation not given for one publication:

376: NIPPON & AMERICA

JEWISH
(Hebrew; Yiddish; German; English)

HEBREW AND BI-LINGUAL

	Number of Publications	Circulation
Weekly	3	31,600
Monthly	5	64,960
Quarterly	2	8,100
Semi-annual	1	1,100
Irregular	1	850
(Subtotal)	(12)	(106,610)

YIDDISH AND BI-LINGUAL

Daily	4	106,431
Weekly	1	4,750
Semi-monthly	2	10,350
Monthly	8	57,150
Bi-monthly	6	33,800
Quarterly	6	20,000
Semi-annual	1	4,000
3 times/year	1	3,500
Irregular	2	28,000
(Subtotal)	(31)	(267,981)

JEWISH (cont'd)

GERMAN

	Number of Publications	Circulation
Weekly	1	31,000
Monthly	1	8,000
(Subtotal)	(2)	(39,000)

ENGLISH

Weekly	50	985,229
Semi-monthly	9	89,860
Monthly	34	1,255,609
Bi-monthly	7	266,500
Quarterly	19	546,730
Unknown	2	110,000
7 times/year	1	19,000
3 times/week	1	6,000
Annual	2	1,900
(Subtotal)	(125)	(3,280,828)
TOTAL	170	3,694,419

Circulation not given for eleven publications:

387. SHEVILEY HAHINUCH
397. KINDER ZEITUNG
401. OIFN SHVEL
403. UNDZER VEG
436. CALL
446. HABONEH
477. JEWISH OBSERVER
499. KENTUCKY JEWISH POST AND OPINION
507. PARENTS' BULLETIN
522. SOUTHWEST JEWISH CHRONICLE
535. WISCONSIN JEWISH CHRONICLE

KOREAN
(Korean; Korean and English; English)

NATIVE LANGUAGE

	Number of Publications	Circulation
Daily	1	2,500
Bi-monthly	1	2,800
(Subtotal)	(2)	(5,300)

BI-LINGUAL

Weekly	1	120
Semi-monthly	1	494
(Subtotal)	(2)	(614)

ENGLISH

Semi-monthly	1	1,154
Quarterly	1	33,000
(Subtotal)	(2)	(34,154)
TOTAL	6	40,068

LATVIAN
(Latvian)

NATIVE LANGUAGE

	Number of Publications	Circulation
Semi-weekly	1	12,650
Semi-monthly	1	500
TOTAL	2	13,150

LITHUANIAN
(Lithuanian; Lithuanian and English; English)

NATIVE LANGUAGE

	Number of Publications	Circulation
Daily	3	47,090
Semi-weekly	3	21,200
Weekly	3	9,328
Semi-monthly	3	9,336
Monthly	7	14,650
Bi-monthly	3	490
Quarterly	5	550
Semi-annual	1	900
Annual	2	1,685
Bi-annual	1	200
Irregular	1	
(Subtotal)	(32)	(105,429)

BI-LINGUAL

Monthly	4	11,750
Bi-monthly	1	1,950
(Subtotal)	(5)	(13,700)

ENGLISH

Monthly	2	12,000
Bi-monthly	1	2,110
Quarterly	1	5,000
3 times/year	1	1,000
(Subtotal)	(5)	(20,110)

TOTAL	42	139,239

Circulation not given for nine publications:

557. AKECIOS
567. I LAISUE
571. LAISVE
577. MUSU SPARTAI
581. SANDARA
582. SEJA
584. SVIESA
585. TAUTOS PRAEITIS
586. TECHNIKOS ZODIS

LUXEMBOURG
(English)

ENGLISH

	Number of Publications	Circulation
Monthly	1	650
TOTAL	1	650

NORWEGIAN
(Norwegian; Norwegian and English; English)

NATIVE LANGUAGE

	Number of Publications	Circulation
Weekly	1	4,840
Monthly	1	2,465
(Subtotal)	(2)	(7,296)

BI-LINGUAL

Weekly	3	19,856
Monthly	1	1,510
(Subtotal)	(4)	(21,336)

ENGLISH

Semi-monthly	2	9,800
Monthly	2	44,300
Bi-monthly	1	1,005
Quarterly	1	25,000
Irregular	1	1,155
(Subtotal)	(7)	(81,260)
TOTAL	13	109,922

Circulation not given for one publication:

604. THE AUGSBURG NOW

POLISH
(Polish; Polish and English; English)

NATIVE LANGUAGE

	Number of Publications	Circulation
Daily	3	42,633
Weekly	8	44,956
Semi-monthly	4	34,248
Monthly	7	30,808
Bi-monthly	2	15,225
Annual	1	15,387
(Subtotal)	(25)	(183,257)

BI-LINGUAL

Weekly	6	49,850
Semi-monthly	5	305,368
Monthly	2	10,000
Bi-monthly	2	8,000
Quarterly	1	
Annual	1	1,000
(Subtotal)	(17)	(374,218)

ENGLISH

Weekly	4	18,200
Semi-monthly	1	26,639
Monthly	3	13,000
Quarterly	7	10,700
Semi-annual	1	
(Subtotal)	(16)	(68,539)

TOTAL	58	626,014

Circulation not given for ten publications:

631. MORZE
633. NASZE SPRAWY
641. POLKA
644. POSLANIEC MATKI BOSKIEJ SALETYNSKIEJ
645. PRZEWODNIK POLSKI
660. THE NATIONAL P.L.A.V.
662. POLISH AMERICAN
663. POLISH AMERICAN CONGRESS NEWSLETTER
666. POLISH AMERICAN STUDIES
670. THE QUARTERLY REVIEW

PORTUGUESE
(Portuguese; Portuguese and English; English)

NATIVE LANGUAGE

	Number of Publications	Circulation
Daily	1	7,263
Weekly	1	5,250
Semi-monthly	2	18,600
3 times/month	1	3,970
(Subtotal)	(5)	(35,083)

BI-LINGUAL

Weekly	1	3,700
Monthly	1	
(Subtotal)	(2)	(3,700)

ENGLISH

Monthly	1	10,550

TOTAL	8	49,333

Circulation not given for one publication:

671. BOLETIM DA S.P.R.S.I.

ROMANIAN
(Romanian; Romanian and English; English)

NATIVE LANGUAGE

	Number of Publications	Circulation
Semi-monthly	2	5,970
Monthly	1	2,000
Bi-monthly	1	
(Subtotal)	(4)	(7,970)

BI-LINGUAL

Semi-monthly	1	4,350
Monthly	1	
(Subtotal)	(2)	(4,350)

ROMANIAN (cont'd)

ENGLISH

	Number of Publications	Circulation
Monthly	1	
TOTAL	7	12,320

Circulation not given for three publications:

> 681. LUMINATORUL
> 684. UNIREA
> 685. ROMANIAN BULLETIN

RUSSIAN
(Russian; English)

NATIVE LANGUAGE

	Number of Publications	Circulation
Daily	2	31,323
Semi-weekly	1	1,650
Weekly	2	4,254
Semi-monthly	1	1,600
Monthly	8	6,045
Bi-monthly	1	200
Quarterly	3	4,480
3 times/year	3	500
5 times/week	1	2,500
Irregular	2	550
Unknown	1	656
(Subtotal)	(25)	(53,758)

ENGLISH

	Number of Publications	Circulation
Monthly	1	5,020
Bi-monthly	2	3,200
Quarterly	2	3,150
Semi-annual	1	
(Subtotal)	(6)	(11,370)
TOTAL	31	65,128

Circulation not given for five publications:

> 687. EVANGELSKOYE SLOVO   695. PODSNEZHNIK
> 699. RODNIYE DALI   701. ROSSIYSKAYA NEZAVISIM
> 716. TOLSTOY FOUNDATION NEWSLETTER

SERBIAN
(South Slavonian; Serbian and English; Serbian; Serbo-Croatian and English)

NATIVE LANGUAGE

	Number of Publications	Circulation
Weekly	1	2,000
Semi-monthly	1	
Bi-monthly	1	3,500
(Subtotal)	(3)	(5,500)

BI-LINGUAL

Monthly	1	1,700
3 times/week	1	9,100
Unknown	1	16,160
(Subtotal)	(3)	(26,960)
TOTAL	6	32,460

Circulation not given for one publication:

718. RADNICKA BORBA

SLOVAK
(Slovak; Slovak and English; English)

NATIVE LANGUAGE

	Number of Publications	Circulation
Weekly	5	50,530
Monthly	6	20,032
Bi-monthly	1	981
Quarterly	1	1,000
(Subtotal)	(13)	(72,543)

BI-LINGUAL

Weekly	2	30,200
Semi-monthly	1	10,000
Monthly	6	53,963
Quarterly	1	
(Subtotal)	(10)	(94,163)

SLOVAK (cont'd)

ENGLISH

	Number of Publications	Circulation
Irregular	1	2,240
TOTAL	24	168,946

Circulation not given for two publications:

723. AVE MARIA
727. FLORIDSKY SLOVAK

SLOVENIAN
(Slovenian; Slovenian and English)

NATIVE LANGUAGE

	Number of Publications	Circulation
Daily	1	5,000
Semi-monthly	1	8,578
Monthly	1	3,529
(Subtotal)	(3)	(17,107)

BI-LINGUAL

Daily	1	8,832
Weekly	1	16,770
Semi-monthly	1	7,500
Monthly	3	26,283
Quarterly	1	1,700
(Subtotal)	(7)	(61,085)
TOTAL	10	78,192

SPANISH
(Spanish; Spanish and English; English; Spanish, English, and Italian—tabulated under bi-lingual)

NATIVE LANGUAGE

	Number of Publications	Circulation
Daily	5	188,205
Weekly	4	18,496
Semi-monthly	2	9,500
Monthly	10	736,220
Bi-monthly	1	2,500
Quarterly	1	
(Subtotal)	(23)	(954,921)

BI-LINGUAL

Daily	2	30,800
Weekly	8	86,536
Semi-monthly	1	25,000
Monthly	1	40,000
(Subtotal)	(12)	(182,336)

ENGLISH

Semi-weekly	1	1,843
Weekly	3	3,530
(Subtotal)	(4)	(5,373)

TOTAL	39	1,142,630

Circulation not given for four publications:

757. ALIANZA
763. CORPUS CHRISTI AMERICANO
774. EL MUNDO DE NUEVA YORK
790. COSTILLO COUNTY FREE PRESS

SWEDISH

(Swedish; Swedish and English; English)

NATIVE LANGUAGE

	Number of Publications	Circulation
Weekly	4	25,817

BI-LINGUAL

Weekly	1	11,000
Semi-monthly	1	1,050
Monthly	2	4,700
(Subtotal)	(4)	(16,750)

ENGLISH

Weekly	1	2,200
Semi-monthly	3	55,689
Monthly	7	73,550
Quarterly	3	8,625
Irregular	1	500
(Subtotal)	(15)	(140,564)
TOTAL	23	183,131

Circulation not given for one publication:

811. SCANDINAVIAN-AMERICAN BULLETIN

SWISS

(English and German; English, German, and Italian; English)

BI-LINGUAL

	Number of Publications	Circulation
Weekly	2	5,000

ENGLISH

Monthly	1	3,600
TOTAL	3	8,600

TURKISH
(Turkish and English)

BI-LINGUAL

	Number of Publications	Circulation
Quarterly	1	4,697
TOTAL	1	4,697

UKRAINIAN
(Ukrainian; Ukrainian and English; English)

NATIVE LANGUAGE

	Number of Publications	Circulation
Daily	1	20,500
Weekly	2	3,270
Semi-monthly	1	1,700
Monthly	14	29,600
Bi-monthly	9	13,575
Quarterly	15	11,575
Irregular	11	10,935
(Subtotal)	(53)	(91,155)

BI-LINGUAL

Daily	1	6,500
Weekly	3	23,356
Semi-monthly	1	4,250
Monthly	2	4,600
Bi-monthly	1	2,000
Quarterly	3	2,450
Irregular	2	2,000
(Subtotal)	(13)	(45,156)

UKRAINIAN (cont'd)

ENGLISH

	Number of Publications	Circulation
Weekly	2	27,000
Monthly	1	
Quarterly	2	6,450
Semi-annual	1	1,500
Irregular	1	1,000
(Subtotal)	(7)	(35,950)
TOTAL	73	172,261

Circulation not given for five publications:

834. KRYZA
846. NAZARETH
848. NOTATNYK
860. SUMIVETZ
891. DIGEST OF THE SOVIET UKRAINIAN PRESS

WELSH
(Welsh)

NATIVE LANGUAGE

	Number of Publications	Circulation
Monthly	1	
TOTAL	1	

Circulation not given for one publication:

896. DRYCH

INDEX TO THE PUBLICATIONS